what is the true

his bloody Crew

and golden voa

but what says y

uman Kind

will ever find

Creation Knows

rcy to its foes

ods the Throne a

with peace and a

ced to place and P

avenging hour

discard

THE LINCOLN
MAILBAG

THE LINCOLN MAILBAG

America Writes to the President

1861–1865

Edited by Harold Holzer

SOUTHERN ILLINOIS UNIVERSITY PRESS

Carbondale and Edwardsville

Frontispiece: Lincoln (detail), Feb. 5, 1865, the last time he posed in a photographer's studio and a week before his fifty-sixth and final birthday. The portrait was made in Washington by Alexander Gardner. Courtesy Library of Congress. Endpapers courtesy Library of Congress.

Library of Congress Cataloging-in-Publication Data

The Lincoln mailbag : America writes
to the president, 1861–1865 /
edited by Harold Holzer.
p. cm.
1. Lincoln, Abraham, 1809-1865—Correspondence.
2. United States—History—Civil War, 1861-1865—Sources.
I. Holzer, Harold.
E457.962 1998
973.7′092—dc21
97-42164
CIP
ISBN 0-8093-2072-X (cloth : alk. paper)

For Brian Lamb,
America's Greatest Reader

Will you permit me an humble individual to address a few words to you the Chief Magistrate of this Great Republic.

—Poughkeepsie, New York citizen to Abraham Lincoln January 28, 1864

Contents

Illustrations

Preface

Virtually from the day the book *Dear Mr. Lincoln*[1] was published in the fall of 1993, I have been urged to undertake a second volume of citizen correspondence to America's sixteenth president. And I have been armed with so much wonderful material ever since that the challenge has become a most welcome opportunity.

Dear Mr. Lincoln opened a window onto citizen sentiment during the Civil War, but could not hope to provide the final word. Thousands of remarkable letters remained all but hidden within the microfilmed reels of Abraham Lincoln's private papers, unread except by historians and archivists. Thousands more had been separated from the official White House files when they were dispatched by clerks to other branches of the government for action. Later they were found or purchased by souvenir hunters desperate to possess relics of the martyred president. Not included in the official Abraham Lincoln Papers in the Library of Congress, they have ended up scattered among private and public collections across the country. They revealed constituent yearning then and deserve no less attention today.

Unavoidably, the first book omitted as much as it included. The economic constraints of commercial publishing limited the size of the book and compelled its editor to delete many of the letters to Abraham Lincoln that deserved inclusion. Such material was anything but dross. In many cases, a rationale driven only by the vagaries of page layout dictated last-minute decisions to cut worthy and compelling letters. They remained unpublished, available only to scholars.

Soon added to this stockpile of valuable material were new letters urged on me by friends and colleagues. Letters came, too, from Lincoln enthusiasts I had never before met. For as I toured cities around the country to promote *Dear Mr. Lincoln*, I was often approached at the end of such events by members of the audience who had brought their own favorite letters to Lincoln to share with me.

For example, I first learned about an unpublished letter from the president of Harvard reporting son Robert Lincoln's unsatisfactory work at school from a physician and Harvard alumnus, who came to a dinner in Jersey City to hear me speak. Earlier, at a meeting of the Lincoln Group of the District of Columbia at Ft. Leslie McNair—the military installation where the Lincoln assassination conspirators were tried and executed in 1865—a longtime collector approached me with intriguing letters from his own personal archive. A journalist visiting the Metropolitan Museum of Art, where I serve as Vice President for Communications, brought me an authoritative copy of a letter to Lincoln from Karl Marx and his fellow European "workingmen," congratulating Lincoln on his reelection in 1864. So the letters trickled in, hardly enough yet to fill a book, but certainly intriguing enough to serve as the nucleus of a new project.

Without really trying, I had assembled a compelling and historically important core of material—letters I had been unable to publish in 1993, together with new material brought to my attention by friends old and new. Now, my own pursuit of Lincoln letters began again in earnest. I had already searched the Lincoln Papers in the Library of Congress (although, ultimately, I would return to that collection, determined to mine it anew for untouched material). I needed to look in uncharted directions.

I found a new research compass quite by accident—over dinner in 1994. It was the evening of the Lincoln Prize banquet, hosted annually by my old friend, Professor Gabor Boritt of Gettysburg College, to honor notable scholarship in the field of Civil War studies. On this April evening, Professor Ira Berlin was being cited for producing the multivolume archive, *Freedom: A Documentary History of Emancipation, 1861–1867*, which brings together letters from both black and white Americans who lived through the era that ultimately redefined their relationship to one another.

As I well knew, the Berlin volumes included several letters to Abraham Lincoln, letters that I had earlier considered, but ultimately chosen to exclude from *Dear Mr. Lincoln*. My rationale at the time was that the only letters to Lincoln truly worth featuring were those which Lincoln unquestionably saw and read for himself. Although he received as many as five hundred letters a day, the White House ultimately retained only ten to twenty letters daily for the president's personal review. Even these were first examined by correspondence secretaries, then briefly summarized in a few words on the back of their refolded pages so Lincoln might know their contents before opening them (or so he might need never open them at all). With few exceptions, it was from this archive—filed away by the secretaries and then preserved by Lincoln's son Robert until he donated them to the Library of Congress in the twentieth century—that I drew the material for *Dear Mr. Lincoln*.

In so doing, I had rejected outright the overwhelming majority of the surviving letters written to Abraham Lincoln: those forwarded to the various federal departments for action or recommendation. At the time I reasoned that these had less claim to inclusion in a volume of presidential correspondence than that which was retained and read, and certainly that which was answered, by Lincoln himself.

My view of this self-imposed restriction changed on the evening I witnessed the tribute to Dr. Berlin. The experience reminded me anew that nearly every letter written to President Lincoln during the Civil War by an African American was routinely, often mindlessly, sent on to the War Department's Bureau of Colored Troops. In many instances such was their fate, even if the letters had nothing at all to do with military affairs. I began to ask myself at that Gettysburg Prize dinner, whether the White House clerks' refusal to lay them before the president diminished the sincerity of the sentiments they expressed or the importance of those sentiments in illuminating black citizen concerns during the Civil War. The answer was "no," I belatedly concluded. What was truly important about these letters was what they revealed of their writers' hopes, fears, anger, and admiration. Purged once from the White House mailbag, I had unwittingly purged them again a century and a quarter later in assembling *Dear Mr. Lincoln*. I now had the precious opportunity to correct my mistake.

So I returned to the National Archives to begin a search for the earnest letters to Lincoln that had found their way into official government files, presumably unread by the man to whom they were addressed. They had been received at the White House, reviewed by secretaries, and sent on through the bureaucracy—formidable even then—where they were sometimes answered by functionaries, but often merely filed away and forgotten. Here were letters from black soldiers and their families seeking justice and recognition. In other dusty files, I found correspondence from slaveowners furious over emancipation, from job- and favor-seekers demanding special attention and employment for which they were not qualified, and from would-be inventors certain that they had developed the weaponry that could miraculously bring the rebellion to a merciful end.

In addition, I went back to the collections of the Minnesota Historical

Society; the Lincoln Museum in Fort Wayne, Indiana; the Chicago Historical Society; and other repositories to renew the hunt for letters that ended up in their archives, which I had too quickly dismissed in my original search for such material. I also returned, ultimately, to the ninety-six microfilm reels of the Lincoln Papers, dazzled by what I could still uncover from that extraordinary resource. This trove continues to be harvested by historians for the correspondence it contains from prominent, rather than everyday, citizens.

This new book thus gathers together more of the yet-unheard, authentic voices of Lincoln's America, presented in letters bringing congratulation and condemnation, invitation and warning, advice and instruction, and even out-and-out threats. On one occasion, for example, an overjoyed abolitionist can devise no better way of thanking Lincoln for issuing the Emancipation Proclamation than to send him some fresh hams. On another, a Union officer writes to complain about the vexing inaction of the Army of the Potomac, warning that frustration might prove more dangerous than enemy fire. In yet other letters, an imprisoned "privateersman" writes from his dank cell in New York City to complain that he has been unlawfully detained; would-be inventors send proposals for chain-mail armor, electric-shock weaponry, portable "ironclad" shields, and other flights of fancy; a pro-Union pamphleteer demands $50,000 for her propaganda; and a black woman from a border slave state writes to ask, directly and plaintively, whether or not she is free. One unschooled admirer is so sure that Rebel sympathizers at his flour mill are conspiring to murder the president that he hides in a wheat bin to eavesdrop on their scheming, and then writes, clumsily but endearingly, to report the plot to its intended victim.

With such material now at hand, I wanted to demonstrate the sheer variety of the letters that competed for Lincoln's attention in a typical month, week, or even day. When I found myself unable to resist a particularly rich cache of letters that came to the White House in the second week of January 1864, I knew at once that this collection must be allowed to reveal itself in strict chronological order.

On the pages that follow, every month of Lincoln's presidency, as well as the weeks leading up to his 1861 inauguration, are represented by at least one letter and often by several. "Public sentiment is everything," Lincoln once said.[2] Just as these letters reflect the wide variety of their authors' opinions, interests, priorities, fears, joys, and resentments, they also hold up a priceless collective mirror onto public opinion about Abraham Lincoln during the brightest and the darkest moments of the long, costly struggle to preserve the Union. Reading them now in day-by-day order, we can better picture the beleaguered Lincoln and his overworked staff sifting through a numbing variety of pleas, importuning, flattery, and complaints. At a single reading they might handle requests for political appointments (from an ex-president, a New York archbishop, even Lincoln's own minister); suggestions for how better to manage the war; requests for autographs, locks of hair, and personal appearances; presumptuous political advice; hymns, epistles, and rhymes, including sixteen pages of vicious abuse in verse, from amateur poets; and gifts that included food, drink, clothing, pictures, and sculptures—to name but a few of the categories of correspondence that arrived at the Executive Mansion each day.

Through these letters the modern reader is able to travel the full gauntlet of citizen sentiment during the Civil War—not the kind that was reflected, and often molded, by newspapers, but rather that which sprung, heartfelt and uninvited, from the pens of ordinary Americans. Here, finally, are the voices of African Americans who had been denied their hearing before Lincoln by an office routine that effectively barred them from inclusion in the screened mail set before the president each day. Here, too, are letters from notables that stimulated important replies from Lincoln. Their inclusion in this collection serves to demonstrate the full range of priorities and concerns aimed at Lincoln daily by subordinates, political leaders, literary figures, and ordinary Americans he never knew: supporters, opponents, friends, enemies, and the inevitable, out-and-out crackpots.

Although this book re-opens the White House mailbag, retrospectively, to the unheard concerns of black correspondents, it bears no new evidence that any solace ever arrived from members of Lincoln's own family. Not a single greeting or good wish unencumbered by a request for some favor can be found among the letters from in-laws, cousins, and distant relatives that arrived at the White House during Lincoln's presidency. One can only imagine Lincoln's embarrassment when a highly personal letter to his wife, Mary, was discovered by a soldier in the field and returned to the president months after it was sent.

No one is absolutely certain how many letters Lincoln received in the daily deliveries to the Executive Mansion, because the secretaries themselves disagreed about the volume, with estimates ranging from 250 to 500 pieces a day. Whatever the total, the volume of mail to Lincoln pales before the mind-numbing amounts reported by modern presidents. Appearing on National Public Radio in 1993 with the Assistant to the President for Correspondence, I learned that Bill Clinton routinely received 9,000–12,000 letters *per day* in what the White House refers to as "low season." In "high season," during the school year when students organize group letter-writing efforts, or in the heat of public debate over the budget or other explosive issues, the number swells to an astronomical 25,000–30,000 letters a day. During the debate over health care, I learned that the Clinton White House received 82,000 pieces of mail on one morning alone! Even Socks the Cat, the presidential pet, was getting five pieces of fan mail daily.

Of course, the raw numbers need to be put into perspective. There were 31 million people in the United States in 1860, nearly 9 million of whom seceded the following year, leaving a pool of some 22 million letter-writers to Lincoln. Using the most generous estimate of the contents of the Lincoln mailbag (five hundred letters daily) that means that one in 44,000 wrote to Lincoln each day. In today's America of more than 250 million people, one in 25,000 writes to the president on any given day. But this total includes faxes and e-mail, and counts as individual letters the preprinted post cards distributed to potential "letter-writers" by lobbying groups and special interests. Taking this into account, along with vastly increased literacy, the development of typewriters and personal computers, and the greater participation of women in today's body politic, it is not unreasonable to conclude that things have not changed all that much since Abraham Lincoln occupied the White House, at least not where the yearning to be heard is concerned. People then wrote to their president nearly as often, and always as passionately, as they do today.

One thing that *has* changed a great deal is the staff that is employed to handle presidential correspondence. Lincoln was authorized by law to hire only one personal secretary. He managed to triple his staff to a total of three aides by appointing them to posts in the federal departments and ordering them assigned to the Executive Mansion.[3] As of 1993, Bill Clinton's correspondence staff included two assistants, seven letter-writers, sixty secretaries, the aforementioned Assistant to the President for Correspondence, and up to three hundred volunteers (some of whom work, coincidentally, from the Soldiers' Home, which Lincoln used as a summer residence during the Civil War).

In addition, today's chief executives also employ resident pollsters who can take the pulse of public opinion in a heartbeat. Abraham Lincoln had only constituent mail with which to measure citizen confidence.

Through this daily dose of praise, reverence, insult, sanctimony, and exhortation, whatever the limits on his time to read such letters, and whatever limits on the access that his secretaries afforded him, Lincoln learned what his public thought about war, race, and politics. Most of all, he learned what they thought about their president.

These are the letters Abraham Lincoln read, as well as those he had neither the time nor the opportunity to read, during the most dramatic era in American history. Together, they provide new insight into public sentiment and political culture during the Civil War. As Lincoln understood so well even before he took office as president, "in a government of the people, where the voice of all the men of that country, substantially enters into the execution . . . of the government . . . what lies at the bottom of all of it is public opinion."[4]

If that belief has not changed since, neither has the ethic guaranteeing public access to our presidents, although today's citizen-correspondents are likely to find their efforts to communicate with the White House even more frustrating than did their Civil War counterparts.

I have known the frustration myself, although I found the experience more amusing than offensive. In September 1994, President Clinton visited the Metropolitan Museum to attend a reception marking the 49th United Nations General Assembly. The president was scheduled to enter through the American Wing and to pause and be greeted privately by museum officials. While there, he was to be presented with the obligatory stack of gifts. Earlier, Mr. Clinton's "advance" team had recognized me from a C-SPAN appearance and, knowing that the president is a student of Lincoln, asked if I would like to include a copy of *Dear Mr. Lincoln*, which they proposed I autograph for Mr. Clinton on the spot. Flattered and honored, of course I agreed.

On the big night, the president entered and was led to the table laden with museum presentations. As promised, the friendly aide pointed to my book and whispered in Mr. Clinton's ear as I, along with my Metropolitan colleagues, hovered in the background. Unexpectedly, Mr. Clinton announced in a loud voice, "I already have this book in my presidential library." Then he added, "Would the author like *me* to autograph it to *him* instead?" I stammered something about how thrilled I would be, and the president obliged with an inscription that I still treasure: "To Harold Holzer, with appreciation for this fine work. Bill Clinton."

But if the experience left me with delusions of celebrity, they were quickly shattered when I received a presidential thank-you note a few weeks later for the gift never tendered. "Thanks so much," it read, "for the copy of your book, *Dear Mr. Lincoln.* I am grateful for your kind words and thoughtful expression of support." As if that were not enough, I received yet another unanticipated presidential communication a few weeks after that—this time a preprinted card with a stamped Clinton signature. Beneath the gold seal of the president came this message: "Thank you for your kind words and your gift. The American people have given me the opportunity to lead our country in a new direction. I will depend on the diverse talents of every citizen to make the American dream a reality once again. I am grateful for your support." In barely a month, I had fallen from the heights of supposed intimacy to the depths of anonymity.

Every correspondent to a president should be prepared for the delay, the seeming indifference, the occasional neglect, and even the confusion that will likely greet their most heartfelt letters. It was ever thus.

At least where Lincoln was concerned, there was a desire to keep the lines of communication open. "For myself," he told a New York newspaper editor, "I feel—though the tax on my time is heavy—that no hours of my day are better employed than those which thus bring me again within the direct contact and atmosphere of the average of our whole people."[5] Lincoln was speaking of the regular office hours he reserved, twice weekly, for meeting citizens and hearing their complaints personally. He called them "my '*public-opinion baths*.'" But he might just as well have been referring to the hours he devoted to reading letters from his vast constituency. "Many of the matters brought to my notice are utterly frivolous," he admitted, "but others are of more or less importance, and all serve to renew in me a clearer and more vivid image of that great popular assemblage out of which I sprung, and to which . . . I must return."[6]

The men and women who wrote to their president during the Civil War seemed to sense this welcoming spirit and drew from it encouragement and inspiration. As one of the president's private secretaries put it years later, there was something unique about Abraham Lincoln "calculated to draw forth communications from the trustful and sincere."[7]

On the following pages, those trustful and sincere communications are communicated once again.

Notes

1. Harold Holzer, ed., *Dear Mr. Lincoln: Letters to the President* (New York: Addison-Wesley, 1993).

2. Roy P. Basler et al., eds., *The Collected Works of Abraham Lincoln,* 9 vols. (New Brunswick, NJ: Rutgers University Press, 1953–55), III: 27.

3. William O. Stoddard, for example, was on July 20, 1861, appointed to the Department of the Interior, but to serve as "Secretary to the President to sign patents for lands." See William O. Stoddard Jr., ed., *Lincoln's Third Secretary: The Memoirs of William O. Stoddard* (New York: Exposition Press, 1955), commission reproduced opp. p. 74.

4. Basler, *Coll. Works,* III: 441–42.

5. Francis B. Carpenter, *Six Months at the White House with Abraham Lincoln: The Story of a Picture* (New York: Hurd & Houghton, 1866), 281.

6. *Ibid.*

7. Theodore C. Blegen, ed., *Abraham Lincoln and His Mailbag: Two Documents by Edward D. Neill, One of Lincoln's Secretaries* (St. Paul: Minnesota Historical Society, 1964), 46.

Preface

Acknowledgments

IN UNDERTAKING THIS VOLUME, I have been blessed by assistance, support, and encouragement from friends and colleagues who have earned much more gratitude than I can begin to express. Most of all, I am indebted to my close friend, Judge Frank J. Williams of Hope Valley, Rhode Island, who again made available to me the vast resources of his incomparable Lincoln and Civil War library. More than once, in response to some urgent call for help, he traveled uncomplaining, to his Hope Valley office after a long day in court at Providence, to search through his archives and gather material to air-ship to me the following day at his own expense. Such manifestations of friendship truly go beyond the call. Reels of microfilm, copies of documents, passages from books, photocopies from the *Official Records of the Rebellion*, all flowed to New York as if on a conveyor belt. To say that this book could not have been written without Frank Williams's help would be a gross understatement. All I can do is thank him, again and always, for his support, generosity, patience, and enthusiasm.

Along the path from conception to publication, a number of curators, archivists, and librarians helped me track down documents, and then obligingly granted permission for their publication here. I am grateful in particular to Gerald Prokopowicz, historian of the Lincoln Museum in Fort Wayne, and his research assistant, James E. Eber; Michael Musick and Dee Ann Blanton at the Military Reference Branch of the National Archives; William J. Walsh at the Archives' Textual Reference Branch and Budge Weidman at its Civil War Conservation Corps; Illinois State Historian Thomas F. Schwartz and Kim Bauer, curator of the Lincoln Collection at the Illinois State Historical Library; Don McCue of the Lincoln Shrine in Redlands, California; and Steve Nielsen, Jean H. Brookins, and Dallas R. Lindgren of the Minnesota Historical Society.

At the Library of Congress, James R. Gilreath offered the resources of his Department of Rare Books and Special Collections, Civil War Specialist John R. Sellers helped much, Clark Evans provided expert guidance and much forbearance, and Yvonne Brooks provided special help with the William T. Sherman Papers. Larry Hackman, former New York State Archivist, now director of the Harry S. Truman Library in Independence, Missouri, pointed the way to important papers. Theresa McGill of the Chicago Historical Society generously shared important material, and Malcom S. Forbes Jr. granted permission to reprint material from the Forbes family's superb Lincoln collection.

Among the many private collectors who identified unpublished material, or made letters available from their own collections, were Malcolm S. Forbes Jr. (and Catherine S. Thomas, Registrar of the Forbes Collection); Dr. Jules Ladenheim of Jersey City, New Jersey; and William W. Layton of Washington, D.C. I must thank Bill Alexander of Alexander Autographs, Inc., in Connecticut, and Daniel Weinberg of the Abraham Lincoln Book Shop in Chicago. I owe a special debt of gratitude to Thomas Brencick, managing director of Transfertex in Kleinostheim, Germany, for the copy of the letter to Lincoln that hangs at the Karl-Marx-Haus, and to Burton Gerber of Washington and Gene Rubin of Beverly Hills for identifying and supplying choice material.

Uncovering the letters to Lincoln represented only part of the research challenge. There are few more daunting tasks than the examination and transcription of original nineteenth-century handwriting. There are times when words and sentences appear so stubbornly illegible that an editor is certain that a fabulous entry will have to be discarded because it simply cannot be read authoritatively.

Fortunately, my wife, Edith, and my younger daughter, Meg, now at Yale but then at home, were always available to cast fresh eyes on the most unyielding passages and almost never failed to comprehend something I had failed to grasp. Many a superb letter was saved for inclusion in this book thanks to their patient readings and re-readings. My close friend and frequent coauthor, Mark E. Neely Jr., of St. Louis University is the most accurate reader of documents I have ever known and was always able to decipher words that none of the Holzers could fathom. Finally, even though she was seldom at home during the preparation of this book, our older daughter, Remy, generously offered crucial words of encouragement even as she was focusing on her senior thesis at Harvard.

Further indispensable help came later from Carol A. Burns, managing editor of Southern Illinois University Press, and my skillful copyeditor, Alexandria Weinbrecht. It was John F. "Rick" Stetter, director of SIU

Acknowledgments

Press, who convinced me early on to undertake this volume and enthusiastically supported its preparation, a task I know took longer than he had hoped. It was the pride of SIU, Professor John Y. Simon, who introduced me to Rick Stetter and who became the first, and most steadfast, advocate of this project. He also became a loyal, supportive friend and colleague. In the end, while I owe significant debts of appreciation to people in all parts of the country, much of it resides in Carbondale, Illinois, with Rick and John.

Acknowledgments

Introduction

Omnium Gatherum: The Lincoln Mailbag,
by the Private Secretaries Who Opened It

DURING THE CIVIL WAR, responsibility for the White House mailbag fell to a succession of staff aides: first, to John M. Hay, the future secretary of state who served as assistant private secretary throughout the Lincoln administration; then, when Hay required help, to the young Illinois journalist, William Osborne Stoddard; and, finally, when illness forced Stoddard to take a leave of absence, to the Minnesota minister and historian-turned-secretary, Edward Duffield Neill.

Not surprisingly, each of these men recalled his experiences with presidential correspondence somewhat differently. But they all remembered that Lincoln had entrusted them with complete authority in the handling of mail. They could summarize, forward, re-route, or destroy the incoming correspondence at will, and their judgment would never be questioned. They could draft responses and, as one secretary suggested, even sign Lincoln's name to them.

Ultimately, responsibility bred a certain cynicism. The oppressive burden of opening and reading up to five hundred letters each day was bound to exhaust and irritate even the most devoted of clerks. Stoddard, who inherited the job of correspondence clerk and handled it for more than two years, always seemed prouder of the letters he destroyed than those he summarized and passed along to Lincoln. Of the three, Neill seemed the most methodical and least self-aggrandizing, both in his role as correspondence clerk and in remembering his experiences later. Among Lincoln's correspondence secretaries, he seems to have sympathized most deeply with the men and women who wrote to their president with such high expectations during the Civil War.

Following are the firsthand recollections of each of these men, describing the White House office routine under Lincoln exactly as they remembered it. John Hay's reminiscences are excerpted from a letter he wrote after the war to Lincoln's former law partner and future biographer, William H. Herndon. Stoddard published his story, which has been all but forgotten since, in a New York newspaper in 1866. Neill composed his story for a publication he originally entitled, "Peeps into President Lincoln's Mail Bag."

Together, these reminiscences shed considerable light on the rather informal system under which citizen letters to Lincoln were received, sorted, and then either forwarded to federal departments or bureaus, destroyed, or passed along to the president himself. Stoddard was probably correct when he guessed that most letter-writers would have been outraged had they known of the fate that their letters often received at the hands of Lincoln's secretaries. But even if the overwhelming majority of correspondence failed to elicit personal responses from the president of the United States, the amount of letters, as Neill asserted, grew steadily as the years went by. By the end of his presidency, Lincoln was receiving twice the amount of mail that he had at the beginning.

Although Abraham Lincoln's clerks did not always allow the president to listen, the correspondents themselves wanted, and apparently needed, to express themselves in increasing numbers. As Edward Duffield Neill recognized, in a nation divided by civil war and wracked by the unprecedented casualties and deprivation it brought, the Union's deeply troubled citizens had only two ways of "unburdening themselves": either in prayer "to the Unseen" or in letters "to the official head of the Republic." Neither prayers nor letters were always answered. But that did not stop America from praying to God—or writing to Abraham Lincoln.

John M. Hay Remembers[1]

He [Lincoln] was extremely unmethodical: it was a four-years struggle on [presidential secretary John G.] Nicolay's part and mine to get him to adopt some systematic rules. He would break through every regulation as fast as it was made. Anything that kept the people themselves away from him he disapproved—although they nearly annoyed the life out of him by unreasonable complaints & requests.

He wrote very few letters. He did not read one in fifty that he received. At first we tried to bring them to his notice, but at last he gave the whole thing over to me, and signed without reading them the letters I wrote in his name. He wrote perhaps half-a-dozen a week himself—not more.

Nicolay received members of Congress, & other visitors who had business with the Executive Office, communicated to the Senate and the House the messages of the President, & exercised a general supervision over the business.

I opened and read the letters, answered them, looked at the newspapers, supervised the clerks who kept the records, and in Nicolay's absence did his work also.

William O. Stoddard Remembers[2]

A vast amount of business—and the reverse—came to the office through the mail, and of this I had charge, "with full power," for about two years and a half. The packages and envelopes, of all sorts and sizes, sometimes numbered hundreds in a day, and sometimes dwindled to a few dozens. They related to all imaginable interests and affairs: applications for office, for contracts, for pardons, for pecuniary aid, for advice, for information, for autographs, voluminous letters of advice, political disquisitions, religious exhortations, the rant and drivel of insanity, bitter abuse, foul obscenity, slanderous charges against public men, police and war information, military reports—there never was on earth such another *omnium gatherum* [a collection of miscellany—Ed.] as the President's mail.

The spiritualists favored him constantly, and I still have in my possession urgent epistles signed with the *fac-simile* signatures of half the dead worthies in our history, not to speak of sundry communications from the Apostles and the Angel Gabriel, of the correctness of whose signatures I am not so certain. As a general thing, during the war, we believed that so soon as a man went clean crazy his first absolutely insane act was to open a correspondence, on his side, with the President. As to the letters of advice, I am truly glad that the writers of many bulky and labored documents do not know what became of their precious productions, and in any event cannot accuse me of any dereliction from duty. One more point is, in the light of subsequent events, especially worthy of note, and that is, the large number of threatening letters. It is quite within bounds to say that they averaged one per diem. Most of them were manifestly merely intended to harass and provoke the President, while others but too evidently breathed a spirit that only needed courage and opportunity to have anticipated Wilkes Booth. It was impossible to secure the attention of Mr. Lincoln to any of these, except as a matter for contemptuous ridicule; and when his friends, especially Mr. [Edwin] Stanton [secretary of war], insisted on his permitting himself to be accompanied and surrounded by a guard, he consented finally only under protest. It was hard for a heart like his to comprehend the venomous vindictiveness and cruelty of too many of his opponents.

After a proper examination almost all business letters were promptly referred to the special office, war, navy, &c., to which their matter related; another large class—indeed, the largest, as a general thing—went into my willow waste-basket, a few were filed in the office for future reference, and a small per centage, three or four in a hundred, properly briefed and remarked upon, were laid on the President's desk. This though exciting the furious wrath of sundry unthinking people, was unavoidable; for if every day had been a month it would have been impossible for Mr. Lincoln to attend to all these things in person.

Another huge mass of documents was daily transferred from his table to mine—the accumulation of the offerings of the day's caravan of personal petitions—though these were generally of a class to demand and receive careful attention. Any paper of real importance was pretty sure to do its work, and in due time to make its appearance from the proper pigeon-hole [Lincoln worked at a pigeon-hole desk—Ed.].

Again and again I have experienced the liveliest amusement in having local politicians and others boast of the effect their advice has evidently had upon the mind of the President, and describe the course which they had marked out for his future action. More than one has asked me if I had ever heard Mr. Lincoln speak of his letters, and if such and such a one was not read in Cabinet council. Dante should have seen my willow basket before he completed his list of limbos. Its edge was truly a bourne from which no traveler returned.

One day a well-dressed gentleman—a judge, or something of the kind, at home—sat in my room looking on at the performance of my morning job of destruction. Twisting uneasily in his chair and changing from red to pale with indignation, until he could contain his gathered wrath no longer. He had evidently indulged in letter-writing himself.

"Was that the way in which I dared to serve the President's correspondence? Was this the manner in which the people were prevented from reaching Mr. Lincoln? He would complain of me to my master at once! Teach me a thing or two about my duties! See if this was to be allowed! A mere boy in such an important place as that!" And so on for some moments, until I looked up and requested him to be still for a moment, while I read him a few of the precious documents I was destroying.

Of course, I made judicious selections to suit the occasion, for he was evidently intensely respectable and patriotic. I began with an epistle full of vulgar abuse that "riled" the old gentleman fearfully. Next I put in a proclamation "written in blood," and signed by the "Angel Gabriel;" and wound up with a horrible thing from an obscene, idiotic lunatic—a regular correspondent. The last was too much for him, and he begged me to stop. It was, indeed, sickening enough. I told him that if he insisted on the President's giving his time to such things he must take them in himself, as really I was forbidden to do so. The old gentleman, however, thought better of me by that time, and leaned back in his chair to moralize on the total depravity of human affairs.

Complaints did frequently get to the President; but as he never interfered with me in any way and refused to reverse my decisions, I concluded he was satisfied even with the willow basket. No doubt they have one there now, and in these times it may well be a large one.

The applications for autographs were innumerable, but received very little encouragement, as the President had other things to attend to.

Colonel Hay imitated the signature of his Excellency very well, and I strongly suspect that some of the autographs distributed by my enterprising friend were very good indeed. On leaving the White House I had a fine collection, but they now adorn the portfolios of other men and women.

Edward Duffield Neill Remembers[3]

The mail-bag of President Lincoln, brought daily by a messenger, from the Post Office to the Executive Mansion was always filled, especially during the last year of his life. Its contents were different from those that had been hitherto received as communications to Presidents of the United States. The country was engaged in a momentous struggle for existence; a heart rending civil war was being waged of such magnitude as to elicit the attention of all the nations of earth. Every patriot became intensely interested in the strife, and many after unburdening themselves in prayer before the Unseen, felt that they must give their thoughts on public affairs to the official head of the Republic.

Then the organization of the man was calculated to draw forth communications from the trustful and sincere. He was what we term a natural man. The prominent traits of his character had not been curbed nor repressed by scholastic discipline, nor had he ever studied the art of etiquette. In the Presidential chair he appeared to his neighbors essentially the same Abraham Lincoln that they had known when they volunteered together, as soldiers to check the movements of the Indian Chief, Black Hawk, or as he sat on the porch of the Country Inn telling stories on the evenings of Court Week.

The sobriquet of "honest old Abe" was bestowed no one exactly knew when, but it became as valid as a baptismal name, and inseparable from the man as the tunic of Nessus.

In the tour from his Illinois home at Springfield to the National Capital previous to his inauguration as President, he passed through many cities and towns and as eager crowds gazed upon his tall spare form, sad but kindly eyes, by no means handsome face, and observed his want of manner, although there was at first a feeling of disappointment, because he did not "look every inch" a President, yet that very absence of official dignity, led to a personal interest, and by the time he was domiciled at the Executive Mansion, loyal men of all parties began to think that he was a patriot who had the welfare of his Country, close to his heart, and that he would rule "with malice toward none, with charity toward [*sic*] all."

The fact that he never with "official awe" glanced at any one, and frequently relieved embarrassment by a little story, caused thousands of the sanguine and unsophisticated to take the liberty to write to him not only on the conduct of the war, but to unfold their tale of woe and personal misfortune. To have read all the letters directed to him would have been a Sisyphean labor, never completed, and it was necessarily delegated to another person.

Good and true men without foresight would mail twenty or thirty pages of anxious thought as to the course which they would pursue if in his place, and timid ones would forward manuscripts equally voluminous on the subject of peace at all hazards.

School girls would mail their pretty photographs and in the sauciest little notes ask for his *pretty* face in exchange. College students afflicted with the autograph mania, stormed him with requests for his signature.

An applicant for entrance as a student to the Military Academy at West Point forwarded an accurate description of himself, and stated that he did not possess a form like Apollo, and moreover was *very near-sighted* but added that in reading Plutarch's Lives he had learned that some of the ancient heroes were deformed; he further stated that he was a young Christian, and lifted up with the pride of a novice he strongly urged his appointment, on the ground that the army was much in need of officers of good moral character.

After the day of his election to a second term of office, a wag in New

York City wrote, that he had walked his boots out, in securing votes on the previous day, and desired a new pair to be sent by *return mail*. An old Kentuckian sent a large plug of tobacco, as an evidence of his high respect, not knowing that the President though a Kentuckian by birth, eschewed the ancient habit of the Kentucky gentlemen, of rolling a "quid" under his tongue, like a sweet morsel.

The lunatics did not forget him, and the pigeon hole of the letter desk labeled "Crazy and Poetry" an odd if not true conjunction, was always filled with contributions. These epistles came not only from Maine and Oregon, but the uttermost parts of the earth, and while many were complimentary, others were imprecatory.

A denunciatory and hortatory religious poem of sixteen foolscap pages came from New Zealand written by a "messenger of the King of Kings and Lord of Lords."

The author stated that he had been absent from England twenty seven years, most of which period was passed in sailing on the coast of New Holland. The insertion of a few lines of the poem will enable each reader to judge whether the inspiration that dictated it was celestial, or derived from the letters of Bull Run Russell [a reference to William Howard Russell, the war correspondent—Ed.] in the London Times, and copied into all the papers of the distant outposts of the British Realm.

> "At first, the tyrant legions drilled,
>   And led by men in war, well skilled,
> In numbers, they did far exceed
>   Those, Beauregard against them led;
> Numbers don't always win the strife,
>   Freedom's far more dear than life,
> And so it happened on that day,
>   The tyrant's legions ran away.
> And when the Yankees grew so bold
>   Again to boast, it shall be told,
> Long as the Sun shall rule the day,
>   That at Bull Run, they ran away.
>
> Like curs they bark, but cannot bite,
>   No courage have they for the fight."

A woman on the distant Pacific coast requested that her husband might be made the postmaster of a small village in Oregon, and in her application stated that the President would remember *her*, as the daughter of a plain and strict Presbyterian, at whose house he used to tarry when a young man, while going or returning from County Courts, and that one night, just before her father commented his too lengthy evening prayer, he whispered that he wished she would go up and bring him a pillow for his knees, as he feared they might give out, before her parent finished.

A deaf and dumb man who as married had fallen in love with a young girl and supposing that it was in the President's power begged for a divorce promising that if his petition was granted he would go to Church with the new love every Sunday morning.

Some letters were so full of the deepest heart sorrows that the eyes of the reader flooded with tears. A lad eighteen years of age states that his parents are heart broken and no longer smile; that his elder brother whom he believed was a brave boy under some unaccountable infatuation had deserted from an Ohio regiment and that for two years he had been marked as a deserter; that his parents were mortified that such a word should be written after the name of one of their sons.

After this statement the heroic self-sacrificing brother offered himself as a substitute and to lift the load off of his father's and mother's heart agreed to serve out the unexpired term of his brother and make up the time since he disappeared on condition that the word *deserter* was expunged from his brother's name on the regimental roll.

The last mail bag for President Lincoln was received at the Presidential Mansion some hours after his body lifeless from an assassin's hate had been stretched upon a bed in one of the chambers.

It was opened amid an awful stillness and two of the last letters read were from Major General Burnside and Chief Justice Chase. The former tendered his resignation as an officer of the army and expressed his willingness to again buckle on his sword if the liberties of the Country should be again endangered.

The letter of Mr. Chase had been written on Friday night in Baltimore where he was holding Court and but a little while before the fatal pistol ball had been fired at Washington. It was a long and earnest letter urging the President to recede from his position relative to suffrage and adopt the views of the Chief Justice.

Mr. Lincoln's view that only colored soldiers and freedmen who could read should at first be allowed to vote, has not been adopted while Mr. Chase's theory has become a law of the land.

Notes

1. John M. Hay, *Abraham Lincoln* (Pamphlet, n.p., n.d.), "reproduced from the original in the collection of Lincolniana formed by Wm. H. Herndon now in the possession of Gabriel Wells."

2. William O. Stoddard, "White House Sketches by One of Lincoln's Secretaries," Sketch No. IV, *New York Citizen*, September 8, 1866.

3. Reprinted from *Abraham Lincoln and His Mailbag: Two Documents by Edward D. Neill, One of Lincoln's Secretaries*, edited by Theodore C. Blegen (St. Paul: Minnesota Historical Society, 1964), pp. 46–50. Copyright 1964, 1992 by the Minnesota Historical Society.

Introduction

A Note on Editorial Methods

THE LETTERS on the following pages are presented chronologically, rather than by topic, to best provide a sense of the broad range of subjects that Lincoln's correspondents addressed daily. The editor has made a determined effort to preserve the letters in their original state. Misspellings are not corrected, and the warning flag, *sic*, is employed only to alert modern readers to the most egregious and potentially confusing errors. Nor is standard punctuation imposed; even if nineteenth-century authors eschewed periods and commas, they are not corrected here. Perhaps most important of all, underlined passages are not changed into italics—the modern editing method of choice. Such passages are allowed to remain underlined here, just as their original authors intended. Editorial impositions within the texts are kept to a minimum: only the names of important persons and events are identified in bracketed commentary. Sources for letters, editorial notes, and/or Lincoln's replies come at the end of the last editorial note. If no reference is listed, then the source is the Abraham Lincoln Papers, Library of Congress.

Whenever responses from Lincoln are available, they are presented following each citizen letter, and these also appear with no editing. Secretarial endorsements and comments are given when they can be found.

Only one major concession has been made to the modern standards of documentary reproduction. To avoid a cacophony of design, salutations and return addresses have been standardized, with the former placed at the left-hand corner of each letter with no indentation and the latter placed at the right. Correspondents of the day might use four or five lines to write a flamboyant salutation, and these were tightened and restricted to a line or two. But readers of this book should feel confident that no other alterations have been permitted.

Views of Lincoln
and His Inner Circle

Lincoln in his office at the White House, Apr. 26, 1864. This is the exact spot where he presided over cabinet meetings, where he signed the Emancipation Proclamation, and where, occasionally, he opened his daily correspondence. No doubt, some of it was dispatched to the trash: note the wicker wastebasket beneath the table. This rare on-site picture was taken by cameraman Anthony Berger as a model for artist Francis B. Carpenter, whose legs are visible at right. Reprinted by permission of Lloyd Ostendorf.

The First Reading of the Emancipation Proclamation Before the Cabinet, the engraving of Francis B. Carpenter's 1864 painting, shows all of Lincoln's ministers gathered in the cabinet room Lincoln also used as a private office and reception area to welcome visitors. Today it is the so-called Lincoln Bedroom, but the original furnishings actually used here by the working president have long since vanished. Reprinted by permission of The Lincoln Museum, Fort Wayne, IN (Ref. 151).

This work by pro-Confederate artist Adalbert Volck of Baltimore, ca. 1864, represents a different view of Lincoln in his private office. He envisioned the president working at a cloven-foot desk and dipping his pen into a devil-held inkwell, inside a room decorated with pro-Abolitionist art, with hard liquor at the ready on a nearby table. Reprinted by permission of The Maryland Historical Society, Baltimore.

John George Nicolay (1832–1901) served as Lincoln's private secretary from 1860 to 1865, and later coauthored a multivolume biography of his famous chief. The German-born Nicolay ended his long career in public service with a fifteen-year stint as marshall of the U.S. Supreme Court. Reprinted by permission of The Lincoln Museum, Fort Wayne, IN (Ref. 1321).

John Milton Hay (1838–1905) was assistant private secretary to Lincoln throughout his presidency and for several years had charge of the White House mailbag. Indiana-born and Brown-educated, he later served as U.S. secretary of state and, with John Nicolay, was a biographer of Lincoln. Reprinted by permission of The Lincoln Museum, Fort Wayne, IN (Ref. 1322).

William Osborne Stoddard (1835–1925) served as White House correspondence clerk from mid-1861 until he contracted typhoid fever and took sick leave in 1864. He wrote more about the Lincoln mailbag than any other observer. Reprinted by permission of The Lincoln Museum, Fort Wayne, IN (Ref. 4282).

Edward Duffield Neill (1823–1893) was a forty-one-year-old clergyman and historian when he joined the staff of young White House secretaries in 1864 to replace ailing William O. Stoddard. Reprinted by permission of The Minnesota Historical Society.

A mute surviving relic from Lincoln's White House desk, this handsome paperweight was probably employed to hold down the incoming mail that Lincoln intended to file or answer. Since his pigeonhole writing desk was positioned near a window that was often left open in good weather, the paperweight would have been needed to keep order on the desk. Reprinted by permission of The Lincoln Museum, Fort Wayne, IN (Ref. 3129a).

THE LINCOLN
MAILBAG

This first studio photograph of Lincoln as president was made by an unknown cameraman in Washington sometime before the end of June 1861. Reprinted by permission of The Lincoln Museum, Fort Wayne, IN (Ref. 0-55).

Warning of "Midnight" and "Noonday" Assassins

Cincinnati Jan 24/61

Hon A. Lincoln

My Dr Sir

I venture none of your friends inclined to congratulate you, and our country, and thank God of the grave utterance to the feelings of my full heart in a line to you lest I should add to the weight of your numerous and perplexing cares.

I now beg your indulgence while I submit a few words for your consideration. I have no opinion to express—no suggestion to make about <u>men</u> or <u>measures</u>   I rest perfectly easy and well satisfied that your department of the government will be administered with prude & skill, as well as firmness and efficiency according to well matured and <u>fixed principals</u> [*sic*]. And if I can have any influence at the court of heaven you and your constitutional advisers will be guided by wisdom from above and divinely assisted in your difficult and important duties.

What I now desire to say is, that, in these times of <u>political traders</u>, stock jobbers, and panic makers, as well as numerous desperados and traitors both north and south, I fear your precious and valuable life <u>is in danger</u>. And it may be possible that many in <u>secret associations</u> have bound themselves by an oath, as in the case of St. Paul, to take your life

The midnight or noonday assassin may be in wait for you.

There may be corrupt men who would be willing destroy many lives to reach your plate with poison. "<u>Watch</u>."

I hope the Lord will make you immortal until the 5th of March 1865 as he did George Washington until <u>his</u> work was done.

I am dear sir with much respect and sincere esteem

your <u>friend</u>
John F. Wright

Hon A. Lincoln
Springfield Ill

Mr. L. may recognize my name as the same person who wrote him last Septr to whom he kindly replied

---

There is no record of replies to either of Wright's letters—this warning or the letter he had written the previous September. (Letter, The Lincoln Museum, Fort Wayne, IN)

1861

Fearing Lincoln Will Be Poisoned

January 25th 1861
Washington Washington County Penna

Mr Lincoln

I take the liberty of sending a few lines to you with my respects to you and your familys welfare The time has arrived that every good Citizen should look out for himself   It is a duty incumbent on us   You sir are on the eve of being placed in a very important situation before the American people as President of the United States   Now sir what i wish to say that a great many of our friends are fearful you will not receive fair play with respect to your Occupying the Presidential Chair during your term of office   Now sir we the people have not had a Republican officer to occupy that post for several years [actually, Lincoln was the first Republican to be elected president—Ed.] General [William Henry] Harrison [a Whig—Ed.] livd but a Short time after he was Installd in office General [Zachary] Taylor [also a Whig—Ed.] livd but a short time after he took his seat   A great many wise heads believe he was not fairly dealt with after his arrival at Washington City   When he passed through our town he was a hearty robust man for his age with a florid complexion

You Sir be careful at the Kings table what meat and drink you take there might be poison in the ink   Your life and health are precious   Sir I hope you will form a Cabinet around you that will be an ornament to you and your country of men Fearing God and hating covetousness excuse the liberty i have taken it is for your welfare

I am Sir with sentiments of respect your Humble Servant
David Wylie

For generations some Americans believed that President Taylor had been poisoned. There is no record of a reply to this dire warning that the same fate might await Lincoln when he reached Washington. (Letter, The Lincoln Museum, Fort Wayne, IN)

1861

"God Help Old Abe"

Peoria [Illinois,] Feb 3 1861.

To Abraham Lincoln

When I read over from time to time your views as to the policy our Government should pursue in reference to slavery, I say God help Old Abe. Coming generations will bless you and say a prouder inheritance could not be left to your children. I write this because [Congressman William] Kellogg proposed resolutions looking to the amendment of the Constitution perpetuating the Slave Power. Lincoln dont fear to stand straight up to this line of duty of conscience; to Back down will disgrace us demoralize the party and set back the sun of freedom. Better die right here. I will die with you if necessary, but the cause is ruined if we take counsel of our fears. I shall not trouble you much. My heart is in the cause & you are its representative. Hold the banner aloft it will at last triumph. No offensive movement is required. You have been fairly elected. When inaugurated it will be time enough to concede. But Abe be president untramelled or die with your fame unclouded. Old Abe Good bye

H. Grove

Henry Grove was an ardent Republican who had supported Lincoln for the Senate in 1854, declaring himself to be "pretty sure for Abe" as long as the candidate's views continued "to harmonize with mine." Illinois Congressman Kellogg, to whom Grove referred, was a member of the House Committee of Thirty-Three, formed to seek a compromise solution to the secession crisis before Lincoln's inauguration. One of its proposals was a constitutional amendment guaranteeing no interference with slavery in existing slave states. This is one of the many last-minute letters the president-elect received from new admirers and old friends during his final days in Springfield. They brought a dizzying array of contradictory advice, caution, encouragement, and warning. (Letter, The Lincoln Museum, Fort Wayne, IN; Ed. note, Grove to Lincoln, November 1854)

1861

Proposals for Editing His Inaugural
Address—Completely Ignored or Dramatically Improved

Suggestions for a closing paragraph

[February 1861]

However unusual it may be at such a time to speak of sections or to sections, yet in view of the misconception & agitations which have strained the ties of brotherhood so far, I hope it will not be deemed a departure from propriety, whatever it may be from custom, to say that if in the criminations and misconstructions which too often imbue our political contests, any man south of the capital has been led to believe that I regard with a less friendly eye, his rights, his interests or his domestic safety and happiness, or those of his State, than I do those of any other portion of my country or that I would invade or disturb any legal right or domestic institution in the South, he mistakes both my principles and feelings, and does not know me. I aspire to come in the spirit, however far below the ability and the wisdom, of Washington, of Madison, of Jackson and of Clay. In that spirit I here declare that in my administration I shall know no rule but the Constitution, no guide but the laws, and no sentiment but that of equal devotion to my whole country, east, west, north and south.

[William H. Seward]

———————

When President-Elect Lincoln arrived in Washington, he had the draft of his Inaugural Address set in type and gave a newly printed copy to the man he had appointed secretary of state, William H. Seward, inviting his comments. Seward obliged by submitting the above conciliatory insert, which Lincoln chose to ignore. The original memorandum, in the handwriting of Seward's son and private secretary, Frederick Seward, was preserved in Lincoln's papers, as was a subsequent proposal from Seward for a dramatic closing paragraph. This time Lincoln accepted his advisor's suggestions but improved them markedly. Following is Seward's draft language, then the edited peroration Lincoln actually used for his inaugural. The subtle changes Lincoln imposed demonstrate his remarkable feel for dramatic language and his ability to write and rewrite in his own, original voice. By altering Seward's well-crafted peroration, Lincoln turned a very good closing paragraph into something sublime and unforgettable.

———————

———————
1861
———————

6

I close. We are not we must not be aliens or enemies but fellow country-men and brethren. Although passion has strained our bonds of affection too hardly they must not, I am sure they will not be broken. The mystic chords which proceeding from so many battle fields and so many pa-triot graves pass through all the hearts and all the hearths in this broad continent of ours will yet again harmonize in their ancient music when breathed upon by the guardian angel of the nation.

[Lincoln re-write of Seward draft]

I am loth [sic] to close. We are not enemies, but friends. We must not be enemies. Though passion may have strained, it must not break our bonds of affection. The mystic chords of memory, stretching from every battle-field, and patriot grave, to every living heart and hearthstone, all over this broad land, will yet swell the chorus of the Union, when again touched, as surely they will be, by the better angels of our nature. (See Roy P. Basler et al., eds., *The Collected Works of Abraham Lincoln*, 9 vols. [New Brunswick, NJ: Rutgers University Press, 1953–55], IV: 261–62; [hereafter all volumes cited as *Coll. Works*]; Lincoln's final address, *Coll. Works* IV: 271)

Near-Unanimous Approval for the Inaugural

16 Wall St. New York
March 5th 1861

His Excellency Abraham Lincoln

My Dear Sir,

I read your Inaugural approving every argument it contains, and my heart responded "Amen" to every patriotic sentiment therein ex-pressed—I took it home and read it to my wife, and she seemed de-lighted with it—This morning I called on a Breckenridge Democrat and put the question "How do you like the Inaugural?" "First rate, It is short and full of pith, was the reply"— I then called on a "Silver Gray" [a supporter of the defunct Whig Party—Ed.] friend and asked him. "How do you like the Inaugural"? ["]Splendid It could not be bettered" he answered.

1861

I then stepped into the office of a staunch Douglass [*sic*] man and inquired "How do you like the Inaugural?" "All right & if Mr Lincoln will stand firm to his position I am with him heart and hand" was his answer— It being about lunch time I dropped into the restaurant of the black man across the street and says, "Well Mr Ray how do you like the Inaugural["] "I think he has hit the nail on the head, our folks will all stand by him" said he— Lastly I called on a stock broker and asked the same question, and added "how does the Inaugural effect the stock market" "We are afraid there is too much fight in it, the market is feverish" was his answer— From these indications I think the honest portion of the American people are with you and will hold themselves subject to your direction whether it be storm or sunshine that may follow

I am very Respectfully

Your Obedient & Humble Servant,
H. D. Faulkner

This was one of the very first letters Abraham Lincoln received as president of the United States. It brought the heartening news that New York supporters of two of his recent rivals for the presidency—Democrats John C. Breckinridge and Stephen A. Douglas—were now voicing approval for the Inaugural Address he had delivered the day before. But no reply to the ringing endorsement is known. The letter was filed with the notation: "H. D. Faulkner 1861 New York Political."

Job Candidate from Former President

Buffalo, March 8, 1861.

His Excellency Abraham Lincoln

Sir,

The bearer, E. C. Sprague, Esq. visits Washington on business and has requested me to give him a letter of introduction to your Excellency which I do with great pleasure, as I have known Mr. Sprague from his childhood, and have a very high regard for him as a gentleman of intelligence and high moral character.

He studied law in my office and is now a partner of my son, and occupies a high rank in his profession, and I may add (without being suspected of partisanship) that he is a devoted Republican.

1861

I am Respectfully & Truly yours
Millard Fillmore

There is no record of a reply to this letter from ex-president Fillmore, but it is likely that Lincoln forwarded his recommendation to one of the federal departments. The evidence for this supposition is the Fillmore letter itself; it was not retained in the Lincoln Papers. It is owned today by The Lincoln Museum in Fort Wayne, IN, whose collection of letters to Lincoln comes principally from the scattered archives of the various federal departments.

A "Dear Old Friend" Asks a Judgeship

Danville Ills March 12th 1861

Hon A. Lincoln

My Dear old Friend I have not had the pleasure of seeing you since your nomination to the position you now so Honorably Fill; I have Been Rather unfortunate in my attempts to see you. I was at Springfield on the memorable 8th of August Last, when the whole world and his wife was there [thousands of supporters marched past Lincoln's home on August 8, 1860—Ed.]. But I was taken sick on the way Down & was unable to be out of my room on the 8th and I was again sick when you passed through our place on your way to Washington [President-Elect Lincoln had spoken briefly at Danville on February 11—Ed.]. I am truly Rejoiced to see that you have taken the stand you have upon the great questions that now agitate the country: there are a great many things that I would Like to say But I will not Bore you with a Long Communication for I see by the papers that you have an abundance in that Direction. I will come at once to the point & you Excuse me for addressing you plainly & as I would have some years ago. you are Doubtless aware that I have always been an uncompromising <u>Lincoln</u> man & Shall undoubtedly Remain so. Satisfied that I Shall have no Reason to be otherwise, whether you are a Peters man in this particular or not. I have Some Desire to Emigrate west and I therefore ask of you to give me an <u>associate Judge Ship</u> in one of the new Territories in which a Territorial Government has Been Recently Established. you are acquainted with me & have Been for Twenty years & have Been a citizen of Illinois for Twentyfive years and if in your kindness & goodfeeling to me you can

---

1861

give me Such an appointment it will help me verry much & will be greatfully Received & you Shall never have any cause of Regret so far as I am concerned. I do not wish to beg you But now my Dear old Friend you can now help me in time of need & will you not Do So. I have been Investigating the Duties to some Extent & I am Satisfied that I can Discharge the Duties & that there will be no cause for Dissatisfaction on this point. I Do not hold that Because a Lot of men assembling at Washington Besieging the president one for the other for office, Entitle them to precedence over other men who Stay at home attending to their Business, & who present their claims the president being acquainted with them. in this light I therefore present my claim & Leave the matter with you Relying on your ability to Decide for yourself, without setting on a host of papers. I can present a host of politicians if necessary from this & various other parts of the State & will take a pleasure in Doing so if necessary & Dont Deem it necessary to say anything more on the Subject Relying on your kind Feelings towards me I leave the matter in your hands & believe me your Friend & well wisher for your health & prosperity in your present position.

Joseph Peters

There is no record of a reply to, or an appointment for, Peters. (Letter, courtesy of William W. Layton, Washington, D.C.)

Greetings from an Indiana "Cousin"

Indianapolis Ind.
March 28 1861

Mr. Lincoln

Dear Cousin,

You will doubtless be surprised, when you glance at the signature of this letter. But when I tell you I dont want office, and am a democrat, you will feel encouraged to read what I may write. I had thought to defer my writing 'till some future day, but then concluded that a <u>disinterested</u> letter among so many office begging ones, would relieve the monotony, and be more acceptable now than in the future. I called on you when at

Indianapolis (Lincoln passed through that city en route to his inauguration on February 11 and 12—Ed.), but the crowd was so great, I merely said, cousin Abram, and passed on. You will think, another relation because I am President!! Well your thoughts will be precisely correct in this case. For had I not thought that it was quite an honor to be even distantly related to the highest Executive Officer in the U.S. I should not have gone to the trouble of writing.

I am not very good at tracing out relationships, but if I read grandfather Shaver's letter correctly, he said his mother and your grand mother were sisters. Their names were Cassner. With the exception of my father's family, all my relatives live in Virginia. Grandfather Shaver is the only cousin by the name of Shaver that you have. He is 77 years of age. Were you to see him you would not be at all ashamed of him as a relative—only his politics. His grand-daughter is rather an ordinary personage, but with vanity enough to think Cousin Abram will answer her letter.

I am connected with our Blind Inst. and have been for six years. There is a political jurisdiction exercised over all our benevolent institutions; and as I was placed here by democratic directors, I am informed I will be removed by the opposing power.

I spend my summers in Va. I shall with or without an invitation call and see you when I pass through Washington.

I hope in answer to this, to receive a letter written by yourself—recollect by your own self.

Accept my best wishes for your wisdom in governing the distracted politicians, and believe me

E. Wertha Bowman

P.S. Present my regards to Mrs. Lincoln & family.

E.W.B.

Mrs. Bowman may have been distantly related to Lincoln, but her father's recollections were incorrect. Lincoln's grandmothers were Lucy Shipley Hanks (maternal) and Bathsheba Herring (paternal). Although much confusion reigned during the president's lifetime, and in most of the years since, concerning his ancestry, the name Cassner has never figured in the story. (Ed. note, Louis A. Warren, *Lincoln's Youth: Indiana Years[,] Seven to Twenty-one[,] 1816–1830* [New York: Appleton, Century, Crofts, 1959], 7)

1861

Slippers from a Little Girl, Prayers and Advice from Her Father

Chillocothe Ohio April 2nd 1861

Hon. Abraham Lincoln
President of the U.S.

Dear Sir

I have this day Sent to you per the Adams Express Co one Box inclosed you will find one pair of Slippers worked by my Little Daughter as a present for you from her—you will also find a few lines inclosed in Box Well now in regard our National trubls=I Sometimes think we are giving them Traitors too much time they are working with a will to do and in a Short time will I fear be the Strongest Government of the two—though I Still hope that you may Be able to restore the Government   But if the Country is Lost the Democratic Party must bare the blame for it is them that made all this truble we know you have a hard time of it and I often think of you in those trublesome times and Pray God that he may give you Wisdom and Strenght [*sic*] to guide the Ship of State into the harber of Safty— I am but a poor humble Mechanic and Seek no office But I Love my Country and would Die in its Defence though I must not intrude on your time with a Long Letter will you please let me know if you receive the package and oblige
Yours truly
S. Shreckengaust

To A. Lincoln
President U.S.

Lincoln may well have received little Miss Shreckengaust's hand-made slippers and obliged with an acknowledgment, but if so, the family never brought it to light. A secretary endorsed this "poor humble" correspondent's letter: "Slippers/1861."

1861

Handwriting Expert Wants Sample

New York April 3. 1861.

Sir

I take the liberty of presenting the request of a Lady in Ireland for a small specimen of your handwriting.

She is a worthy person, who supports a large school from an income derived from giving delineations of character from hand writing.

Pray pardon the liberty I take in this trespass upon your time.

Very Truly Yours

A. Baird

His Excellency S. Lincoln.—&c &c &c

There is no surviving record of a reply, but Lincoln probably complied with the request. He sent autographs to countless admirers over the next four years.

Offering the White House a Flag

Brooklyn May 9th. 1861.

Respected Sir,

It is with feelings of sadness, I have just noticed in a papers, that Our Flag, floats not upon, or over Our Presidents Mansion. This should not be, it shall not be any longer, if you will allow me the privilege, the honor, the glory, of presenting one that will be suitable and appropriate for the place. I most respectfully ask your permission and consent to furnish one, as a slight expression of my feelings and sympathies for the honor and welfare of our country in this her hour of trial and trouble. If you will permit me that privilege, I will forward one immediately, upon hearing from you what sised one will be proper, for the place you intend to hoist it. Please forward me a few lines, to the care of Messrs. Wm. C. Bryant & Co. New York Evening Post. N.Y.

I remain with great respect

Yours most truly

Robert G. Thursby

1861

No reply is known, but period descriptions and sketches certainly indicate that the White House very soon boasted its own American flag.

Temperance Movement Wants His Name

Illinois Band of Hope & Union
Box 1844 Chicago, Ill.
13 May 1861.

To the Right Honble Abraham Lincoln
President. United States;

At this time when politics and the various vicissitudes that attend war possess your attention the only excuse that we can offer for addressing you is that we too are about to Commence a War against an enemy as hateful as that which has arisen against us in the South.

We are about to form in Chicago a Band of Hope & Union, an organization for the enrolment of the young under the standard of Total Abstinence, to teach them the outside of the public house is the best side and knowing your principles and the potency of a great and good name, we earnestly and respectfully solicit yours, as the Patron of our Temperance Union.

We do this because we feel that it is due to you and because we know it will be a powerful assistance in our endeavors to do good.

We do not desire to trouble you with a long petition but if you will kindly give us permission to head our list with your name, a name that we associate with all that is good & noble.

We will ever pray that the God who said "Suffer the little Children to Come unto me" will throw around your head a halo of glory and victory here and a Crown of glory hereafter an inheritance uncorruptible and that faceth not away.

Your <u>devoted</u> and obliged Servts.

Frederic Hudson
George Charles Betts

We take the liberty of enclosing addressed envelope

The letter was filed away on May 13, and no record of a reply was indicated. Lincoln had always been interested in, but not obsessed with, the temperance movement, urging in a hometown lecture back on Washington's Birthday in

1861

1842 that chronic imbibers should instead try drinking "the sorrow quenching draughts of perfect liberty." (Ed. note, *Coll. Works* I: 271-79)

A Good-Luck Piece as a Gift

Rochester, N.Y. May 16, 1861

President Lincoln

I hope you will pardon me for writing a few lines to you it is not to your injury but I trust for your good. I have thought of it for some time but being a poor old woman I feared you would not notice it I am an old woman in my 72 year. I have seen war before and had a husband two years in the War 1812 on board of the President a frigate and when she was taken by those five English ships the Barrett masters mate who was directing the steersman was shot the first broad side my husband was called to take his place and stood four hours and a half a mark to shoot at and such as I send you in this letter to wear about your person is such as I had my husband wear about him to protect him from danger as he was not wounded in the least during the action   I am perfectly satisfied it is a proof against fire and water and I have great faith to believe it will be a great protection to you in the dangerous situation in which you are placed it is a thing not often found I have sent you the Largest part of what I had and if you should think it not worth noticing please return it to me again   That with the long ribbon is for you to wear and the other piece is to put in the Capitol to protect that for I have papers in that Capitol which Mr. Ely took there and never returned and I should be sorry to lose them. My husband died in Charleston in the spring 1813 and his remains there reposed in peace ever since but it troubles me much to think his grave is amongst such a set of rebelous traitors to this country. If you dont think this worth retaining please return it to me as I value it very highly. I should not have taken the trouble if it had not been from a sincere wish that you might overcome your enemies.

Mrs. Sarah Post

A White House clerk noted on the top of this letter: "Mrs. Sarah Post sends two charms to the President, to assure him against being shot." If an acknowledgement was sent for this heartfelt good-luck offering, it has never been located.

1861

Prince of the Church Seeks Patronage

New York June 17, 1861

His Excellency Abraham Lincoln, President of the U.S.

Mr. President:

A gentleman whom I have known for many years, John B. Murray Esq. writes to me that he is an applicant for some office or position at the disposal of the Government, but the position itself he does not particularly describe.

Mr. Murray is a highly respectable man. He has built up for himself a reputation which, in all the relations of life, is unblemished. He is industrious, sober, devoted to his business, and in my opinion, there are few to be found better qualified to discharge any trust that may be confided to him with honor to himself and advantage to his country.

It will be very agreeable to me if Mr. Murray should be selected by Your Excellency for the post to which he aspires.

I have the honor to remain with profound respect,

Your most Obedt. Serv.
John Abp. of New York

Lincoln is not known to have replied to this letter from Archbishop John J. Hughes. Several months later, however, he did write the archbishop to ask him to recommend candidates to serve as Catholic chaplains in army hospitals—"a sort of quasi appointment," Lincoln made clear, since, he conceded, "I find no law authorizing the appointment of Chaplains for our hospitals." Murray was applying for the position of surveyor of the Port of New York. (Ed. note and reply, *Coll. Works* IV: 359)

You Are "Slaughtering Your Friends"

Boston, Mass. 20 June 1861

Hon. A. Lincoln,

Sir.

I dont know as you will see this letter, or that it will do any good if you should, as it only seems to be necessary for Col. Baker to recommend a man, to secure his appointment by you. I have just learned that one Matlock is likely to be Receiver of the Land office in Oregon City, and as when I go home Republicans will ask why you were not told the truth about him and saved from a grievous blunder, I intend to be able to say that <u>I am clear of even the responsibility of Silence</u>.

Matlock is ignorant, discourteous and very unpopular—knowing no more of the duties of the office, than a bear does of arithmetic. He is too old to learn any thing and too bigoted and obstinate, if he were younger. If he is appointed, we shall lose a hundred votes in the county, when appointments ought to make us stronger.

Hon. George Abernathy, first Governor of the Territory is an applicant for the same office—he is intelligent, competent, influential and a sound and true Republican: his success would please men of all parties—but alas—he was not <u>a Baker man</u>—and so stupidity is pushed into a place which wisdom and good sense ought to fill.

My duty is done—you will appoint whom you please, but I assure you that the time will speedily come when you will regret so much reliance upon Bakers statements as to appointments in Oregon and California. While rewarding his tools, you are <u>slaughtering</u> your friends and your party on the Pacific Coast. We should have been glad to boast of your judicious and patriotic selection, but if we say any thing we can only apologise and excuse you for being imposed upon by one who used you for his own purposes.

Respectfully yours
Amory Holbrook of Oregon

Holbrook, an Oregon state legislator who had first met Lincoln in 1848 in Massachusetts, wrote this frank warning a week too late. On June 13, Lincoln had forwarded to the secretary of the interior a list of Oregon Senator Edward D. Baker's recommended appointments, with the instructions: "Please make out and send me Commissions according to it." (*Coll. Works* IV: 406–7.) The roster included the name of William T. Matlock for receiver at Oregon City. Baker's influence with Lincoln was far greater than Holbrook's. He had been closely associated with Lincoln years before in Illinois, and though the two did not always agree on issues, their relationship was sealed when the Lincolns named their second son, Eddie, in his honor.

1861

A "Widowed Mother Prayer"

President U States
Hon A. Lincoln

Dear Sir

Will you excuse my daring to address, you, and enclosing this petition for my eldest son, for, your kind consideration   It will tell you all I need, and allow me to say a few words. I know you will listen to them for you have a kind <u>heart</u>, and my story is a sad one. I am a widow left with only these two sons, who have left, me, to fight, for the good cause and I am proud to send them forth although they leave me desolate, and my heart broken, as they are all I had, for my support, and are my only hope in this world, but I have given them up, but trust in God's mercy to return them to me, some day. My eldest son is a first Lieut in the 15th Regiment and educated for the Army holds a permanent place in it my youngest son, is a Private Soldier in Gen Duryea's [no doubt General Abram Duryée—Ed.] 5th Regiment Advance Guards, now at Fort Monroe, he is a druggist by Profession and almost a Physcian he was my only stay because the youngest—and to have him perhaps forever taken away from me almost kills me, my health is extremely delicate and if he could only have a higher place, than a private in the Regiment, would make me feel better if he could assist in the Medical Staff in the Hospital, perhaps I am wild to ask such things but I know you can do ALL THINGS. As for my family I can refer to Gov Seward [now secretary of state—Ed.] who was an old friend of ours. And also a great man. I could refer, but it is useless. Dont dear Mr Lincoln refuse to listen to a Widowed Mother prayer. Will you look favorable upon this petition. Let me ask your forgiveness for trespassing but you will excuse a broken hearted woman—

Cornelia Ludlow Beckman

Hon A Lincoln
President U States.

No reply has come to light to this heartfelt plea for a son's army reassignment. The day the widow wrote this letter, Lincoln delivered a special Independence Day message to Congress, declaring—no doubt with citizens like Mrs. Beckman much in mind—"this is essentially a People's contest." (Ed. note, *Coll. Works* IV: 438)

Astral Warnings

Philada. July 5th 1861.

2 h 17 m PM.

To His Excellency,

President Lincoln,

Convinced of the earnest sincerity of your objects and desires, and the correct purposes of your heart, I write with the one solitary object of benefit to yourself, and the Country you represent, I wrote you a few days ago; the letter may have been too long and required too much time, let me assure you of its importance, For the present let me call your attention to the following.

Predictions Fulfilled.

From July Horscope, 10th, 1858.

REPORTERS FOR THE PRESS.—In the hands of Providence, you will ere long have the lead of bringing about the distribution of the evil Rulers of Philadelphia. Arm yourself for the contest, as it will be a fierce one.

1859 will commence the dawn of a new political era in the United States; and we boldly predict that 1860 will witness almost an entire new Congress at Washington. Enough for the present.

At the time the aboved [*sic*] was penned, your name was scarcely whispered, whilst every one deemed the Astrologer in error, Who would have thought, in 1858, of the clean sweep of 1859 and 1860? Let the Stars proclaim it!

Here is another from Horscope of August 1st. 1858.

SECRETARY COBB will have a harder time of it in counting Uncle Sam's money than any Secretary during the last 36 or 37 years. When he waits the office, the Treasury will be filled with borrowed hold and the country at war. [Cobb, a Georgia native, went south at the outset of the Civil War and became a Confederate major general—Ed.]

This requires no comment! The facts are patent.

1861

And still another from Horoscope Sept. 1. 1858. These were considered bold predictions in 1858, but the Stars said it, and events from that we read in the Stars aright.—

VOICE OF THE STARS,
FOR SEPTEMBER, 1858.

JAMES BUCHANAN and Stephen A. Douglas, both claim the 23d of April for their birth day. When "the blind leads the blind, both fall into the ditch;" so say the stars for 1860.

FILLMORE'S horoscope will be afflicted in 1860 and 61 . . .

Here is still another from the Horscope of the 1st September 1858.

So, of course, from August 1858 until the latter part of August, 1860, the prospective period for the next Presidential Election, there will be more caucusing by letter between Statesmen, and more violent, obstinate Cabinet disputes, internal warrings between chartered companies, and disorder in our Legislative Halls than can now be foreseen by the most observing politician.—It is Hague the Astrologer who is to explain the handwriting on the walls, printed by the Eternal when he incepted the universe.

Latter part of August, 1860, Saturn enters Virgo, the last of the northern signs, and he progresses tardily through, sometimes retrograde, and sometimes direct, to the middle of July 1863, when he enters the southern sign Libra, and when, too, the northerners must succumb to the south to an extent not now dreamed of, while the southern people become partially northernized in temperament, and victorious in a majority of their plans.

This prediction was penned before your name was dreamed of for President, and when any thing like the present state of affairs was considered altogether visionary. Confident in the Astral Science, and our ability to read and comprehend, we were willing [to] be laughed at, for the certain triumph to come. As past has been fulfilled to the letter, so will the balance. The voice of God proclaims it, through those instruments which constitute his Celestial Telegraph, to this sublunary sphere, through which we have Biblical proof he from everlasting communicates to man, his mind and will towards Creation.

Yours Respectfully
Thomas Hague
No. 525 Callowhill Street Philadelphia

Not surprisingly, Lincoln wrote no known reply to this bizarre offer of divine predictions—one of a surprisingly large number of lunatic letters that still survive in the Lincoln Papers. It is entirely possible that every so often, his clerks would allow such diatribes to reach the president to amuse him, perhaps to relieve him of the burdens he otherwise faced unrelentingly throughout his term.

A "Photograph" of a Founder

N. Y. Dobbs Ferry July 12. 1861

To the President of the U States
Washington

Dr Sir

Allow me to hope that you will accept the enclosed Photograph of my Father Alexander Hamilton. The likeness is a very good one, as a mark of my respect and regard for you. I have the honor to be With respect and regard

Your obt sv
James A. Hamilton

Photography was not invented until long after Alexander Hamilton's death. What James Hamilton sent was a carte-de-visite photograph of a Hamilton painting, published by Rintoul & Rockwood of New York. He inscribed it on the reverse: "Presented to Abrm. Lincoln/President of the U States/by James Hamilton." Lincoln filed it, along with the letter, in the envelope in which they were sent, endorsing it simply: "Likeness of Alex. Hamilton." The next month, James Hamilton wrote again, this time seeking a patronage appointment.

Raising Lincoln's "Spirits"

Private
Boston August 9/61

Mr President Lincoln

Dear Sir

I sent you a very long letter on spiritualism—if the subject is unpleasant to you I have no desire to annoy you, in the midst of your arduous duties, and I shall feel no mortification if this [is] returned to me unopen'd.

But if the matter is not offensive to you and you read it at your leisure & if you ever have such a moment I think you will be amply repaid for so doing.

Respectfully Yr. Obt. Sr

J. S. Hastings

If there was one constant among Lincoln's varied reactions to his correspondence, it was his distaste for long, long letters; he seldom read them, and occasionally chided their senders for burdening him with them. Thus it is not surprising that he did not reply to this letter, merely filing it under the heading: "Spiritual communications." The following year, Mary Lincoln became involved with spiritualists after the death of son Willie and was said to have held seances in the White House in an effort to contact him in the afterworld.

Wife Seeks Post for "Modest" Husband

Jay Homestead [Katonah, New York]

August 12, 1861

Dear Mr. Lincoln

I have such a modest husband he never will do anything for himself and I hope you will excuse the liberty I take without consulting him in writing directly to you about giving him the Austrian Mission. I am very sure you would have no better or truer man in any position and you will excuse his wife for saying it. Chief Justice [John] Jay was a model statesman and his grandson is very like him.

Believe me with great respect

Very Truly Yours

E. Jay

Eleanor F. Jay was the wife of John Jay, grandson of America's first chief justice. The younger Jay eventually won the coveted diplomatic post of minister to Austria-Hungary, but not until 1869, four years after Lincoln's death.

1861

A Displaced Kentuckian Seeks a Job

Paris, Kentucky
September 5th 1861.

Sir,

For the sin of having given my best support to your claims to the exalted position you occupy, and because of my persistent profession of uncompromising loyalty to the Government of the United States, and to your own admirable administration of it, I have been for the last five months, and am still, an exile from my home and family. My residence is in the city of Paducah in the first congressional district of the State, where, until the 6th day of May last, I was engaged in the practice of law. The accompanying letters will show, that I was appointed by the Republican Central Committee Elector for that district, during the presidential campaign—an office that was declined with regret. A victim now of the bitter prejudices engendered by the course that an honest judgment obliged me to pursue, I venture to ask the relief that may be found in Executive patronage. Testimonials of a character beyond impeachment can be furnished if needed; for the present I will merely refer to your old acquaintance, Judge G. S. Trimble of Paducah—late Union candidate for Congress in the first district of Kentucky. He is, already, I believe in Washington; and will, probably, mention my name to your Excellency.

Temporarily sojourning here, I hope to receive a favorable response to this application at this place; remaining, with assurances of highest esteem

Your Excellency's humble servant
F. M. Murray
Paris, Kentucky

Tp Hon. Abraham Lincoln
President of the United States/Washington D.C.

Judge Trimble sent a recommendation for Murray on October 6, on the back of which Lincoln wrote: "Whenever a Paymaster-Quarter-Master or Commissary, can be appointed for Paducah, Ky Mr. Murray ought to be the man." But there is no record that the candidate was ever named to such a post, the president's recommendation notwithstanding.

1861

Proposing a Steam Gun
to Protect Coastal Cities

[Late 1861]

To His Excellency Abraham Lincoln, President of the United States, and Hon. Simon Cameron, Secretary of War.

The defence of the country through every appliance of modern science and skill is of such paramount importance at the present time that we beg leave to ask your attention to Messrs. Perkins' invention of the Steam Gun, as presented in the brief description brought from London by Mr. Pliny Miles. The statement of the results of the trial of their last gun of moderate size with a rifled barrel and super heated steam, together with the illustrative facts and arguments adduced of its vast power and great utility if constructed on a large scale, seem to us to justify the very moderate expenditure required ($5,000) for the construction of a twelve pounder gun with every modern improvement. If the results of Messrs. Perkins' last experiments are correctly given there seems no reason to doubt that an armament of steam ordnance placed in forts at the entrance of harbors like New York, Boston, and Philadelphia would render these otherwise exposed sea coast cities utterly impregnable against any naval force that could be brought against them by all the naval powers of the world. We would therefore respectfully ask that you give such attention to the Perkins' Steam Gun as would seem to be justified by the statement of the inventors, and as just and reasonable towards an invention that already occupies a prominent place in the history of American inventive genius.

Abram Wakeman [et al]

Altogether, thirty-eight like-minded citizens joined Wakeman, the U.S. postmaster for New York City, in signing this letter. Among the petitioners was the Massachusetts poet, William Cullen Bryant. No reply to the suggestion of a steam-gun defense for Atlantic coast ports has been uncovered. (Letter, Ordnance files, National Archives)

1861

Illinois Foe Seeks Patronage Job

Washington
Sept. 5, 1861

His Excellency A. Lincoln
President U.S.

Sir,

By your permission I address you this note to which you promised to respond.

You will recollect that I desire to obtain the position of Pay Master in the Army. I feel competent to perform the duties of that office entirely to your satisfaction and will be much gratified to receive the appointment. But if there should be obstacles in the way I shall feel grateful for whatever.

I am the more emboldened to thus approach you from the fact that I met with no favors from the last administration, and from our long and favorable acquaintance, and fully rely upon your kindness & friendship for a favorable consideration of my request.

I am very respectfully

Your obdt Servt.
William G. Flood

Lincoln could hardly honor all the job requests he had from fellow Republicans, much less those from Democrats. William Flood of Illinois was a longtime supporter of Lincoln's arch-rival in politics, Stephen A. Douglas. But Lincoln evidently had a soft spot for Flood. More than twenty years earlier, when both men were serving in the Illinois general assembly, Lincoln balked when his fellow Whigs introduced a resolution barring legislators from holding "lucrative" federal or state offices while serving in the legislature. Lincoln liked the idea in principle, but not the fact that it was timed to prevent Flood from assuming the Quincy Land Office. Now Flood was seeking Lincoln's help again. Douglas himself had died three months earlier after campaigning tirelessly to prevent disunion, and Lincoln must have felt more nostalgic than usual about the old days in his home state. The day after receiving this letter, Lincoln endorsed it to the secretary of war.

[To Secretary of War Simon Cameron]

The writer of the within is a good Unionman though not a Republican. He was with me in the Ills. Legislature more than 25 years ago. He is a reliable man, and if there were a place for him he would fill it well.

Sep. 6, 1861   A. Lincoln

A record of Flood's appointment has not been located, but there is no reason to believe that he was not awarded a job of some kind. Flood letter to Lincoln, Illinois State Historical Library; Ed. note, *Coll. Works* I: 138)

Desperate for a Presidential Appointment

Baltimore September 21. 1861

To His Excellency Abraham Lincoln,
President of the United States

My Dear Sir,

When I wrote to you ere the election, you replied I was entirely too early. Since you have become the Chief Magistrate of the Nation, you refer me to the heads of Departments. I have tried the different Departments, their reply is, there is no vacancy except for those already pledged to be provided for.

As all offices are filled directly or indirectly by the Executive, I appeal to you again, to know whether you would be kind enough to give me the office of Messenger, or even the lowest office I would accept. I voted for you, in consequence I am not allowed to see my parents who reside in Virga. Please let me hear from you, and for <u>God</u> sake do not disappoint me.

Yours truly
Geo. A. Wenck

There is no record of a reply to this desperate plea. Lincoln did not usually react favorably when correspondents demanded patronage so blatantly.

Old Friend Wants a Quartermaster Named

[Near September 23, 1861]

To His Excellency
The President of the United States

Sir

I will be personally very much obliged by the appointment of Francis G. Young as Brigade Quarter Master.

He has performed the duties of the office for sometime past and is well qualified.

Very respectfully
E. D. Baker

British-born, Illinois-raised Colonel Edward Dickinson Baker was a longtime friend of the Lincolns; they had named their second son, Edward Baker Lincoln, in his honor. Not surprisingly, Lincoln obliged Baker by forwarding his request to Secretary of War Simon Cameron on September 23 with the following endorsement: "If consistent with the public interest, let the appointment be made." Young became a captain in Baker's famous California regiment. The colonel was killed at the Battle of Ball's Bluff on October 21—a loss deeply felt by all the Lincolns, inspiring middle son Willie to write and publish a tribute in verse. In a tragic irony, the man whom Baker had recommended to Lincoln, Captain Young, was suspected of failing to do his duty to prevent Baker's death and was court-martialed. Lincoln intervened in the case with the following letter to the commanding general of the Army of the Potomac.

Executive Mansion. Dec. 6. 1861

Majr. Genl. McClellan:

My dear Sir:

Capt. Francis G. Young, of the California regiment (Col. Baker's) is in some difficuly—I do not precisely understand what. I believe you know I was unfavorably impressed towards him because of apparently contradictory accounts he gave me of some matters at the battle of Ball's Bluff. At length he has brought me the paper which accompanies this, showing, I think, that he is entitled to respectful consideration. As you see, it is signed by several senators and representatives, as well as other well known and respectable gentlemen. I attach considerable consequence to

---

1861

the name of Lt. Col. [Alexander] Shaler, late Major Shaler of the New-York 7th [the number of the regiment was added later in pencil—Ed.]. These things and his late connection with Col. Baker, induce me to ask you if, consistently with the public service, the <u>past</u> whatever it is, can not be waived, and he be placed in service, and given another chance?

Yours truly
A. Lincoln

McClellan did not offer another chance to Captain Young, since he did not get to see Lincoln's letter. When Young first read it, he was so disappointed that he wrote to Lincoln on December 7 to say he would not hand it to the general. "You have misunderstood my case & . . . unintentionally done me injustice," Young protested. "I did not know that you thought me untruthful." A court-martial subsequently convicted Young of leaving camp without permission, and McClellan ordered him dismissed from the service on January 2, 1862. As late as April 11, 1864, Lincoln was again looking into the case, writing to the Judge Advocate General to say: "What I want is the record of the trial" (*Coll. Works* VII: 294). There is no indication that the verdict was overturned or that Young was welcomed back into the service. The death of the man who had recommended him to President Lincoln effectively ended his military career. (Baker letter to Lincoln, Illinois State Historical Library; Ed. note, *Journal of the Abraham Lincoln Association* 17 [Winter 1996]: 50; Lincoln's reply, *Coll. Works* V: 60)

A Slain Hero's Comrades Send His Flag

Washington D.C. Oct 6th 1861

To His Excellency Abraham Lincoln

We the former members of <u>Ellsworth's Chicago Zouaves</u>, being desirous of presenting our Stand of Champion Colors as a memento to us of <u>our lamented Colonel</u>.

We would most respectfully solicit permission to place these at your disposal.

Most Respectfully
Your Obt. Servants
Capt. J. G. True, <u>Secy</u>
Leit Chas H. Hosmer, U.S.A.
Major Frank F. Yates

1861

Colonel Elmer Ephraim Ellsworth, a young friend of the Lincoln family, had been killed at Alexandria, Virginia on May 21, after ripping down an offending Confederate flag from a local hotel. As the first Union officer to die in the Civil War, he was widely mourned by northerners, and honored by poets and artists alike. A bereaved Lincoln gave him a White House funeral and sent his parents a touching condolence letter. The flag refered to here was once flown by Ellsworth when he commanded the U.S. Zouave Cadets of Chicago before the war. Although no acknowledgment of this memento has been located, Lincoln most likely accepted it with gratitude.

Nine Choices for Spoils

[October 10, 1861]

A List of Offices
Any One of which I shall be very glad to accept.

1.—Secretary of the Territory of Nebraska.
2.—Consulship of Glasgow, Scotland
3.—Congressional Librarian.
4.—Indian Agency at Omaha, Nebraska
5.—Commissioner of Public Buildings, Washington
6.—Assistant Congressional Librarian
7.—Captain of the Capitol Police
8.—Any $2,000 a year Consulship in Scotland, England, or Ireland.
9.—A Clerkship in Washington—3rd or 4th Class preferred

B. J. F. Hanna
Alton, Illinois.

Among the innumerable requests for jobs Lincoln received in the early months of his administration, few were as thorough as this list of ever-declining expectations from a citizen of his home state. There is no record of a reply.

1861

A Weapon to Set Man and Beast Afire

Elmira [New York] Oct 11th 1861

Abraham Lincoln
President of the U.S.

Dear Sir:

I have got up an Explosive Shell that I am desirous might be used in our army   I think it novel and Surley it is Verry Simple in Construction and it is my opinion as well as the opinion of all who have Examined its principles that it would prove very destructive to life and property   I use Small Magazine of Powder in the Cinter of the Shell and filling the balance of the Shell with Explosive fluids using the Same kind of fuse that are now used in order to Set fire to the powder at the moment the Shell Strikes or explode[s] at a Certain distance the powder taking fire in the magazine in the Shell and being Surrounded by explosive fluid the fluid takes fire at the Same time the Shell explodes and producing a Complete blaze of liquid fire and Setting on fire man & beast and anything Else that it Comes in Contact with   I have tried it using a small Shell filled with one quart of fluids most of it Camphine powder magazine one and a half by three inches   The Shell burst Complete Setting the fluid on fire and it was one blaze of fire for 20 feet around the Shell when it burst Setting all on fire that Came in Contact with it

I also send a Sketch of a double Cannon for throwing Chain Shot this has been tried and it worked well on a Small Scale this Cannon was executed and Patented to William M. Jeffers and myself on the 21st day of June 1859 the model being in the Patent office at Washington where it may be seen all Scientific men that have examined it think it the most destructive gun ever invented We should have had a Cannon of this kind made at our own Expense if we had the means to do so if the Government will make a gun on this plan and try it we will be glad to give them the Right for this invention for this war to difeit the Rebels   I hope that you will answer this letter that I may know what you think of the Shell and double Cannon for Chain Shot

Truly Yours
W. L. Gibson

Lincoln began receiving proposals for new weaponry almost as soon as he took office as president. Gibson's letter, one of many that flooded the White House in 1861, was referred to the Ordnance Department. Lincoln seldom replied personally to such unsolicited suggestions. (Letter, Ordnance Files, National Archives)

His Old Hero's Son Seeks Patronage

Washington City Octr 17th 1861

Hon A. Lincoln

My dear Sir

In the interview which I had the pleasure of holding with you on yesterday evening, I took the liberty of requesting you to make appointments of two Paymasters in the Army in Kentucky, viz. that of Hiram Shaw of Lexington Ky and William Venon Wolfe of Louisville Ky.

I herewith enclose several letters which are testimonials of the fitness of Mr. Shaw for the position. As to the qualifications of Mr. Wolfe, I, myself bear willing testimony. Both the gentlemen are possessed of every requisite to fit them for the offices which I ask for them at your hands.

It would afford me the highest gratification to know that I had been instrumental in promoting both the public interest and the wishes of those gentlemen in securing for them those appointments. I have the honor to be

Yr friend & obt Servt.
Thos. H. Clay

P.S. Should you not find it compatible with the public interest, to appoint two Paymasters, I would ask for Mr. Wolfe the office of Captain of the regular army, he being well qualified to discharge the duties.

Lincoln wrote the following endorsement on the back of this appeal from the son of Henry Clay, the man he once referred to as his political "*beau ideal*": "For the sake of Kentucky and the memory of Henry Clay I would like these appointments to be made as soon as practicable. A. L." (*Coll. Works* IV: 557–58). Research has yielded no record of a paymaster's appointment for either man, although Wolfe did become a first lieutenant in the Kentucky Infantry. Thomas H. Clay ultimately fared better for himself. Lincoln named him minister to Nicaragua the following year. (Ed. note, *Coll. Works* III: 29)

1861

A Cannon to Destroy Whole Battalions

Oct 24th, 1861

To his Excellency Abraham Lincoln
President of the United States
and to the Hon Simon Cameron
Secretary of War

Gentlemen:

I beg leave respectfully to inform you that I have invented a cannon which will destroy a whole battalion at a single shot, and in naval warfare it cannot fall to cripple the largest ship on the first discharge. As you will easily perceive by the accompanying drawing and description which I herewith send you, I have tested the gun by a small model. Should the War Department think proper to adopt this gun I will proceed immediately to Washington and exhibit the working model before you. With great respect I have the honor to be Gentlemen your most obedient servant

John D'Arcy
San Francisco

Would-be inventor D'Arcy enclosed a drawing of his proposed twin barrel gun. Letter and drawing alike we referred to the Ordnance Bureau, which took no further known action on his idea. (Letter, Ordnance Files, National Archives)

Imprisoned Pirate Seeks Freedom

New York City Prison
Cell No. 110, 3d Tier, Nov. 12, 1861.

Hon. Abraham Lincoln.
President United States of America:

Sir,—

I, J. P. N. Calvo, a South Carolina Secessionist and Privateersman, take the liberty of expressing myself freely to you in regard to the im-

---

1861

prisonment of the Privateersmen in the above named place, however feeble and incorrectly written it may appear. We are not Pirates, and it is a sin and a shame that an intelligent Government should tolerate such an idea and have us entombed in damp Cells, eight by six feet, with food only fit for hogs. (I here enumerate a few of the meals allowed us: some mornings we have mush and something looks like molasses, but taste and smells quite different—when mixed together would make any body vomit; other mornings we have coffee sweetened with this molasses, also a couple pieces of bread a week old; the same at dinner, except occasionally we have meat that a dog refused to touch the other day when I was good enough to offer it to him. We have two meals a day of such stuff.) You can no more make us out Pirates than you and the Army Prisoners of the Confederate States, or those of the Federal Navy and Federal Army, or the Privateersmen and Army of America when she was in her infancy and rebelled against England. The Seceded States have as much right to have her private armed vessels on the seas, if they have no Navy, as the United States have with Naval vessels. Our forefathers thought it was only right and acted accordingly when they were in arms against Great Britain. If they thought so then when these States had comparatively nothing that they could call their own, why should the Southern Confederacy or the Seceded States be backward now in having Privateers, especially that they own all in their possession and even an equal portion of what the United States Government claims as her own. Allow me to remark that as long as this civil war lasts between the two sections, North and South, it will be "dog eat dog"—"steal any dog I will steal your cat." If we, as Privateersmen, are considered and treated as Pirates, those belonging to the Army and Navy on both sides, North and South, should be considered and treated the same. It is useless, however, for me, who is a poor man and who had no chance to but [sic] his head against a College wall, to bandy words with you and others at the head of affairs on this subject for my (our) defence. In conclusion allow me to say for myself, if you still think and will have it that I am a Pirate for serving my country, (Southern Confederacy) as a Privateersman, in God's name have me indicted, tried, sentenced and hung, instead of having me imprisoned as above stated. Do you suppose dragging us from pillow to post in irons as have been done, and confined and fed as we are now, will make us loyal subjects under the Stars and Stripes any quicker? If so, you and those in power are and will be deceived! It is calculated to make us worse— yes, it will make us hate the Banner that our forefathers gained their independence under!

1861

33

With all due respect, I am
Your Prisoner,
J. P. N. Calvo

Lincoln and his staff were apparently unmoved by this plea. A secretary endorsed the communication with, "Letter from J. P. N. Calvo a S.C. Pirate," and filed it away.

Sending Busts of Rival Generals

[December 12, 1861]
V. J. Magnin Guedin & Cie.
New York

To His Excellency Abraham Lincoln
President of the U.S. of America &c &c &c

Sir

Having through the exertions of our friends in Europe, obtained, what we consider are accurate resemblances of Generals "Scott" and "McClellan," we take the liberty of tendering to you, two first proofs of these busts, asking of you, Sir, the favor to accept them as a feeble token of our appreciation of your patriotism, moderation and firmness
With our highest respect
We remain, Sir,
Your most obedt Servants
Magnin Guedin & Co.

New York Decemb 12 1861
These busts will be forwarded by Adam's Express

If the busts subsequently arrived at the White House, and if they prompted a presidential acknowledgment, there is no record in the Lincoln Papers. Nor would it have been particularly appropriate to display the two busts side-by-side. Two months earlier, Scott had retired from the army, exasperated by the brash young McClellan.

1861

1862

Lincoln in a contemplative mood, captured at Mathew Brady's Washington photographic studio sometime in 1862, the year of the Union defeat at Second Bull Run and the bloody victory at Antietam. Courtesy Library of Congress.

Protesting an Abolitionist Speech at the Smithsonian

Washington, D.C January 5th 1862

Mr. President.

Dear Sir:

Allow me with all due respect, to protest against the use of the Smithsonian Institute (of which you are one of the Regents) for the purpose of advancing the political Sentiments of any party. I regard the lecture of Mr. Horace Greeley delivered at the Institute on the evening of the 3d inst. So far as it related to the question of Slavery highly objectionable. I think the Institution was not endowed for partizan purposes, If we are to avoid the fatal consequences of division amongst our Selves, these Abolition lectures at the Institute Should be immediately stopd. I have given your Administration a cordial Support, and my best efforts in its defence with the understanding that your policy was, to put down this wicked Rebellion, to save the Constitution, and the Union, and re-establish the Supremacy of the laws, without reference to the Slavery question, or in other words, the <u>object</u> of the war was to save the Union, and <u>not</u> to free the Slaves.

The deep Solicitude I feel for our bleeding Country is the apology I have to offer for thus freely advising you. I am impressed with the immense responsibilities of your position, and I feel the destiny of this Nation is in a great degree in your hands. May God give you wisdom to direct, and Controll it for our good. It may not be proper for me to intrude my opinions on your consideration, but trusting that no harm will result, I hope to be excused for Saying, that it is my firm opinion that if we fall in putting down this Rebellion it will be the result of our having acted unwisely on the Negro question. I think the very best we can do under all the circumstances, is to let that Subject alone, and if Slavery Suffers under the laws of war, we can not help it and as we did not begin this war, we Should not be held responsible for its legitimate consequences. Let us not close our eyes to the fact, that if we change the policy of the war, and attempt through its instrumentality to Emancipate four millions of Slaves, we Shall immediately loose all the border Slave States and Send them into the vortex of Revolution, Soon to be followed by all the border free States, whose Natural Channels of trade and Commerce is, and must for ever be, with the South. We can not

---

1862

afford to make any blunders in the present distressed condition of our country. We must gird up our loins like men, and look our destiny in the face. Abolitionism and Secessionism must be met and crushed or we must prepare for a long and bloody war which will at last, end in Seperation, or consolidated despotism, these are the Sentiments of the Democracy without any official authority on my part to give them, and I believe they are the Sentiments of all Conservative Republicans. Whilst Conservatism marks the policy of your Administration on the war question I am prepared to sustain it. Any change to radicalism blasts the last hope of putting down the Rebellion.

. With the best wishes of my heart that you may be instrumental in Saving the Union, I am Your Obt. Servt.

J. A. Cravens, M. C.

There is no record of a reply from Lincoln to Congressman Cravens, a Democrat. The letter was returned to its original envelope, and the following file notation was added by a secretary, probably John Hay, in pencil: "Indignantly protests against abolition lectures at the Smithsonian."

General Sherman's Wife Pleads for His Transfer East

Lancaster Ohio; Jan 9. 1862.

Mr. Lincoln

dear Sir;

Having always entertained a high regard for you and believing you to possess the kindest feelings as well as the truest honor I appeal with confidence to you for some intervention in my husband's favor & in vindication of his slandered name.

Left, for several weeks, in an enemy's country, with but thirty thousand raw recruits to protect an extent of territory, larger than that which General McClellan held his choice & immense force to protect; with miserable arms, for the few men he had; with no arms to give the East Tenesseians, could he have sent a force through Cumberland Gap; he was almost ignored by the Military Authorities at Washington. The public were given to understand, by the report of Adj. Genl. [Lorenzo] Thomas, that a demand for a large force, in Kentucky, was considered,

---

at headquarters, <u>absurd</u> and <u>ridiculous</u>; and that he was expected to advance, with his inadequate force. Being of a nervous temperament, he shrunk from the responsibility of his position, which secured him <u>no</u> adequate means of protecting those under him. His request to be relieved was very <u>cooly</u> compiled with, & much <u>more readily</u> than any request for men and arms had been. His successor was immediately reinforced, by three or four times the number of men he had when he was notified that he "would be relieved;" and with <u>this</u> & <u>many other</u> advantages, he has been there <u>longer</u> than Gen. Sherman and has moved but seven miles. Yet nothing from Adj. Gen. Thomas has been telegraphed over the Union holding him up to the ridicule of men or announcing that he is "expected to push into Tenessee."

He was ordered to report to Gen. [Henry W.] Halleck at St. Louis & was, by him, sent to Sedalia, to inspect the troops there & "if necessary, take command." Finding the troops too much scattered, not within supporting distance and badly situated in regard to water & fuel, he ordered a change of position. Suddenly, & <u>in consequence of reports that were made to him</u> Gen. Halleck telegraphed Gen. Sherman to return to St. Louis. I had just arrived in St. Louis, and knowing my husband to be worn out, with anxiety & labor, I wished him to come home with me for a short visit. Gen. Halleck readily gave his consent.

A week after he left St. Louis and when the conspirators against him (with newspaper correspondents as tools) had time to arrange their plans, the statement that "Gen W. T. Sherman was a <u>madman</u>" was telegraphed from <u>Sedalia</u> to St. Louis, from St. Louis to Chicago, from <u>Frankfort</u> Kentucky to Cincinnati & from <u>Washington City</u> to New York, all about the same day.

An article appeared in the Cincinnati Commercial the Louisville Journal and the St. Louis Democrat, on the same subject, about the same day, and all emanating from the same source. Contradictions were immediately published but who gives credence to these? Not more than half of those who read a slander, ever see a contradiction, & of the number of those who read this, the greater part will consider it "an effort of his friends to conceal his misfortune."

No <u>official</u> contradiction has yet appeared, & no official act has yet reinstated him. As the minister of God, to dispense justice to us, and as one who has the heart to sympathise as well as the power to act, I beseech you, by some mark of confidence, to releive my husband from the suspicions now resting on him. He is now occupying a <u>subordinate</u> po-

---

1862

sition in Gen. Halleck's department, which seems an endorsement of the slander. I do not reproach Genl Halleck as Mr. Sherman's enemies may have shaken the confidence of the men in him, by the suspicion that he is insane & thus rendered it impolitic to appoint him to a command there. His mind is harassed by these cruel attacks. They were started in the west; he is exposed to their influence there, and his subordinate position gives sanction to the belief. Newspaper slanders are generally insignificant, but this you will perceive, is of a peculiar nature and one which <u>no</u> man can bear with stoicism—particularly one who is nervous and sensitive.

Will you not defend him from the enemies who have combined against him, by removing him to the Army of the East? If I were sure there would be no forward movement of the Missouri troops down the Mississippi, I would ask you to telegraph him to come on to Washington where you could dispose of him in your wisdom.

I take the liberty of enclosing some of the articles that appeared in the papers. The charge which he ordered in the disposition of the troops at Sedalia excited the publication; and a subsequent investigation showed that he saw and fixed, at a glance the true position for the troops, which was determined on after a careful survey by Lieut. Col. McPherson under a subsequent order of Gen. Halleck. This fact I have from Gen. Halleck's own letter which came for my husband after he had left, and which I opened and have kept.

Adj. Gen. Thomas has shown himself, <u>more than once</u>, an enemy of my husband. He had it in his power and he seized the occasion, to present him in an unfavorable light, to you. As malice cannot prevail, where justice rules, I look for a speedy relief from the sorrow that has afflicted me in this trial to my husband. That your name may be handed down, with undiminished honor, to posterity, and that eternal joys may be your portion hereafter, is the wish of

Yours, most respectfully,
Ellen Ewing Sherman.

As promised, Mrs. Sherman enclosed newspaper clippings reporting "the painful intelligence . . . that Gen. W. T. Sherman . . . is <u>insane</u>." On January 13, she sent a copy of the letter to her brother-in-law, Senator John Sherman, after she learned that he had visited Lincoln "in regard to Cump"—the family name for the beleaguered William Tecumseh Sherman. "I am very anxious to know

1862

40

the result," Ellen added, for "Cump . . . is under a cloud." Modern biographers tend to believe that the general indeed suffered some sort of nervous break-down under pressure from hostile newspaper correspondents, whom Sherman loathed. But Lincoln did not agree to Mrs. Sherman's plea that her husband be transferred to the eastern theater of the war. Within three months, Sherman would play a major role in a Union triumph in the west at the Battle of Shiloh in Tennessee. (Mrs. Sherman's letter to John Sherman and an imperfect copy of her letter to Lincoln, Sherman Papers, Library of Congress)

Minister Recommends Marine

Washington Jan. 10. 1862.

His Excellency Abraham Lincoln

Dear Sir

Permit me to introduce to your acquaintance & commend to your kindness and confidence the bearer of this note, Mr. Robert H. Thompson of Maryland. He is connected with a large & highly respect-able family, all of whom have been true to the Union since the com-mencement of our troubles. He desires an appointment in the U.S. Ma-rine Corps. Hoping you will favor his wishes,

I am yours truly
P. D. Gurley

Reverend Phineas D. Gurley was pastor of Washington's New York Avenue Pres-byterian Church, which the Lincoln family often attended. The President obliged with the following, previously unpublished endorsement: "Mr. Thompson, named within, as I understand, has papers on file, for an appoint-ment in the Marine Corps. He is well recommended, & if he can consistently be appointed, I shall be glad for it to be done. A. Lincoln." A month later, Gurley would conduct the funeral service for the president's eleven-year-old son, Willie, and in 1865, it was Gurley who preached the oration at Lincoln's own funeral. (Letter, courtesy of Alexander Autographs)

1862

41

A Warning about His Harvard Son

Cambridge, [Mass.,] Jan. 20, 1862.

Hon. Abraham Lincoln,
President of the United States, Washington, D.C.

Dear Sir,

Your son has received a requisition to make up during the vacation. I take this occasion to say a word or two about him and his pursuits. Since he entered College his conduct and studies have been unexceptionable until recently: and I do not think he has even now gone far astray. But, of late, the Professors have been pained to notice that he has seemed to be on intimate terms with some of the idlest persons in his class. His studies generally have suffered detriment: and in the department of Chemistry, his failure has been complete.

I trust this is only a temporary aberration: and I write to you, though I have no vote of censure to communicate, but in order that you may know how the case stands with him. He is a good, ingenuous, frank and pleasant young man: with the ability to do well in every department. But he must guard gainst "good fellowship". I have no doubt a word or two from you will set every thing right; for I feel quite sure that he has no bad habits as yet.

I have the honor to be, with the greatest consideration,

Yours,
C. C. Felton, Pres. H[arvard].
C[ollege].

No reply from the president is known, nor was this letter from Cornelius Conway Felton preserved in the Lincoln Papers, at least once Robert T. Lincoln gained control of them after his father's assassination. Undoubtedly, father did have "a word or two" with son when they next met in Washington, although neither left any record of their confrontation. Later that same year, Lincoln received yet another complaint from Robert's school, this time from Felton's successor as president, asserting that the young man known as the "Prince of Rails" had been caught smoking in Harvard Square. Robert graduated from the college in 1864 and went on to attend Harvard Law School. (Felton letter, courtesy of the Harvard University Archives)

1862

Condolences for His Son

Washn Feby 22 1862

My dear Sir

I have not felt authorized to intrude upon you personally in the midst of the deep distress I know you feel in the sad calamity that has befallen you & your family—yet I cannot refrain from expressing to you the sincere & deep sympathy I feel for you.

You have been a kind true friend to me in the midst of the great cares & difficulties by which we have been surrounded during the past few months—your confidence has upheld me when I should otherwise have felt weak. I wish now only to assure you & your family that I have felt the deepest sympathy in your affliction.

I am pushing to prompt completion the measures of which we have spoken, & beg that you will not allow military affairs to give you one moment's trouble—but that you will rest assured that nothing shall be left undone to follow up the successes that have been such an auspicious commencement of our new campaign.

I am very sincerely & respectfully your friend & obt svt
Geo B McClellan

His Excellency Abraham Lincoln
Presdt, US.

Even in a letter offering condolences, General George B. McClellan could not resist the bragging that characterized so much of his wartime correspondence to his commander in chief. The death of the Lincolns' middle, and favorite son, eleven-year-old Willie, sent both parents into protracted mourning. The president recovered only with great difficulty, and Mary remained embroiled, as she put it, in a "fiery furnace of affliction." Life at the White House would never be the same for the Lincoln family.

_____1862_____

Urging the Use of Black Troops

Canal, Venango Co. Pa.
March 12, 1862

His Excellency A. Lincoln, L. L. D.
President of the United States:

Dear Sir:

I have the honor to enclose herewith a Petition for emancipation, signed by 92 citizens—the majority of whom reside in this county. Praying that the Almighty may assist and guide you in the performance of your arduous duties, I remain

Yours most respectfully,
John Gregory
Wesleyan Methodist Minister

The petition from rural, Western Pennsylvania urged more than mere emancipation. It called on Lincoln as chief magistrate to proclaim, in the words of Leviticus, " 'liberty throughout all the land, unto all the inhabitants thereof.' " It also urged him, as commander in chief, to "call on all the inhabitants of the United States, of all conditions, bond and free, to aid in supporting the Government, assured of its protection, under the flag of our national Union and freedom." Rev. Gregory's letter was filed, appropriately: "Petition of Pennsylvanians urging use of Negroes in army."

Explaining "Incorrect" Accounts at the White House

Treasury Department
Comptrollers Office
March 12th 1862.

President Abraham Lincoln

My Dear Friend.

As I was leaving my office yesterday at four O'clock, I received your esteemed favor of that date, requesting if any accounts from the Mansion should appear wrong, to make it known to You, directly.

1862

I have been deterred from communicating with you personally on that, and on other subjects, from my knowledge of the mighty matters, that engross your attention.

If you have a constituent or fellow citizen, more sincerely devoted to You than myself, I am not aware of it. Your request shall be observed.

Most Respectfully and Sincerely Yours,
Elisha Whittlesey.

Whittlesey, who had been serving as first comptroller of the Treasury since the days of Zachary Taylor, was then seventy-nine years old and in the final year of his life. No doubt worried over reports of fraudulent accounting at the White House, Lincoln wanted the aged Whittlesey to guard the Executive Mansion's books more scrupulously. His vague response surely gave Lincoln little comfort, especially the frank admission that the fiscal watchdog was in the habit of leaving work at 4 P.M. The comptroller was responding to the following private letter, sent to him by the president the day before. (Ed. note, *Journal of the Abraham Lincoln Association* 17 [Winter 1996]: 45, 52; Lincoln's reply, Lincoln Shrine, Redlands, California)

Private

Hon. Elisha Whittlesey   Executive Mansion

My dear Sir: Washington, March 11, 1862

Once or twice since I have been in this House, accounts have been presented at your Bureau, which were incorrect. I shall be personally and greatly obliged to you if you will carefully scan any account which comes from here; and if in any there shall appear the least semblance of wrong, make it known to me directly.

Yours very truly
A. Lincoln

1862

Capture of New Orleans

[April 28, 1862]

Glory to God and the President—
Forts Jackson & St. Phillip are taken and New Orleans is ours—
Abraham Lincoln
President of the United States

This infernal machine was captured at Fort Jackson April 24th 1862. It could only have been invented for your Excellency's special destruction. May God preserve you many years.

I am with all respect Your Exxcellencys Most Obt Servt.

John D. Camp
Comdr. U.S. Navy

Comdg. U.S. Steam Sloop Iroquois
New Orleans April 28th 1862

Commander Camp was probably referring to the Confederate ram *Manassas*, which terrorized Admiral David Farragut's fleet as it stormed past Forts Jackson and St. Phillip en route to its capture of New Orleans. But in truth, the *Manassas* was not captured; it ran aground and burned after ramming several Union warships on the Mississippi River.

Recommending a Methodist Chaplain

Lebanon Ohio May 19th 1862

To his Excellency A Lincoln
President of the United States.

Dear Sir

The meeting of Ministers which forwarded the accompanying memorial, appointed a committee to recommend a suitable person for the post.

After a full & free interchange of views, & considering not the claims but the adaptation to the work of the several gentlemen whose services could be secured, all of whom were personally known to us, the committee unanimously recommended for your appointment

---

1862

Rev John Floyd of
Springfield Ohio,
His experience in similar work added to his adaptation to it render him
in the opinion of the committee eminently fitted for it. He is an efficient,
earnest laborer, in any field assigned him.

We only add that Mr. Lloyd does not seek the place but the place seeks
him.

He is a regular ordained minister of the Methodist Episcopal Church
connected with the Cincinnati Conference.

In behalf of the Committee
Geo. W. Harris Secretary

The undersigned, Ministers of the Methodist Ep. Church in Cin. O.
most cordially concur in the recommendation of Rev. J. F. Lloyd of the
same church as a person admirably adapted to the work of a Hospital
Chaplain.

Signed

Jno. T. Mitchell
D. W. Clark
C. Kingsley
Erwin House
Adam Poe
S. Hitchcock
D. J. Starr

This well-organized recommendation was sent on to the War Department. But
the White House staff endorsed it without comment: "John F. Lloyd of Ohio/
Petition to Lincoln." Candidates for chaplain positions were often submitted to
Lincoln, but few arrived with the blessing of so many ministers as this one.
(Letter, The Lincoln Museum, Fort Wayne, IN)

Advice on the Conduct of the War

[Memorandum from General Winfield Scott, June 23, 1862]

The President having stated to me, orally, the present numbers & positions of our forces in front of the rebel armies, south & South west of
the Potomack, has done me honor to ask my views, in writing, as to the

---

1862

further dispositions now to be made, of the former, & particularly of the army under [Gen. Irvin] McDowell, towards the suppression of the rebellion.

Premising that, altho' the statements of the President were quite full & most distinct & lucid—yet from my distance from the scenes of operation, & not having, recently, followed them up, with closeness—many details are still wanted to give professional value to my suggestions—I shall, nevertheless, with great deference, proceed to offer such as most readily occur to me—each of which has been anticipated by the President.

I consider the numbers & positions of [Gen. John C.] Fremont & [Gen. Nathaniel] Banks, adequate to the protection of Washington against any force the enemy can bring by the way of the Upper Potomack, & the troops, at Manassas junction, with the garrisons of the forts on the Potomack & of Washington, equally adequate to its protection on the South.

The force at Fredericksburg seems entirely out of position, & it cannot be called up, directly & in time, by McClellan, from the want of rail-road transportation, or an adequate supply train, moved by animals. If, however, there be a sufficient number of vessels at hand, that force might reach the head of York river, by water, in time to aid in the operations against Richmond, or in the very improbable case of disaster, there, to serve as a valuable reinforcement to McClellan.

The defeat of the rebels, at Richmond, or their forced retreat, thence, combined with our previous victories, would be a virtual end of the rebellion, & soon restore entire Virginia to the Union.

The remaining important points to be occupied by us, are—Mobile, Charleston, Chattanooga. These must soon come into our hands.

McDowell's force, at Manassas, might be ordered to Richmond, by the Potomack & York rivers, & be replaced, at Manassas, by [Gen. Rufus] King's brigade, if there be adequate transports at, or near Alexandria. Most respectfully Submitted

Winfield Scott

On June 23, 1862, frustrated by General McClellan's lack of progress along the Virginia peninsula in his ambitious campaign against the Confederate capital of Richmond, Lincoln began an unpublicized visit to retired General in Chief Winfield Scott at West Point, New York, to seek the old veteran's advice. Returning to Washington on June 25, Lincoln encountered a crowd of well-wishers at the railroad station in Jersey City, New Jersey, where he was called upon to deliver the only comments he ever made public on the West Point conference with Scott. Based on these vague remarks, it is clear that the president had no intention of divulging the advice the general had proffered both orally and in the confidential memorandum above. The day after delivering his comments at Jersey City, the Seven Days Battle began in Virginia. McClellan's campaign ultimately failed. Following is Lincoln's extraordinarily unrevealing speech at Jersey City. (Lincoln's speech, *Coll. Works*, V: 284 [incorrectly dated as June 24, 1862]).

REMARKS BY PRESIDENT LINCOLN
AT JERSEY CITY, JUNE 25, 1862

When birds and animals are looked at through a fog they are seen to disadvantage, and so it might be with you if I were to attempt to tell you why I went to see Gen. Scott. I can only say that my visit to West Point did not have the importance which has been attached to it; but it conceived matters that you understand quite as well as if I were to tell you all about them. Now, I can only remark that it had nothing whatever to do with making or unmaking any General in the country [Laughter and applause.] The Secretary of War, you know, holds a pretty tight rein on the Press, so that they shall not tell more than they ought to, and I'm, afraid that if I blab too much he might draw a tight rein on me.

Pro-Union Virginians Want
Captured Husbands Released

Fredericksburg Virginia
July 14th 1862,

To the President of the United States

The petition of the undersigned Union women, residing in the vicinity of Fredericksburg respectfully shows

That on the 25th of April 1862, Moses Morrison, and Thos. Morrison the husbands of two of your petitioners, were arrested on their farms in this vicinity and carried off to prison in Richmond by the rebels, their only offence being their Union sentiments. That several others among them Peter Cousse another union farmer were arrested and also carried to prison by the Rebels and that since that day your petitioners have been

---

1862

left with their farms injured and going to waste and their families exposed to great sorrow and suffering on account of their absence. Your other petitioner Mary Wheeler would state that on the 8th of March 1862 her brother Major Chas. Williams was arrested as a Union man, and has been since confined either in Richmond or North-Carolina greatly to the suffering and distress of herself and her six children, of whom he took sole care—That James Maguire, Chas. Brown, Beverly Gill, and Mr Bradley now living in Fredericksburg were mainly instrumental in his in his [sic] arrest, and are now enjoying the protection of United States laws— Your petitioners would state that another Union man, arrested on the 28th of April—Jas. Morrison arrived yesterday from Richmond, having been compelled to take the oath of allegiance and reports that eight Union prisoners were lately unconditionally released by the Confederate authorities in exchange for eight Rebel citizens arrested as hostages by the United States authorities.

They pray the President of the United States that the same method may be employed for the release of their husbands and brother and respectfully beg that Thos. Barton, Thos. J. Knox, H Clay Roe, John S. Mayer, C. H. Welford, James Maguire Charles Brown & Beverly Gill the most noted leaders in the secession movement in Fredericksburg may be at once arrested and held as hostages for the safe return to their families of Moses Morrison, Thos. Morrison Major Charles Williams and Peter Cousse.

This we beg as those who have suffered everything we could suffer on account of the determined loyalty of our friends in the good cause

Mrs Amanda S Morrison
Mrs Mary Morrison
Mary M Wheeler

Letters to Lincoln proposing prisoner exchanges are extremely rare; this example, and the scheme it proposed, may be unique. The authors, the wives and a sister of captured pro-Union Virginians, demanded that local secessionists be arrested so they could be exchanged for the imprisoned Union men. Lincoln referred this letter to Secretary of War Edwin M. Stanton, who evidently agreed with the petitioners. He endorsed the letter: "Referred to Major General [John] Pope with recommendation that he take as hostages disloyal persons of the same vicinity and hold them until the return of the within named persons to their homes. Edwin M Stanton Sec of War July 17. 1862". The fate of the hostages, however, remains unknown. Union sentiments in this part of the Confederacy may have been stronger than heretofore believed. A few months after the above letter was written, for example, Hazard Stevens, son of the martyred Union general Isaac Ingalls Stevens, was emboldened to organize the "1st Regt Loyal East Virginians," and began raising troops from among "those who wish to remove the stigma of past disloyalty" from the region. (Letter, Daniel E. Weinberg, Abraham Lincoln Book Shop and Gallery, Chicago; Ed. note, Richard Nelson Current, *Lincoln's Loyalists: Union Soldiers from the Confederacy* [Boston: Northeastern University Press, 1992]), 25.

Consolation from Switzerland

Orbe, Canton de Vaud
Switzerland—18 July 1862

Sir—

It is in moments of difficulty that friends should show themselves.

The check sustained by the federal army before Richmond [McClellan's Peninsular Campaign had just ended far short of its goal of conquering the Confederate capital—Ed.] was certainly a situation of difficulty for the United States. Learn that your friends in Europe do not lose courage, and that they pray for you.

This, besides, is not a Bull Run. There is nothing in it like defeat. The mischief, please God, will soon be repaired.

Why is it that the North with her great armies, so often is found, without inferiority in numbers, face to face, with the armies of the South? You know that battles are won by the feet!! and that the great principle of war is to concentrate forces in place of scattering them. It is necessary that at important points the national troops should always outnumber those of the rebel forces. It seems that the contrary has too often taken place [McClellan's frequent complaints of superior Southern forces in fact proved untrue—Ed.].

Have you received, recently, the volume and the letter I had the honor to address to you? I have attempted to sustain in Europe a struggle which is not always easy. There, assuredly, the greatest peril of America is to be found; without Europe; without the chances of European intervention, or mediation, the revolt—in fact—would have been at an end long since.

That ideas of intervention may be counteracted in our old world, there is need not only of military successes achieved by you, but more

---

1862

than that, a continuation of your wise policy; avoid, I entreat you, the complications you may find in Mexico, [where the following year French forces would impose Maximilian as emperor of that conquered country—Ed.]—avoid also, revolutionary measures—confiscations—capital punishments—appeals to the negroes—precipitate emancipation. [Six days after this letter was written, Lincoln read a preliminary Emancipation Proclamation to his cabinet, then tabled it until Union forces could win a victory—Ed.].

You have traced a programme which every upright mind must applaud. Whilst developing it in the spirit of liberty, it tends to the preservation of fundamental principles. On the day when it can be said in Europe that your Government is, either indifferent to abolition, or carried away by the extreme abolitionists, the partizans of intervention, in favor of the South, will succeed in effecting it.

Pardon me for writing these things to you, my excuse lies in the interest which I take in the cause of which you are the worthy representative.

Accept Sir the assurance of my devotion and of my respect

A. de Gasparin

Count Agénor-Etienne de Gasparin—author of *Un Grand Peuple qui se relève: Les États-Unis en 1861*, a prescient book about the coming of the war—had long warned his fellow French liberals of the international implications of the American rebellion. Lincoln's reply to Gasparin follows. (Ed. note, Jay Monaghan, *Dilplomat in Carpet Slippers: Abraham Lincoln Deals with Foreign Affairs* [New York: Bobbs-Merrill, 1945], 92, 241; Tyler Dennett, ed., *Lincoln and the Civil War in the Diaries and Letters of John Hay* [New York: Dodd Mead, 1939], 53; Lincoln's reply, *Coll. Works* V: 355–56)

Executive Mansion, Washington
August 4, 1862

Dear Sir:

Your very acceptable letter dated Orbe Canton de Vaud, Switzerland 18th of July 1862 is received. The moral[e] effect was the worst of the affair before Richmond; and that has run its course downward; we are now at a stand, and shall soon be rising again, as we hope. I believe it is true that in men and material, the enemy suffered more than we, in that series of conflicts; while it is certain he is less able to bear it.

1862

With us every soldier is a man of character and must be treated with more consideration than is customary in Europe. Hence our great army for slighter causes than could have prevailed there has dwindled rapidly, bringing the necessity for a new call, earlier than was anticipated. [After the failure of the Peninsular Campaign, Lincoln had confided to secretary John Hay that the troops in fact "dwindled on the march like a shovelfull of fleas pitched from one place to another."—Ed.]. We shall easily obtain the new levy, however. Be not alarmed if you shall learn that we shall have resorted to a draft for part of this. It seems strange, even to me, but it is true, that the Government is now pressed to this course by a popular demand. Thousands who wish not to enter the service are nevertheless anxious to pay and send substitutes, provided they can have assurance that unwilling persons similarly situated will be compelled to do like wise. Besides this, volunteers mostly choose to enter newly forming regiments, while drafted men can be sent to fill up the old ones, wherein, man for man, they are quite doubly as valuable.

You ask "why is it that the North with her great armies, so often is found, with inferiority of numbers, face to face with the armies of the South?" While I painfully know the fact, a military man, which I am not, would better answer the question. The fact I know, has not been overlooked; and I suppose the cause of its continuance lies mainly in the other facts that the enemy holds the interior, and we the exterior lines; and that we operate where the people convey information to the enemy, while he operates where they convey none to us.

I have received the volume and letter which you did me the honor of addressing to me, and for which please accept my sincere thanks. You are much admired in America for the ability of your writings, and much loved for your generosity to us, and your devotion to liberal principles generally.

You are quite right, as to the importance to us, for its bearing upon Europe, that we should achieve military successes; and the same is true for us at home as well as abroad. Yet it seems unreasonable that a series of successes, extending through half-a-year, and clearing more than a hundred thousands square miles of country, should help us so little, while a single half-defeat should hurt us so much. But let us be patient.

I am very happy to know that my course has not conflicted with your judgement, of propriety and policy.

I can only say that I have acted upon my best convictions without

---

1862

selfishness or malice, and that by the help of God, I shall continue to do so.

Please be assured of my highest respect and esteem.

[A. Lincoln]

Welcoming the Draft

(Near) Boston. Aug. 5. 62.

Dear Sir:

I take the liberty to assure you that the draft for 300.000 men is welcomed in this section by <u>all classes</u> of citizens.

The sentiment has been strengthening here that the army should be increased to 1000.000 by Nov. Next. A petition has been prepared, & would have been ready tomorrow for signatures throughout the N Eng. States asking you to adopt this measure. Your action makes this popular appeal unnecessary. But it is nevertheless the common belief of our people that this step is necessary to save the credit of the Govt. & the lives of our citizens.

Your Obt Servt
Amos A. Lawrence

His Excelly
Prest Lincoln.

The day before Lawrence wrote this letter to the president, Lincoln had ordered a draft of 300,000 militia to serve for nine months. Gratified by this statement of support, Lincoln replied to the Boston merchant on Aug. 7: "My Dear Sir[,] Allow me to thank you sincerely for your kind letter" (*Coll. Works* V: 362). Still worried that the president might alter his conscription policy, however, Lawrence took up his pen to write again on the same subject five days later.

(Near) Boston. Aug. 12. 62.

Dear Sir:

A desire is expressed here by some gentlemen in official positions to have the drafting for troops delayed. This is not the desire of the mass of our citizens. It is the certainty of the draft which has given confidence

---

1862

to all. The letters received from our troops indicate a restored & an increased faith in the action of the Govt. On this account.

An intimation that an <u>additional levy for an army of reserve</u> would be hailed with enthusiasm in this section.

Respecty Yr Obt Servt
Amos A. Lawrence

His Excelly
The Prest of the
Ustates.

(No answr expected.)

Lincoln did not write again to Lawrence, whose worries proved well-founded. Perhaps alarmed over reports that able-bodied, draft-aged men were mutilating and maiming themselves to avoid compulsory service, Lincoln did not put his August 4 militia draft into effect. However, an official Conscription Act was enacted the following year.

Proposing a Constitutional Convention
to Restore the Union

New-York, August 10, 1862

To His Excellency President Lincoln

My Dear Sir:

I have the honor to acknowledge the receipt of your esteemed favor. Its contents bear the stamp of that statesmanship and patriotism which I know to have guided all your actions in the trials which this wicked rebellion has brought upon our once so happy country.

I share entirely your views with regard not only to the duty, but also the policy of the revolted States to return to their allegiance without allowing their unequal struggle against the power of the United States to increase in violence and exasperation, as it reasonably must. Still I think that we might, perhaps, find means to remove the difficulties which the miseries of civil war and the terrorism conjured up by the leaders of the rebellion, have placed in the way of conservative men, who otherwise would most gladly return to the Union.

1862

The words <u>conquest</u> and <u>subjugation</u> have been used to good effect by our opponents. They are words repugnant to the American ear, and while the rebel leaders can keep up to their misguided followers the idea that the North means conquest and subjugation, I fear there is very little hope for any Union demonstration in the revolted States, however great the dissatisfaction against the Richmond government might be.

My own conviction has always been, that sooner or later we would have to come to a national convention for the reconstruction of one government over all the States. I cannot see by what other means, even after a complete defeat of the rebel armies, a restoration of the Union can be effected.

My impression is, that such a solution would at the proper time, be acceptable to the majority of the Southern people, and I sent to Mr. [Thurlow] Weed [New York Republican leader—Ed.] the letter which procured me the honor of receiving your note, for the very reason that I saw in it an indication of the writer's desire for reconstruction of the Union. He is a very wealthy and influential planter, and I have every reason to believe that a large number of his class share his views.

A few weeks ago, and previous to the receipt of that letter, I had written to Mr. Weed, giving him my candid views on our present situation and the means which I thought the government ought to adopt. [He had proposed in his letter to Weed "an amnesty for all political offences during the war, and the calling of a national convention for the purpose of reconstructing the Federal compact, with such modification of the Constitution as our late sad experience has demonstrated to have become necessary."—Ed.] I do not know whether he communicated to you my letter, but as you have been kind enough to evince a flattering confidence in the earnestness of my intentions, which must plead for the shortcoming of my judgment, I take the liberty of inclosing you herewith a copy of my letter to Mr. Weed, hoping that you may deem it worthy of your perusal.

The present moment may, perhaps, not be a propitious one for carrying on a negotiation in the manner in which I suggest. As soon, however, as we shall again have a large army in the field, such as we are sure to have under your energetic measures for recruiting, then I hope that you may find in your wisdom the means of opening negotiations with our misguided fellow-citizens of the South.

They must become convinced that we are fighting <u>only for the Union</u>, and that we cannot, in our own self-defence, as a nation, admit any other solution <u>but the Union</u>. I am certain that ere long reason must prevail over sectional passion, provided that your strong hand will equally crush the secessionists of the South and the fanatical disorganizers of the North, who are equally dangerous to the country and its institutions.

August Belmont

The author, a noted banker, had been minister to the Netherlands during the Pierce administration and later served as chairman of the Democratic National Committee. In 1870, Belmont published this letter, along with his earlier one to Thurlow Weed, because, he explained, his wartime words had been "often misrepresented and sometimes misunderstood." The "esteemed favor" from Lincoln to which the writer referred was a strong response to a Belmont letter to Weed quoting a Southern critic of the president. Weed apparently showed the letter to Lincoln, provoking the following famous reply.

July 31, 1862.

Dear Sir:

You send to Mr. W[eed] an extract from a letter written at New Orleans the 9th instant, which is shown to me. You do not give the writer's name; but plainly he is a man of ability, and probably of some note. He says: "The time has arrived when Mr. Lincoln must take a decisive course. Trying to please everybody, he will satisfy nobody. A vacillating policy in matters of importance is the very worst. Now is the time, if ever, for honest men who love their country to rally to its support. Why will not the North say officially that it wishes for the restoration of the Union as it was?"

And so, it seems, this is the point on which the writer thinks I have no policy. Why will he not read and understand what I have said? . . .

Broken eggs cannot be mended; but Louisiana has nothing to do now but to take her place in the Union as it was, barring the already broken eggs. The sooner she does so, the smaller will be the amount of that which will be past mending. This government cannot much longer play a game in which it stakes all, and its enemies stake nothing. Those enemies must understand that they cannot experiment for ten years trying to destroy the government, and if they fail still come back into the Union unhurt. If they expect in any contingency to ever have the Union as it was, I join with the writer in saying, "Now is the time."

1862

How much better it would have been for the writer to have gone at this, under the protection of the army of New Orleans, than to have sat down in a closet writing complaining letters northward!

Yours truly,

A. Lincoln

Lincoln never responded to Belmont's proposal for a Constitutional convention aimed at restoring the Union "with such modification" to the "Federal compact" as the war had made necessary. Nor did he, apparently, learn the identity of the New Orleans citizen who had "sat down in a closet" to complain about Lincoln's indecisiveness. Neither that writer nor Belmont knew at the time, of course, that the president had already written a draft Emancipation Proclamation and planned to issue it as soon as a Union battlefield victory made it politically expedient. In effect, as Lincoln well understood, the Union would never be recreated again "as it was." His letter to Belmont did give him the opportunity to use the expression "broken eggs cannot be mended." He employed it again on August 22 in drafting his well-known reply to Horace Greeley's editorial, "The Prayer of Twenty Milllons," but crossed it out before sending it. (*Coll. Works* V: 388–89) Belmont wrote yet again on September 4, urging Lincoln to replace Secretary of War Stanton with General Henry W. Halleck. Lincoln did not reply. Instead he rather mischievously sent the "extract . . . which can be construed to allude to you" to Stanton on September 11, offering to show him the entire correspondence "if you wish" *Coll. Works* V: 416). (Letter, August Belmont, *A Few Letters and Speeches of the Late Civil War* [New York: privately printed, 1870], 71–72; Belmont's September 4 letter, John G. Nicolay Papers, Library of Congress; Ed. note, Belmont, *A Few Letters*, 1, 69; Lincoln's reply, *Coll. Works* V: 350–51)

Governor Can't Get "Regiments Off"

Boston, August 11, 1862.

<u>Confidential</u>

His Excellency A. Lincoln:

I can't get those regiments off because I can't get quick work out of the U.S. disbursing officer and the paymaster, and I can't start out men in violation of my authorized proclamation and promises. Everybody here is alive. Men swarm our camps. We will raise regiments until you cry, hold! But why not turn over the funds to me, and we will disburse and account for them and stop delays? I anxiously wait reply to my telegram of last Friday.

Jno. A. Andrew

Desperately in need of troop reinforcements, Lincoln replied to Massachusetts Governor John A. Andrew's telegram the following day. As Secretary of War Edwin M. Stanton explained, Lincoln delayed in answering "in order to obtain information from some other States as to the condition of enlistments." When the information reached him, the president responded as follows, with uncharacteristic impatience and no small amount of sarcastic reproach. (Letter, *Official Records of the Rebellion*, Series III, Vol. II, 353; Lincoln's reply, *Coll. Works* V: 367)

Gov. Andrew   Washington, D.C.,
Boston, Mass.   Aug. 12 1862.

Your despatch saying "I cant get those regts. off because I cant get quick work out of the U.S. disbursing officer & the Paymaster" is received.

Please say to these gentlemen that if they do not work quickly I will make quick work with them. In the name of all that is reasonable, how long does it take to pay a couple of Regts.?

We were never more in need of the arrival of Regts. than now—even to-day.

A. Lincoln.

A Pamphleteer Demands Her Payment

Aug. 14, 1862

Mr. President:

I am just informed that at a public dinner table, in a Washington Hotel, a gentleman, whose name I do not know, stated, that the President had said, "a lady demanded fifty thousand dollars for writing a document," &c; meaning, myself.

I forbear to write, as I desire to forget, the very disparaging manner, in which it was represented by the gentleman, as coming from you.

I saw, Mr. President, that you did not comprehend me, and I said so, at the time of my interview:

1862

But you insisted, that you did, and of course, I said no more.

But the fact that you have given a partial publicity, to that interview, to my prejudice, proved conclusively that you wholly misconceived its object.

It is therefore due to myself, and to you, that, I make this statement plain.

I had a verbal agreement, with Hon Thos A. Scott, as Assistant Secretary of War, to write in defense of the War Policy, of the Government; but before a settlement was had, he left the Dept.

For the writing and circulating of the copies, accepted, under this agreement, there was no question; as I know the Government was legally bound, to pay me, its just value.

But for the circulation of my documents, that I had written under this agreement, and for what I might write, during the war, I was advised by the Assistant Secretaries, to bring the matter before you, as Commander-in-Chief.

And, I was also advised, by many of the ablest men in the nation, that the Government should circulate, extensively, the "Reply to Breckenridge" "The War Powers of the Government". ["]The Relations of the Government to the Revolted Citizens" &c. &c.

They also expressed the belief, that I could render efficient service to the country, by going to Europe, and writing in its defense, and desired me to converse with you, on this subject.

They all understood, that the amount suggested, was to be used in the circulation of my documents among the millions; and to write and publish in Europe, during your Administration; and they deemed it a very reasonable sum.

The statement, reciting the fact of my agreement, which I read to you, had been previously submitted, and approved, by several distinguished friends, of the country:

Among them, Senator [Orville Hickman] Browning [of Illinois, an old friend of Lincoln's—Ed.], whose note I enclosed to you. He called, just before leaving the City, when we conversed fully upon the matter; and it was the result of his remarks, which induced me to see you; for the purpose of bringing the suggestions of my friends, to your consideration in the manner indicated.

Mr. President, Government is something more than a machine, which requires simply the presence of a skillful engineer. It is an <u>institution</u>, which for the successful accomplishment of its ends; depends at last, not so much, upon the skill of the functionaries; as upon the temper and spirit of the people.

Now, this temper of the people is kept right, not by the officials of the Government, but by the leaders of <u>thought</u>, the independent thinkers and actors of the day.

There never was a ruler who neglected to instruct the people, over whom he presided, through these ancillaries, who did not ruin himself, or his country; most frequently, both.

No one understood this better than the great Napoleon. He never adopted a policy, or attempted to carry a measure, without having first, felt the ground, and was assured, that it would meet the approbation of the people:

He caused the people to be instructed, through the independent thinkers, and writers of his time; and he furnished to men and women of that order, every facility for writing and speaking, and rewarded them liberally

When you said to me, that my proposition was "the most outrageous one ever made to any government, upon earth," I remember that, the difference between us, was in our views upon the value of intellectual labor, in the administration of government.

I am satisfied, Mr. President, that we are equally sincere in our views.

But, I fear, that, physical force, <u>alone</u>, however strong it may be, can never bring this war, to a successful termination; unless you avail yourself, of intellect, to make clear to the popular mind, the <u>issue</u>, about which, the country is now, at war.

And, now, without any desire to influence your action upon the matter, I must say, that there cannot be any fair minded man, who knows the value of mental labor, and understands the extent, to which I proposed to apply it; who could believe, the sum I suggested, either absurd, or unjust.

And, I know, Mr. President, that had you heard me, in explanation of the proposition, made in the paper, which I read to you; you could not have deemed the sum exorbitant; however much you may have doubted, the effect of my writing, upon the welfare of the country.

I know, Mr. President, that you, as a lawyer, must decide, that I am legally entitled, under the agreement with the War Office, to compensation, at a fair value, for the writing and circulation of the copies of my document entitled the "War Powers of the Government," and also compensation at a fair valuation, for the writing and circulation of the document, "Defining the Relations of the National Government, to the Revolted Citizens;" whether the Department chooses to give these documents, the extensive circulation, contemplated under the agreement, and continues by services, in the writing of other papers, or not.

If the estimate placed upon my writings, be too high, the error is not mine, but that of the friends of yourself, and of the country.

And although you may differ, from these friends, and perhaps correctly as to the value of my contributions; it shall not dampen my energies in supporting you, Mr. President, in your efforts to save our country.

I shall continue to labor for the salvation of our liberties, to the very extent of my ability; as heretofore, without any pecuniary reward, or the hope of any.

And my only regret, is, that I have not more talent to serve my country better; and and [sic] means, to bring my writings home to the hearts, and the consciences, of the whole people.

Anna Ella Carroll

August 14th, 1862

Maryland-born Anna Ella Carroll had begun her career as a propagandist for the anti-Catholic Know-Nothing Party in the 1850s. When the Civil War began, she freed her family's slaves and began writing pamphlets advocating the Lincoln administration's right to suppress the rebellion. As this extraordinary letter shows, in a personal interview with the president she had demanded a payment of $50,000 both for the writing and distribution of her publications, as well as for continuing to write pro-Union tracts from Europe. But Assistant Secretary of War Thomas Scott, the man Carroll claimed had contracted for her services, insisted that he had acted "under no special authority" in doing so. Anna Ella Carroll never gave up her quest for the $50,000 she insisted the government owed her. She continued fighting unsuccessfully for the payment until her death in 1893. Perhaps shocked by this letter, which practically urged Lincoln to hire a royal court of intellectuals to influence public opinion, Lincoln wrote to Carroll five days later merely to compliment her on her most recent work. He did not even mention the author's fourteen-page letter. This is Lincoln's letter to Miss Carroll, or at least a copy, in Carroll's handwriting, that she sent to President-Elect James A. Garfield in 1880 to renew her claim. The original has never been located. (Ed. note, Sydney and Marjorie Greenbie, *Anna Ella Carroll and Abraham Lincoln* [Manchester, ME: Falmouth Publishing, 1952]; Lincoln's reply, *Coll. Works* V: 381)

1862

Executive Mansion
Dear Miss Carroll   August 19th. 1862
    Like every thing else that comes from you I have read the address to Maryland with a great deal of pleasure and interest.
    It is just what is needed now and you were the one to do it.
                                        Yours very truly
                                        A. Lincoln

Black Support for Colonization

                                        Washington, Augt 16th 1862
His Excellency the President

Sir
    We would respectfully Suggest that it is necessary that we Should confer with leading colored men in Phila New York and Boston, upon the movement of emigration to the point reccommended in your address
    We were entirely hostile to the movement until all the advantages were so ably brought to our Views by you and we believe that our friends and co laborers for our race in those cities will when the Subject is explained by us to them join heartily in Sustaining such a movement.
    It is therefore Suggested in addition to what is Stated that you authorize two of us to proceed to these cities and place your views before them to facilitate and promote the object. We desire no appointment only a letter from your hand Saying you wish us to consult with our leading friends. As this is part of the movement to obtain a proper plan of colonization we would respectfully Suggest to your Excellency that the necessary expenses of the two (or more if you desire) be paid from the fund appropriated.
    It is our belief that such a conference will lead to an active and zealous Support of this measure by the leading minds of our people and that this Support will lead to the realization of the fullest Success. Within the short time of two weeks from our departure the assurance can be Sent you of the result of our mission and that a Success [sic]
    I have the honor to be your Excellencies Obt Svt
                                        Edward M. Thomas
                                        Chairman

1862

Thomas chaired the Anglo-American Institute for the Encouragement of Industry and Art, which at the time was planning a New York exhibition of paintings, prints, and photographs that would compete with the work of "eminent" white "masters" of art. One month before this letter was written, Congress had approved $500,000 to finance the colonization of Americans of African descent. Then, on August 14, Lincoln "gave audience" at the White House to a delegation of black leaders, led by Thomas, to express his own views on colonization. "Your race are suffering, in my judgment," he told them, "the greatest wrong inflicted on any people. But even when you cease to be slaves, you are yet far removed from being placed on an equality with the white race. . . . It is better for us both, therefore, to be separated." Acknowledging that Liberia might be too distant "from the country of your nativity," Lincoln recommended mass black migration to Central America ("The country is a very excellent one for any people"), extolling its natural resources and climate. The president ended his remarks by asking "whether I can get a number of able-bodied men, with their wives and children," to commence emigration immediately. He would settle for a hundred, for fifty, even twenty-five families to start. Chairman Thomas cautiously replied that the delegation "would hold a consultation and in a short time give an answer." Lincoln responded: "Take your full time—no hurry at all" (*Coll. Works* V: 370–75).

Just two days later, Thomas wrote a brief note to Lincoln: "If it is or will be convenient to your Excellency I shall hope to have the honor of a <u>personal</u> interview with you on Monday Morning at 8 1/2 or 9. I am Satisfied that an interview for a <u>few</u> minutes will be requisite to facilitate your object[.]" Oddly, Lincoln apparently declined to see Thomas alone for a follow-up interview. So the committee chairman wrote out the longer letter on the preceding page, indicating that he was impressed by Lincoln's colonization plan, and now proposed testing the idea throughout the North. There is no evidence, however, that Lincoln provided funds for Thomas and his fellow leaders to encourage colonization among African Americans in Philadelphia, New York, and Baltimore. Days after this letter was written, other black leaders from Washington protested the Thomas delegation's early enthusiasm for the president's proposals. Within weeks, the scheme for an experimental colonization in Central America collapsed, and with it Lincoln's enthusiasm for the entire idea of shipping freed blacks to other countries.

Lincoln's much-quoted, exceptionally blunt White House remarks to Thomas and the deputation of black leaders on August 14 have somewhat tarnished his reputation as a liberator. It is often forgotten, however, that at the time he delivered those words, he had already drafted an Emancipation Proclamation, a fact that he did not share with his visitors—or the public at large. A master of political public relations, Lincoln may have intended that his rather harsh remarks, promptly printed in newspapers throughout the North (see *New York Tribune*, August 15, 1862), prepare the white public for emancipation as a military, not a philanthropic endeavor.

Invitation to a New York "War Meeting"

New York Aug 25 1862.

Abraham Lincoln

President

A war meeting will be held in this city on Wednesday next—Particulars hereafter Your presence will render great service to the Union cause—The Committee earnestly request that you will come

> George Opdyke
> Peter Cooper
> Abraham Wakeman

(Please answer)

If Lincoln did answer these distinguished New Yorkers, his reply has not been found. He did not leave Washington the following week to attend the proposed meeting—one of countless invitations to war rallies that he systematically declined.

Missouri Slaveholders Protest Arming of Blacks

Saint Louis Missouri Sep 8 1862

His Excellency Abraham Lincoln
President of the United States

Sir:

There is on the border of our State an armed band of negroes threatening an invasion of the state, and particularly the Counties of Clay and Jackson. In view of the uneasiness felt by our citizens, and to secure peace between Kansas and Missouri the undersigned have come to this City to confer with the Governor of the state in reference to this matter, and now beg leave, also, to address your Excellency, and, respectfully

---

1862

and earnestly, to ask of you an order to have these negroes disbanded, and their arms taken from them, and a further order to put a stop to such things in future. We are loyal, Union men, determined, at all hazards, to uphold the integrity of the Union, and to oppose all its enemies, and Can assure you that, were it not for the threats of [James H.] Lane [whose "Kansas Brigade" had plundered the Missouri border, and who now proposed raising a brigade of black soldiers—Ed.], [Col. Charles R.] Jennison [whose "Jayhawkers," or Kansas raiders, had allegedly attacked Missouri civilians—Ed.] and others to invade us; to despoil us of our property, to burn our Towns and dwellings, murder our Citizens, and run off our negroes, We would be comparatively at peace. At this time We know of no bands of Confederate Guerillas in any part of the state in larger squads than 50 to 100 men, and there are but few of these; none, as we believe, in either Clay or Jackson Counties; whilst our loyal militia are organizing in sufficient numbers to drive them all out of the state, or kill them, and to keep the state Clear of Rebels. We greatly fear, Mr President, that unless these negroe Brigades and Regiments are disbanded and disarmed, and those men who have been instrumental in organizing them are severely dealt with by the Govt the most serious difficulties will take place between Missouri and Kansas—two loyal states—the end of which no man can see. The Officer in Command of the Department of Kansas should be instructed not to suffer the arming or enrollment of Negroes for any such purpose, and if he is not willing to execute such an order a new Commander should be put in his place. We are aware that it is Contrary to your orders, as we believe it is against your wishes, to arm negroes, and have them clothed in the uniform of soldiers, and we beg to assure you that, whilst our people are fast returning to their loyalty, such irritating causes as we have alluded to, are a terrible burden upon the loyal men. We pray you, Mr President, to give these matters your instant attention, and assure you of our very high regard.

> Edward M. Samuel.
> M. Payne
> Patrick Shannon.
> Francis Foster
> E. R. Threlkeld
> Joseph O Boggs

The letter to the president included the following statement from one of its signatories.

1862

Statement of Edward M. Samuel,
of Liberty Clay Co MO

About 15 days ago some 15 persons from the state of Kansas—white men—under the Command of a man calling himself "Jeff Davis," but whose real name is said to be Swain, and who is reported as a desperately bad man, came into the County of Clay, as Swain said, to "recruit negroes for Genl Lanes negro Brigade"—They took forcible possession of some 25 negro men, and about 40 Horses from persons, indiscriminately, and started to cross the Missouri River with them over into Kansas—Hearing of it, Capt Johnson of the MSM, then in Command at Liberty—sent out about 50 men to Capture or shoot the men and retake the negroes and Horses. This Company of Militia succeeded in Capturing 8 of the "Jayhawkers", and recovered all the negroes and Horses. The "Jayhawkers" were lodged in the Jail at Liberty, where they were when I left home on the 4th—A day or two afterwards a white man presented to the Officer at Liberty a written demand for the release of these 8 Jayhawkers signed by "Col Jennison", with a threat that he would "hold the County responsible if they were not released and given up". The demand, of Course was refused— The "Enrolled Militia" of Clay County are sworn into the service of the state, and sworn to fight all the enemies of the state, domestic or foreign". and surely these "Jayhawkers" are enemies. Our people desire to live in peace with the people of Kansas, and I am sure that good feelings and peace between the two states would soon be universal if it were not for these "raids", by unauthorized bands, upon the persons and property of citizens of Missouri, and especially if the Govt of the US would put an effectual stop to the career of "negro stealers", and those who threaten to arm them and come into Missouri to steal other negroes, and to lay waste our property and take our lives.

Edward. M. Samuel.

The bitterly divided border state of Missouri sent 149,000 men to fight in the Civil War—109,000 on the Union side, 40,000 on the Confederate. More than 1,100 battles and skirmishes would be fought within its borders, more than in any other state except Virginia and Tennessee. Lincoln performed a delicate balancing act in Missouri during much of the war, working to keep its pro-Union slaveholders loyal to Washington without offending pro-Emancipa-

---

1862

tion forces in the rest of the country. He chose not to reply personally or directly to this petition, sending it instead on to the War Department. Contrary to its recommendations, Lincoln would eventually move to "arm negroes, and have them clothed in the uniform of soldiers." (Letter and statement, Files of Letters Received for The President and Executive Departments, National Archives; Ed. note, Michael Fellman, *Inside War: The Guerilla Conflict in Missouri During the American Civil War* [New York: Oxford University, Press, 1989], 35, 151–52.)

Emancipation Hams

Balto 25 Sepr 1862

Hon Abm Lincoln Prest U S A

Dear Sir

I have taken the liberty of sending you per Adams & Co Express, a half barrell containing half a dozen hams, which please accept on the occasion of the "Proclamation" as a slight tribute of respect from one whose Unionism knows no compromise. [Lincoln had announced his preliminary Emancipation Proclamation on September 22—Ed.]

My associations are mainly with <u>earnest</u> Union men I and have had conversations with dozens of them since the "Proclamation", and I scarcely meet one of <u>this class</u> but who cordially approve of the measures of this Proclamation.

I have long believed the Proclamation a military necessity, have recently believed it the most efficient, if not an indispensable means of crushing out the rebellion, and you will believe that my motives are not Abolition when I tell you that during the 27 years I have been voting I never even split my ticket but voted for Democracy—strait through, my last important vote having been for my friend Judge Douglass [Lincoln's opponent for the presidency in 1860—Ed.]

The Proclamation will create the necessity for prudent traitors to go home to protect their wives children & property,—and stay there, it will show to the world that we are willing to lose what has been the greatest interest, and which has controlled the country—rather than lose our <u>Nationality</u>.

It will prove to the earnest men of our country that prompt and vigor[ous] measures are to be inaugurated that scoundrelism is to be put

---

1862

down by every available means, that instead of the earlier policy of "developing Union sentiment"—treason is to be punished.

I have felt much assured, and a host of other men echoed it here with regard to the governmental policy, knowing the pernicious influence sought to be brought to bear by well meaning but humbly mistaken "Border State" men, but this act of the President makes us feel that the Jackson spirit is still in the land and that the rebllion will be crushed

With Great Respect I am Truly
George Cassaru

No acknowledgement is known; the letter was filed under the peculiar dual-heading: "Proclamation/half-barrel of hams." It is possible that Lincoln did write a thank-you note that has yet to be made known.

Congratulations for the Emancipation Proclamation

Anti-Slavery Office
Philada Sept. 27th 1862

To Abraham Lincoln
President of the United States

Honored Sir:

It is made my duty to convey to you the enclosed resolutions; a duty which I perform with unfeigned pleasure.

The joy which your great proclamation imparts is not of a kind that shows itself in noisy demonstration, nor is its extent and depth to be judged of by outward appearance. The virtuous, the reflecting, the intelligently patriotic, the people in whom inheres the nation's life, the people who make—not those who speculate in, public opinion, these are they who, as one man, hail your edict with delight and bless and thank God that he put it in your heart to issue it.

Without trespassing on your time and attention with further words I beg to subscribe myself, with sentiments of the sincerest respect,

Your obedient servant
J. M. McKim
Corresponding sec'y
Penna Anti-Slavery Society

1862

At a Meeting of the Executive Committee of the Pennsylvania Anti-Slavery Society, held in this City on the 24th inst. James Mott, President of the Society in the Chair, the following Resolutions were unanimously adopted:

"Resolved, that we hail, with inexpressible satisfaction, the Proclamation of Liberty just uttered by the President of the United States, and that without qualifying our joy by regrets that it had not appeared earlier, or that it is not more immediate and unconditional in its operation—we tender to him our sincerest thanks, and invoke upon his head Heaven's best blessings.

Resolved, that regarding Slavery as the sole cause of the War and the direst curse of the Country, and not doubting that the effect of the Proclamation will be to put an early, and in the more Southern States, a fixed period to its existence, we cannot but regard the act as one of wise humanity, of enlightened patriotism, and prudent Statesmanship.

Ordered that the Corresponding Secretary be requested to forward to the President a copy of these Resolutions at his earliest Convenience."

A. Kimber
Secretary pro. Tem.
Philada. Sept. 27. 1862.

Surprisingly few congratulatory letters and resolutions about the preliminary Emancipation Proclamation survive in the Lincoln Papers. It is not known whether this means that few Americans favored the act, that only a few chose to write, or that many wrote but few of their letters were retained.

A Poet's Plea for a Brother's Furlough

Pine Grove Oct. 20th 1862

President Lincoln,

Honored Sir,

You will be surprised, doubtless, when you receive this, yet I trust that you will patiently read the following & excuse all seeming presumption on the part of a stranger. My object in writing is simply this. During the Summer of 1861 my eldest Brother volunteered as a <u>private</u> in the Michigan "Seventh," & very bravely has he borne himself, never flinch-

---

1862

ing from his duty, & ever ready to lay down his life if it need be, for his bleeding Country—But now his health has failed, & for sometime past he has been very poorly, & he very much disires [*sic*] to return home to rectify his failing health. In vain does he plead for a Furlough! Furloughs are for <u>Officers</u>, not for the poor <u>privates</u> who are a constant sacrifice to their Military blunders,

You will, perhaps, cite him to the "Hospital" where no <u>kindred</u> voice shall greet him. Whose unfeeling Surgeons will point contemptuously to the dying Soldier, saying as he does so, "You will get your <u>discharge</u> soon, & <u>Uncle Sam</u> will give you a <u>farm six feet long</u>." This was actually said by one of your high salaried Surgeons, in a <u>Union</u> Hospital. Do you wonder that my dear Brother exerts every particle of strength to follow those brave lads, which <u>are kind</u> to him & have fought side by side with him on the Battlefield?

And now I ask you in the name of Heaven & all that is merciful, to procure a Furlough for my Brother!

I ask you because I have a <u>right</u> to make the demand.

Shall I tell you why!

In the Michigan "Seventh" I have a Brother & three Cousins. In the Mich. <u>Twenty third</u> is my Husband & two Brothers in law & <u>three</u> cousins; & I have bidden them <u>all</u> go, to help maintain the Majesty of our National Laws. & now with feeble health, I am left on a new farm, (alone with my two children) where I have to chop my firewood, husk Corn, & dig Potatoes, & I do all this cheerfully, for my Country's sake. And next week, Providence permitting—I shall go to "work out" as a <u>servant girl</u>—(a thing I never yet have done)—to procure money to pay the <u>taxes</u> on my little woodland home, leaving my babes with my aged Mother, this while. My main dependence is on the pittance allowed me by the Editor of a Literary journal for my political contributions to his paper.

So long as I can labor I <u>can not</u> accept assistance from our, already <u>overburdened</u> County.

I have laid my <u>all</u> on Liberty's shrine & I would not withdraw the sacrifice.

While my "Loved Ones" are able to strike for their Country, I do not ask to have them come home; but when worn out with fatigue & disease, I implore you, oh! President Lincoln <u>let them come home to die</u>.

Knowing that you <u>can</u> if you desire to; sincerely believing that you <u>will</u> obtain, & <u>grant</u> my request, I give you my Brother's name & address.

1862

71

Wm. J. Anthony. Company E.
Seventh Reg't. Michigan Infantry
Washington DC.

My own address is, Mrs. Charlotte A. Bentley
Pine Grove Tuscola Co. Mich.

Ps. Enclosed you will find one of my poems written for the Tuscola County Pioneer, & struck off in ballad style for the use of the Twenty third Reg't. Michigan Inftry.

Obediently Your's
C.A. Bentley

Mrs. Bentley's poem was not preserved with his letter in the Lincoln Papers, nor does any evidence survive to indicate that Lincoln furloughed the poet's brother.

A Soldier Craves "Action"

Head Quarters 132d Regt [Pennsylvania].V[ols].
Camp at Bolivar Heights—Va
Oct 20. 1862

Hon A. Lincoln
President of the U.S.

Honored Sir.

I am a soldier in the army. I was a delegate to the Chicago Convention and helped to nominate you for the Presidency and few men worked harder to secure your election than I did. I have left home, friends, business, and all to serve my country. I have been in battle and have witnessed the fearful carnage attending it as well as the suffering and misery. I love my country beyond all earthly objects, and I am willing to die for the preservation of the Constitution—as the supreme law of the land.

In coming into the army I have not yielded my right as a citizen to think and to look at things through the eyes of common sense. I believe the Rebellion can be put down in six months so effectively, that the rebels cannot rally another army to fight us. But to accomplish this we must move on the enemy—we must have action. The present policy of the Army of the Potomac in Virginia as I understand it, in my judgment

---

1862

will not end this war in <u>six years</u>. We are again approaching winter. More than a month has elapsed of splendid weather since the Battle of Antietam and <u>nothing done</u> by this great army! The only event that has occurred deserving a place in history is the raid into Penna of [Confederate General J. E. B.] Stuart's Cavalry [culminating in the burning of Chambersburg on October 11—Ed.]—and their successful retreat in the rear of our own army! Their escape is the most humiliating circumstance of the war

I beseech you Mr Lincoln as a friend who asks nothing at your hands and who has nothing but good wishes and prayers for you not to suffer the fair weather to pass away without an effort to give this rebellion its death blow & before the rebels have again gathered a large force, What are we waiting for? For Heaven's sake let not the policy of last fall prevail. We have a large and growing army. The soldiers all are anxious <u>to do something</u> and cannot comprehend the wisdom which keeps them hugging the miasmatic shores of the Potomac. If the rebels intend to give us battle in this part of Va, then every day gives them the opportunity to strengthen themselves in men, munitions of war and fortifying their positions. <u>They will not attack here—we must attack them</u>. They make most now by not fighting—and we would make most by fighting. This is the condition of the two armies—and it seems to me, he is wilfully blind who dont see it. If the rebels do not intend to give battle, then the sooner we know it and pursue them the better—we can then take fair advantage of the demoralized condition of their army—for nothing but demoralization or weakness will cause them to fall back without a fight. How important then for two reasons it is, that our army should advance. If Generals dont know it let me tell you the facts. Soldiers would rather fight than be idle in camp, contract disease, linger and die or be sent home broken down men. More men are unfitted for the service in camp than in the field.

The soldiers want to go home—but they desire to do their work first—and wish for a chance to do it. Many believe that the way home is through Richmond and over the dead bodies of Rebels. <u>They believe this</u>. Of course the soldiers of the Union army know that many of them will never be gladdened again by the sight of home and the dear ones there. They know that many will find their last resting place under the sod of the "sacred soil"—but they understand that such is the fate of war. Of this they dont ever complain—but they do of <u>inaction</u>—it is our inaction which they do not like. They prefer death in battle, to death in Camp.

1862

Mr Lincoln your Emancipation Proclamation was and is hailed with intense satisfaction by the army except perhaps a few pro-slavery political officers. It is considered the greatest act of your Administration. But it will be without virtue and effect if the Union army does not march through the seceded states victoriously and beat down all opposition—just in proportion as the army is successful—so will your proclamation be effective. The rebels must be annihilated. Shall this done [*sic*]? When! In six months or years? If it is to be years then I despair for the future of the Republic. A short war from this out [*sic*] will be the salvation of the nation. Much, very much depends upon the work between now and the 1st of December. Oh that the great and awful inertia of our army could be overcome. I pray to God that something be done speedily—and I warn you not to let this all pass in Va as did the last. <u>The rebels are not at Manassas now</u>. Why not send contrabands [fugitive slaves not yet freed by the Emancipation—Ed.] into the woods cutting cord wood and save our soldiers from the hard work of felling trees?

I write to you Mr President, not because I have a desire to obtrude anything of mine upon you, but because I have felt it my duty to state a few facts—and impressions which are extensively prevalent in the army. My letter may not be worthy of notice and you may disregard it—may profit or avail nothing—so be it. I have written these few lines out of love for the cause—and I am sure Mr Lincoln that neither you or any of your constitutional advisers love the country more than I do.

I have the honor to be very truly and sincerely

Your Obt Servt

<u>Chas A Albright</u>

Lt Col 132d Regt Pa Vols

There is no record of a reply. The letter was endorsed: "Comments on McClellan's war policy by Lt. Col. Albright." No doubt to Albright's relief, the "great and awful inertia" of the army finally ended in December—but in disaster. The Army of the Potomac, now under the command of General Ambrose E. Burnside, attacked the Confederate army at Fredericksburg, Virginia, and was soundly defeated, suffering a staggering 12,653 casualties.

1862

General Sigel Needed for Election Campaign

Union State Central Committee
Astor House, N.Y. October 20 1862.

To His Excellency Abraham Lincoln

Sir:

I am directed by this Committee to take measures to procure the attendance of Maj Gen Sigel to make some speeches here this Fall for our ticket headed by [James S.] Wadsworth & [Lyman] Tremain ["Union" candidates for New York governor and lieutenant governor, respectively—Ed.] The Committee are of the opinion that if he could make a few speeches here it would make several thousand votes difference in the result The Democrats are making superhuman efforts to elect their ticket! Gen Sigle [sic] would take the Germans by storm! We have much work to do and we must employ all the means within our power to succeed. We trust that you will take immediate measures to have Gen Sigel come here

Very Respy
Your Obt Servant
Ben Field   Sec'ty

The German-born General Franz Sigel was a particular favorite among German Americans. Some historians suggest that his ethnic appeal far outweighed his ability to command troops in battle. But even in the tough mid-year election campaign of 1862, Lincoln was not willing to spare a military commander to do battle in politics. His reply to Ben Field follows. Union candidates Wadsworth and Tremain were defeated. (Lincoln's reply, *Coll. Works* V: 472)

Executive Mansion, Washington,

Ben. Field, Esq., Astor House: October 23, 1862.
    Your letter of 20th received. Think your request cannot safely be granted.

A. Lincoln.

1862

An Electric Shock Weapon Proposed

New York November 14th 1862

Hon Abraham Lincoln
President of the United States

Dear Sir

I received a communication from the Ordnance Department at Washington just as I was leaving this City for the Northern regions of the State I therefor had no opportunity to communicate with the Department. I remained there 3 or 4 months and then started for Washington to see the President and some few others, but my journey overcame me and after remaining there ten days I was obliged to return to New York for Meddical Aid yet I have not given up a perfect trial of my discovery.

Now Sir I am willing to submit this to any man or any number of men with whom the secret will be safe, and I will now give you such an idea of the matter as will enable you to judge something of its practicability. It is simple and certain. It is Electriity generated by a machine confined in a retort [a vessel in which substances are decomposed using heat— Ed.] there being another retort charged with gas when the shell strikes which is like the most of your shells, an explosion takes place which when properly arranged is equal to any shock of electricity in the heaviest thunder storm. Now sir this requires an apparatus that will cost two or three hundred dollars, with that I could prepare and charge quite a number of shells, at any rate sufficient to test fully the invention.

If the President or the Department will give me a little immediate aid for its completion I will engage that it will turn out to be the simplest and most perfect in its operations of any discovery that has yet come before the world. I would like an immediate answer in some form in order that I may make arrangements for myself for the winter if I should live so long. I will remain in New York until I hear from the Department.

Yours Most Respectfully
Winter Palmer

Please address—
Winter Palmer Crook's Hotel 74 Chatham St.
N. York City

It is not known whether Palmer lived long enough to receive his hoped-for answer, or whether the medical emergency he reported claimed his life before his

---

1862

proposals could be studied. His letter to Lincoln—endorsed: "calling attention to his newly invented shell asks aid for its completion"—was forwarded to the Ordnance Bureau on November 21, 1862, and received there the following day. But there is no record of a reply to the "inventor." (Letter, Inventions File, Files of the Chief of Ordnance, National Archives)

Slave-Owning Union Colonel Wants "Property" Returned

Louisville [Kentucky], Nov 27th 1862

His Excellency Abraham Lincoln

Mr President.

I deem it my privilege as a Citizen to make the following Complaint directly to you. While I have been absent from my home serving our Country in the field to the utmost of my humble ability, I have not only suffered large pecuniary loss from rebel depredations but worse still, federal officers, particularly those of the 18th Michigan Infantry Volunteers have taken within their lines and hold the negroes of my loyal neighbours and myself. That regiment has not less than twenty five negroes in Camp at Lexington Ky, who belong to loyal union men who have been masters for loyalty's sake, and among the rest one of mine. I called upon the officer Commanding the regiment and mildly remonstrated against this injustice, particularly to myself, and requested him to have my negro turned out of his lines, which he flatly refused to do, justifying his detention by virtue of Your proclamation and the new article of war. My father-in-law, Col. E. N. Offut had in the mean time, during my absence, as the best means of recovering my slave which they refused him permission to take, issued a writ of replevin for the negro which was duly served by the Sheriff of Fayette County—but was disobeyed by the officer and the Civil authorities defied. Another fact I should mention in this Connection, which is, that our negroes are being taught by the abolition officers from Michigan and other northern states now serving in Kentucky, that on the first day of January next, they are all to be free, and will have a right even to kill their masters who may attempt to restrain them, which has aroused a lively apprehension in the minds of Citizens of Central Kentucky of a servile insurrection at that time unless prevented by such orders as will check the evil—This is nei-

1862

ther slander upon those officers or idle rumor; but a fact for which I and hundreds of citizens can vouch. Mr. President I deem it unnecessary to resort to argument to show to you the magnitude of the injustice in this case to me—When I became a solider I sacrificed a large and lucrative practice as an attorney in Philadelphia and placed my property in this state at the mercy of our enemies—who have revenged themselves largely upon me—and now my utter ruin is to be Completed by our own officers to promote a fanatical partizan theory—which not only ignores gratitude as a principle; but does me and many loyal men of my state bold wrong for supposed benefit to another race. Mr President is this right and will you sanction it? While in opinion I must dissent from your policy of <u>freeing</u> the slaves of rebels, which would result in great wrong to loyal slave owners, as well as to all loyal men burthened with this immense war debt—I approve of the <u>Confiscation</u> of the slaves and all property of rebels to weaken the resources of our enemy and relieve the tax burthen of our friends. Being a soldier whether palatable or impalatable, I am always ready to execute the orders of the President as my Commander in Chief; but Mr President were I Commander in Chief I would never trample upon the Constitutional rights of a loyal people in a loyal state whereby our friends would be estranged and our enemies advantaged. I need not reassure you sir of my abiding faith in your goodness, integrity of purpose and sense of justice of which this appeal is the evidence. I have the Honor to be

Your Obt Servt
M Mundy

Apparently, abolition-minded Union troops in Kentucky assumed, incorrectly, that the Emancipation Proclamation would apply in loyal, as well as rebel states, or, at least, they cited it in freeing local slaves even though they knew better. Slave-owning Colonel Marcellus Mundy served as commander of the 23rd Kentucky Infantry. He wrote this letter on official stationery of the District of Western Kentucky. Lincoln, or one of his secretaries, sent it to the secretary of war, but no reply has been located. Two years later, Mundy was again complaining bitterly of government confiscation of his property—this time land in Illinois that was being used by the government for a military hospital. He regarded it as a "further discourtesy" by the Lincoln administration. On March 7, 1864, Lincoln wrote to Secretary of War Stanton asking that he "fix the rate of Col. Mondays [sic] property." (Letter, Ordnance Files, National Archives; Ed. note, *Coll. Works* VII: 229-30)

1862

Doctor Wants His Own Hospital

[December 17, 1862]

If the President will give me the charge of a hospital or a ward in one to use my owne Medisen in and use on the wounded Soldiers for three months I will insure ninety percent of all the flesh wounds to be well and the Soldiers to be in a healthy condition and fit for duty within thirty days from the time I take them if I can have them within 8 or 10 days from the time they are wounded and I will only ask the same assistance that the other Surgeons are allowed and the Soldiers will not suffer the twentieth part as much as they do in the other hospitals and their general health shall not be impaired from the effects of the wounds.

S. W. Forsha, M. D.

This breathless, one-sentence letter was endorsed by Attorney General Edward Bates as follows: "From the within, it is evident that Dr. <u>Forsha</u> is not much of a Scholar. But he certainly has great <u>curative</u> powers; and really works wonders in relieving pain and healing wounds. I do really wish that more of our poor, suffering soldiers could have the benefit of his successful practice." It is not known how Lincoln handled the request. The doctor's undated letter was retained in the president's files, endorsed merely: "Dr. Forhsa to the President[.] He wants charge of a Hospital, & is Endorsed by the Atty Genl."

1862

1863

A rare full-length camera portrait by Alexander Gardner, taken in Washington on Aug. 9, 1863. Lincoln was so tall that the base of the photographer's immobilizer was placed on a pile of books or boxes so it could reach Lincoln's neck; the feet of its base are visible just below his knees. Photograph courtesy of author.

A Poetic Tribute to Emancipation

[January 1863]

To Abraham Lincoln
After reading his recent Proclamation.

Not often unto mortal is it given—
   Whate'er his worldly rank or state may be—
The power, sustained by principle and truth,
   To set, as Lincoln did, a people free.
He was ordained to do this Christlike deed,
   To snap the bonds of slavery apart;
To break the chains which held the negro down,
   And draw the iron from his bleeding heart.

This Proclamation, stamped with his strong will,
   This writ of Freedom, sealed by his firm hand,
This last, great act, Emancipation's prayer,
   Freeing all bondsmen living in the land,
Will cause Humanity throughout the world,
   To bless and honor Abraham Lincoln's name;
And, more than marble fame or statues could,
   Will crown his memory with enduring fame.
                 Barry Gray.
New York. Jan'y. 1863.

No acknowledgment of this poem is known. It was one of several that were inspired by the proclamation and sent to the White House.

Black Doctor Wants to Serve

Toronto Canada West Jan 7/63

President Abraham Lincoln

Sir,

   Having seen that it is intended to garrison the U.S. forts &c with colored troops, I beg leave to apply to you for an appointment as surgeon to some of the coloured regiments, or as physician to some of the de[s]pots

---
1863
---

of "freedmen." I was compelled to leave my native country, and come to this on account of prejudice against colour, for the purpose of obtaining a knowledge of my profession; and having accomplished that object, at one of the principle educational institutions of this Province, I am now prepared to practice it, and would like to be in a position where I can be of use to my race,

If you will take the matter into favorable consideration, I can give satisfactory reference as to character and qualification from some of the most distinguished members of the profession in this city where I have been in practice for about six years. I Remain Sir

Yours Very Respectfully
A. T. Augusta
Bachelor of Medicine
Trinity College Toronto

Lincoln forwarded this letter to the Army Medical Board, which ruled in March that Alexander T. Augusta could not serve in the American military because he was a British subject and "a person of African descent." But Augusta would not give up. He journeyed to Washington "at great expence and sacrifice" and appealed the decision, arguing that he desired only "to be of some use to the country and my race during this eventful period." The board reversed itself, and Augusta went on to serve as a military surgeon in "the Negro regiment now being raised." (Letter, Service Records, National Archives; Ed. note, Ira Berlin et al., *Freedom: A Documentary History of Emancipation, Series II: The Black Military Experience* [New York: Cambridge University Press, 1982], 354–55)

Gold from the Southwest—with the Promise of More

Santa Fe N. M. Feby 1, 1863

Mr Lincoln

Dear Sir

I send herewith specimens of gold and silver ore from Pino Alto mine in Arizona. They were brought from there by Brig Gen James H. Carleton Commanding the Department of New Mexico, and I send them at his request. Gen Carleton who is an able man and an accomplished geologist, and is perfectly familiar with this whole country declares that when its gold fields are developed they will prove to be richer than those

---

1863

of California—In the Southern part of the Territory near <u>Fort Stanton</u> there are some two hundred Mexicans at work digging gold and with considerable success— The Legislature has asked of Congress an appropriation of one hundred thousand dollars to build a major road from the Rio Grande at or near Fort Craig by way of these Pino Alto Mines which will be nearer than the present route to Western Arizona by one hundred miles, will avoid the Potrillo Mountains so much dreaded by travellers, and should at any time the Country about Mesilla be in the hands of enemies, the new route should be perfectly safe Should the memorial be granted and the road opened, it would at once cause an immense emigration to that Country— The latter part of March Gov Arny and myself intend visiting the Southern part of the Territory and it is my intention to forward you such specimens of gold silver and copper as I may be able to obtain on the ground, with a description of the Country— The people of new Mexico are fortunate in having so able a man as Gen Carleton at the head of the Department. They have every confidence in him and he is an untiring man. The vigorous policy he is inaugurating with reference to the hostile indians satisfies me that in less than one year they will all be glad to sue for peace—He is recommended by the Legislature for <u>promotion</u> to a <u>Major Generalship</u> and I assure the President that no act of his would be more gratifying to the people than granting a request, which was unanimously endorsed by the Legislature.

For one thing, be assured that <u>no people</u> are more loyal than the New Mexicans, and since I have been here I have satisfied myself that representations I heard made at Washington with reference to their being a disposition on the part of many to join the South was untrue—New Mexico will soon I trust become a state and will it is my opinion be republican, for until now they hardly knew what republicanism meant

Truly Yr Friend

Charles Leib

General Carleton's tenure as commander of the Department of New Mexico was laced with controversy, although he did succeed in driving Confederate forces from the Southwest. But not even samples of gold and silver ore, with the promise of more to come, could convince Lincoln to support his promotion. Carleton ultimately became a brevet major general, but was relieved in New Mexico after the war. This letter paid scant attention to the many difficulties being encountered at the time by Union forces trying to administer the large and virtually ungovernable territory.

1863

Medal-Maker Wants a Profile Photo

New York March 5/63

Hon Abraham Lincoln
President of the U.S.

Dr Sir:

We are getting up medals in Bronze 3-½ inches in Diameter—of the Leading Generals same style as the Clay & Webster medals in gold & Bronze which we had the honor to present to Queen Victoria & Louis Napoleon The Webster Medal bears our name & the gold Medals were presented to the Families of Clay & Webster

We wish also to make a medal of yourself & for that purpose would require a perfect profile of yourself   We possess only a ¾ face & front face

You will therefore if agreeable to you send us a profile taken on an Ambrotype plate size of the head about 2 inches in diameter at our expense & forward by express When the medal is finished we shall be most happy to forward one to you & are sure you will be well pleased with it After a certain number of impressions are taken the Die will be destroyed so as to make the Medals rare & valuable   If you should conclude not to favor us we shall have to use the ¾ face which will be rather difficult & we are afraid will hurt the likeness Please reply by return mail & oblige

Yr very respy
M. A. Meade
Reply Meade Bros.
233 Broadway
New York
Established 1841

This letter arrived in an envelope identifying the senders as "Photographers, specialists in cartes de visite, daguerreotypes, and ambrotypes." Apparently Lincoln did not reply quickly enough to the proposal, and some six weeks later an impatient Meade wrote yet again.

1863

New York Apl 24/63

Hon A Lincoln

Pres

We wrote you in reference to a profile for a medal. Would you be so kind as to oblige us with a reply or say if you will sit to us if we come to Washington

Yrs very truly
M. A. Meade
Meade Bros., 233 Broadway

There is no evidence that the president ever complied with the studio's request. However, had Meade merely visited the New York galleries of his neighbor and competitor, Mathew Brady, he probably could have purchased for himself a copy of a profile portrait made the previous year. (Ed. note, Charles Hamilton and Lloyd Ostendorf, *Lincoln in Photographs: An Album of Every Known Pose* [Norman, Oklahoma: University of Oklahoma Press, 1963], 100–101)

Rejected Nominee Demands a Second Chance

Kirkwood House
Washington, Mar. 20. 1863.

To the President

I ask a perusal of the following statement of facts as a matter of sheer justice.

I was appointed Quarter Master on the 16th of October 1861, and was with General Sherman's Expedition in South Carolina. I was rejected by the Senate on the 156th of Jan'y 1862, on mistaken grounds. On my arrival in Washington I appeared before the Military Committee and satisfied them that they had done me injustice. In the representation of Senator Wilson in the presence of Judge Johnston of Kansas you issued an order for my reinstation. This order bears date the 9th of August 1862. On the 11th of the same month I handed it to Secretary Stanton. For a period of seven months therefrom he has kept me idle on hotel expenses, awaiting his action on <u>your written order</u>, giving me from

---

1863

time to time such answers as would seem to preclude my right to leave the city. The very last time I saw him some ten days since, he said that he would attend to it before the adjournment of the Senate.

Now, Sir, I have no complaints to make, no harsh language to use, and had this been an ordinary application I should have long since been attending to my own private affairs. But I was anxious to remove the stigma that attaches to the man who receives an adverse vote of the Senate, more especially as I was assured by Senators King, Wade, Lane, Sherman, Nesmith and several others that there was "not the remotest doubt but that I would go through if my name was again sent in," and as I had your order that this should be done, I suggest that no prudent man would have returned from the field.

I have no disposition to complain of the course Secretary Stanton has seen proper to pursue. I merely state facts. But I respectfully ask if this be proper treatment to a man who has ever been an ardent supporter of this war? Who has proved his loyalty by receiving the notice of his Commander in the official report of the battle of Port Royal Ferry [on November 7, 1861 — Ed.]? Besides, is this course good policy? Is it calculated to arouse the energy of the country in support of your Administration? If Secretary Stanton meant to disobey your order was it not acting in bad faith towards me to keep me in ignorance of it for seven long months?

I have the honor to be

Your obedient servant,
Wm. Lilley

His Excellency Abraham Lincoln, President of the United States

---

Lincoln forwarded Lilley's letter to Secretary of War Edwin M. Stanton on March 25 with the following notation: "I remember nothing about this case; but if there is an order of mine, such as stated within, let the appointed [sic] at once? A. Lincoln." Apparently, Stanton convincingly explained his reluctance to make the appointment. The following week, Lincoln responded to Lilley with this letter.

Capt. William Lilly [sic]   Executive Mansion,

Sir: Washington, April 2, 1863.

Possibly there has been some misunderstanding in your case. You were nominated to, and rejected by the Senate. I have thought it a good rule, and have tried to act upon it, not to renominate any one whom the Senate has already rejected, unless I have evidence that the Senate would do differently on a second trial. In your case I now distinctly say that if any Senator, continuing in the Senate, will say in writing, that he voted against you, and that he has since investigated the case, and would now vote for you, and that he believes you would now be confirmed, I will renominate you. Without this, or something as strong, I can not do it.

Yours truly
A. Lincoln

Within days, Senators Henry Wilson and James W. Nesmith obliged with letters stating that their votes against Lilley had in fact been based on erroneous evidence, and that they were now prepared to vote for his confirmation if renominated. Lincoln directed Stanton on April 20 that "William Lilley be re-appointed a Quarter Master." But the case did not end there. Stanton procrastinated, forcing Lincoln to write on May 9: "I wish you would make out the appointment of Lilley at once. He has my word in writing, and I can not afford to break it. I appreciate your opposition to him; but you can better afford to let him be appointed, than I can afford to break my word with him." Then, more of Lilley's war record came to light, including a statement by General Rufus Sexton that Lilley's "treatment of the poor, defenceless blacks" on campaign had been "such as to outrage all the common feelings of humanity, characterised by the most cowardly and brutal treatment, and apparently in one or two instances by criminal indecency. Habitually in a state of partial intoxication, he grossly insulted the wife of the only loyal white man in South Carolina." Concluded Sexton: "A Court Martial held on the spot where he performed his 'efficient service' . . . justly sentenced him to be cashiered." Within days, "contained by a sense of duty," Senator Wilson withdrew his promise of support for Lilley, acknowledging that his recent endorsement had been "a mistake." (*Coll. Works* VI: 208) The quartermaster was not renomoinated after all. Lilley sent yet another plea to Lincoln on June 8, but this time the president ignored it. The strange case of William Lilley was closed. (Ed. note, *Coll. Works* VI: 181–82; Lincoln's reply, *Coll. Works* VI: 158–59)

1863

A Cane from Africa

Rooms of the American Board
of Commissioners for Foreign Missions
Bible House, Astor Place,
New York, April 7th 1863

President Lincoln,

Honored Sir,

Pardon the liberty I take in asking you to accept an Ebony Cane, which I send you by express, which I brought from the upper banks of the Gaboon [sic] River Equatorial Western Africa, where I have resided as a Missionary during nearly twenty years. In a few days I return to that dark land via England where I propose to stop a few weeks, hoping from my acquaintance with British Philanthropists to be able to exert some influence in behalf of our national cause.

With heartfelt thanks for what you have done, & are doing, to suppress the Slave Trade; & with the assurance of the sympathy & prayers of all the missionaries in Africa, & those of thousands of native Christians in that dark land, I subscribe myself—

most truly & Respectfully yours &c
Albert Bushnell

There is no record of a reply, but Lincoln undoubtedly added the gift to his growing collection of canes and walking sticks sent by admirers.

Impatient Editor on the Military Draft

Willard's Hotel [Washington] May 15, 1863

President Lincoln

Not having either time or inclination to hang round waiting rooms among a wolfish crowd seeking admission to your presence for office or contracts or personal favors, I prefer stating in writing the substance of what I would say verbally.

Your army is melting away rapidly by battle, disease and Expiration of term of service, and there is great delay in putting the Conscription

---

1863

act into effect. The hot weather is near at hand, to be followed by the sickly season.

The act itself will not furnish you with soldiers if you continue the 13th sec. As obligatory on the Gov't to receive $300. Commuation [*sic*] for personal service. You will get but few men under it, and they will consist of the poor, penniless, soulless, ragged loafer class who have neither credit, money, or stake in the perpetuity of the union. The attempt to enforce the ill on the money commutation construction will do your administration immense harm and cause it to lose all the state elections next fall. The Copperheads are gloating over the prospective harvest of votes they will reap against a bill that "puts the rich man's dirty dollars against a poor man's life."

A law ought to be construed in harmony with its obvious purpose. The conscript act is not a revenue measure, but a law to raise <u>men</u>. What is the Sec of Treas to do with twenty or thirty millions of dollars that may be paid over to his agents? They are under no bond nor is he. What is to be done with the money? The law makes no provision, except that it is received for "<u>the procuration of each substitute.</u>"

I contend that the Sec of Treas is not bound to receive any conscripts money unless he has a substitute standing ready to receive it and take the conscripts musket.

If you put this construction on the law you will get exactly as many men as you call for—either as conscripts or substitutes. The country will sustain that construction of the law.

Let me ask, is it constitutional to call for soldiers by conscription and after they are fairly drafted, to let off three fourths of them when payment of a few dollars and force the remaining fourth into the camp and battle field? I think not, and the people will think not when the question comes to be submitted to them. The 13th sec of the act if construed to permit money commutation of service completely nullifies, destroys the purpose, tenor, and intention of the whole law, and will in all probability work the downfall of the administration and the elevation of the Copperheads.

There are two constructions that can be put upon the 13th sec that will obviate all difficulty. 1st Take the ground that it is discretionary and not obligatory—when the sec of Treas to receive money in commutation of service the act says he <u>may</u> appoint a person to receive it. Suppose he doesn't, what then? Why, the conscript must find his own substitute or go himself. What is the short, blunt, Jacksonian method of dealing with it.

1863

91

2nd Order a draft for a given number of men, say 350,000. Next call for volunteers as <u>substitutes</u>, offer them a bounty of $400 each—($100. Provided in the 17th sec. And $300. Paid by the conscript) Let each conscript who wishes to commute deposit his money in bank and enter the doct in a pass book in the office of the enrolling officer, for the inspection of volunteers who are willing to become "substitutes."

Let each volunteer designate from among those depositing money for whom he will serve. Let each volunteer or conscript name the old regiment in the field in which he prefers to serve—naming also his second third or fourth choice, to be restricted however to regiments in his own state.

If this course be adopted the 13th sec. will be complied with to the letter, when a fair construction, and one in harmony with the intention of the act. Let men have a chance to volunteer <u>before</u> the draft is made and tens of thousands will do so, as they will get a large bounty and escape being drafted and obliged to serve without bounty. Republican volunteers will select Republican conscripts to become substitutes; by this means the Republican party will not have to furnish ¾ of the soldiers as they did last summer, and thereby lost the elections in Illinois, Ohio, Pa., New York and Mass.

This is all I propose to write upon this vitally important subject.

The country is impatient at the slow progress making in raising colored regiments. The blacks of our State are clamoring for the privilege of raising a regiment. So they are in Ind. So in Ohio. If you would give commissions in the West to white officers they would raise in the Western free states, in Missouri and West Tennessee ten to fifteen thousand able bodied, robust and brave colored soldiers. The opposition to colored soldiers has passed away. The Republicans are all loudly for them, and the Democrats have withdrawn their opposition. A hundred regiments of blacks can be raised between Chicago and New Orleans if you will resolve to have them. Transportation and rations ought to be provided for each colored volunteer as soon as he takes the Oath. If blacks are to be used at all why not let the Union cause have the full benefit of their powerful aid? The war is dragging too slowly. It is now in the <u>third</u> year. Twelve months hence we should be in the midst of another presidential struggle. If the Copperheads elect their ticket all the fruits of this bloody and costly war will go for naught; all will be undone and the plans and treachery of the rebels will achieve perfect triumph. The value of time and concentration of our armed forces are not sufficiently appreciated.

1863

92

In order to rally the Union sentiment and prepare for the next Presidential struggle I have organized a Union League somewhat secret in its action but at the same time strictly patriotic. I wrote the <u>ritual</u> and the forms and devised most of the signs, and set it going. I have worked hard and zealously on it for eight months. It is now spreading in every state. There are 4,000 members in this city, and there are 75,000 in Illinois. A national convention of my calling meets in Cleveland on the 20th inst. With any sort of decent success on the part of the army the League will keep the people up to the support of the administration. My labors and services may not be appreciated by you now, but no matter; if the Union is saved, the rebellion crushed and the principles of Liberty established I will be content, and die happily.

Very Truly Yours
J. Medill

P.S. I start for Cleveland, to attend the convention, tomorrow. I am chairman of the Illinois delegation.

Medill was editor of the *Chicago Press & Tribune*, longtime backers of Lincoln. His letter is important not only because it reflects a loyal supporter's unhappiness over the controversial Conscription Act, but because it shows how difficult it could be for visitors to see the president—notwithstanding the legendary "public opinion baths" for which he opened his doors to the general public. The Union League movement, which began in Philadelphia and soon spread to other northern cities, functioned as a national organization for the reelection of Lincoln in 1864. (Ed. note, Francis B. Carpenter, *Six Months at the White House with President Lincoln: The Story of a Picture* [New York: Hurd & Houghton, 1866], 281–82)

Requesting Fremont's Return

[Telegraph]
Philadelphia, June 19 1863.

A Lincoln

Fremont & Freedom—Give us Fremont and Siegel [*sic*]—we can whip the devil.

Tewandah

1863

No reply has been found to this wire, nor has the identity of its author been ascertained. General John Pope had been named General John C. Fremont's superior in the West, and General Franz Sigel had been transferred east, where he was destined to fail at the Battle of New Market in 1864.

A "Double Cannon" for Land and Sea

Norwalk 24th June 1863

To His Excellency Mr. Lincoln
President of the U.S.A.

Hond & Respected Sir

Allow me to call your special attention to a Letter from <u>Paris France</u>—published in the New York Times of this morning—First column First page—under the "<u>nom de plume</u>" of "<u>Mala Koff</u>["]

It is stated that the Emperor failing to secure the Cooperation of England has accepted that of Spain—and is preparing to aid the Rebells &c

So far as the South is concerned the Rebellion is for the present nearly at an End—Yet they may for a long period by Gurrilla Warfare oblige us to keep a large Armey in the Field and a Navy on the Sea

Age Excludes me from Volunteering as I have desired to do as a soldier—Yet I may perhaps render some service—I have befor written Stating that I had Designed a piece of Ordnance—That is a Double Cannon Intended both for Land & Sea service which to me appears worthy of <u>Notice</u>. I have received no Response to my Letter, and know not if it has been Received by you—I gave a description of the Gun &c—Also of a Design for a Locomotive-power for propelling such Guns—or any other—as well also the Bagging Waggons, Ambulance &c &c—at much Grater Rapidity or speed than is possible by <u>Horse</u> and at far less Expense—Saving not only Money—Expense—but the Lives of both <u>Men</u> and Horses—as well a Gain in speed which is often essential.

Such Locomotives may be used on all <u>Roads</u> and <u>Fields</u> when Horses with other vehicles may be or can be used—and case of Wet & bad Roads where Horses would be useless—The Locomotive may be used to good purpose and effect—Sandy & Muddy Roads in place of being cut up and made impassable will be made passable—The Wheels of Each Locomotive being 3 in Number are arranged thus. The <u>Tire</u> or Face of

---

1863

94

each Wheel to be 2 feet Wide More or less—thus in passing over a Road the whole Track is covered—The Wheels acting as a Roller to compress and make smooth the Track or Road—Where Five or more could pass Abrest [sic] a Track of sufficient width for Foot soldiers would be rendered passable—which otherwise would be impassable—it mite be for days caussing Delay & Loss of time &c

The Gun is Designed to be Breech Loading for the Charge of powder above the Chamber for the powder the Gun divides and becomes Two—the Balls for this being Connected First by a Bar or Bolt of Iron the length of the Gun attached to Each Ball—The outer Ends—to be connected by Chain The Mouths to be slightly diverge[d] from the Center of the Gun—Thus when Discharged the Chain will at a Given distance be Elongated or Extended to its full length between the two Balls—Sweeping through Rank & File of Men or Horses—If on Shipboard Cutting away Spars & Rigging of Sailing vessells or Smook Stacks—&c of Steamers—One such Gun when properly discharged doing more Executing than a Broadside of Single Guns.

Ware our Merchant Ships furnished with one Such Gun Each—The pirats Sims [probably Raphael Semmes, commander of the Confederate raider, Alabama—Ed.] & others of the like would soon be disabled—To me such Gun appears a Desidratum—Yet I have not the menes to Compleat & Exhibit Such Gun—as Business Intrest ware and have been for a series of years at the South—I am so long as the war continues without Menes or Business if not Entirly Ruined. Yet I hope the nation may be Saved from all Her Enimies at Home & Abroad for the Generations to come to the End of time.

Your Obt Svt & Respectfully
Chs. F. Raymond

Lincoln's office referred this perplexing letter to the War Department, which replied as follows a few days later.

W[ar]. D[erpartment]. W[ashington]. C[ity].
July 31st. 1863.

Sir:

The S[ecretary] of W[ar] directs me to acknowledge the receipt of your letter of the 24th instant, addressed to the President & by him referred to this Department, describing a piece of ordnance which you have designed, as well as a locomotive power for propelling it; and in reply to inform you that the same has been referred to the Chief of Ordnance.

> Very respct
> Chief Clerk
> Mr. Chas. F. Raymond.
> Norwalk. Connecticut

Raymond evidently received a letter sometime later from the Ordnance Bureau, but he was apparently dissatisfied with it, for, again inspired by a report he read in the *New York Times*, he wrote to Lincoln the following spring:

> Norwalk 26th March 1864

To His Excellency Abm Lincoln-
President of the U.S.A.

Hond & Respected Sir

I have noticed in the N.Y. Times of this day—That—His Emperial Highness L.N.B. [Louis Napoleon Bonaparte]—Has—Conferred the <u>Cross</u> of the Legion of Honor—on a Mr. Claxton of Baltimore—for His improvements on and Experiments with an American Invention—<u>Viz</u> Broadwells Breech Loading Cannon.

The French Government paying Mr. C____ <u>Six Hundred Francs</u> per <u>Month</u> to Exercize His own Gun

I have offered our Government not only a <u>Breech</u> But Double Cannon which for <u>Execution</u> in my own estimation would be worth a <u>Score</u> of single Guns— The Chief of The Ordnance Department—Says—this a Breech Loading & Double Cannon is Nothing <u>New</u>—Has been tried and Condemned. I do not know what he refers to—the <u>Breech Loading</u>—or The Double Cannon—or the <u>Combination</u>.

From the Statement referred to—it would appear—that Simply—the <u>Breech Loading</u>—was something new <u>abroad</u> and that a High Value is set upon it—

> Your Obt Servt Respectfully
> Ch. F. Raymond

Raymond wrote once more on July 13, 1864. A clerk endorsed this new plea: "Again calls attention to his double Cannon, submitting further explanation of its principles &c." Once more his request was referred to the Ordnance Deptartment. The irrepressible correspondent wrote to Lincoln yet again on September 12, 1864—another long letter—this time seeking the president's favor

---

1863

96

on political grounds by warning: "We have much to contend with in the coming Election—we shall need all the aid we can get—I fear our Opponants will lieve no measure untried to carry there <u>Peace-War Candidate</u> The <u>Traitor</u> McC___ .... The price of Liberty is Vigilence—constant enduing vigilance." Lincoln evidently felt he could manage his reelection campaign without Raymond's invention to bolster him. (Letter, Ordnance Files, National Archives)

Hero's Mother Worries over Treatment of Black War Prisoners

Buffalo [New York] July 31 1863

Excellent Sir

My good friend says I must write to you and she will send it   My son went in the 54th regiment. I am a colored woman and my son was strong and able to fight for his country and the colored people have as much to fight for as any. My father was a Slave and escaped from Louisiana before I was born morn forty years agone   I have but poor edication but I never went to schol, but I know just as well as any what is right between man and man. Now I know it is right that a colored man should go and fight for his country, and so ought to a white man. I know that a colored man ought to run no greater risques than a white, his pay is no greater his obligation to fight is the same. So why should not our enemies be compelled to treat him the same, Made to do it.

My son fought at Fort Wagoner but thank God he was not taken prisoner, as many were I thought of this thing before I let my boy go but then they said Mr. Lincoln will never let them sell our colored soldiers for slaves, if they do he will get them back quck he will rettallyate and stop it. Now Mr Lincoln dont you think you oght to stop this thing and make them do the same by the colored men they have lived in idleness all their lives on stolen labor and made savages of the colored people, but they now are so furious because they are proving themselves to be men, such as have come away and got some edication. It must not be so. You must put the rebels to work in State prisons to making shoes and things, if they sell our colored soldiers, till they let them all go. And give their wounded the same treatment. it would seem cruel, but their no other way, and a just man must do hard things sometimes, that shew him to be a great man. They tell me some do you will take back the

1863

97

Proclamation, don't do it. When you are dead and in Heaven, in a thousand years that action of yours will make the Angels sing your praises I know it. Ought one man to own another, law for or not, who made the law, surely the poor slave did not. so it is wicked, and a horrible Outrage, there is no sense in it, because a man has lived by robbing all his life and his father before him, should he complain because the stolen things found on him are taken. Robbing the colored people of their labor is but a small part of the robbery their souls are almost taken, they are made bruits of often. You know all about this

Will you see that the colored men fighting now, are fairly treated. You ought to do this, and do it at once, Not let the thing run along meet it quickly and manfully, and stop this, mean cowardly cruelty. We poor oppressed ones, appeal to you, and ask fair play.

Yours for Christs sake
Hannah Johnson

[In different hand] Hon. Mr. Lincoln
The above speaks for itself
Carrie Coburn

Lincoln did not reply to Hannah Johnson; her letter was forwarded to the War Department's new Bureau of Colored Troops established on May 22, 1863. Two weeks before she wrote, her son, along with his comrades from the 54th Massachusetts, had led the fateful assault on Battery Wagner, near Charleston, South Carolina, suffering major casualties. Hannah Johnson did not yet know it, but the very day that she wrote this tautly reasoned demand for equal treatment for black prisoners of war, Lincoln issued publicly the following order of retaliation, written July 30, vowing to enslave a Confederate prisoner for every black Union prisoner enslaved by the enemy. (Letter, Colored Troops Division Files, National Archives; Lincoln's reply, *Coll. Works* VI: 357)

Executive Mansion, Washington D.C. July 30. 1863

It is the duty of every government to give protection to its citizens, of whatever class, color, or condition, and especially to those who are duly organized as soldiers in the public service. The law of nations and the usages and customs of war as carried on by civilized powers, permit no distinction as to color in the treatment of prisoners of war as public enemies. To sell or enslave any captured person, on account of his color, and for no offence against the laws of war, is a relapse into barbarism and a crime against the civilization of the age.

1863

The government of the United States will give the same protection to all its soldiers, and if the enemy shall sell or enslave anyone because of his color, the offense shall be punished by retaliation upon the enemy's prisoners in our possession.

It is therefore ordered that for every soldier of the United States killed in violation of the laws of war, a rebel soldier shall be executed; and for every one enslaved by the enemy or sold into slavery, a rebel soldier shall be placed at hard labor on the public works and continued at such labor until the other shall be released and receive the treatment due to a prisoner of war.

Abraham Lincoln

Rumored Invitation to New England

Washington Aug. 1, '63

To the President

My Dear Sir,

It is said that you contemplate visiting New England this month. I should esteem it a great favor to be permitten [*sic*] to accompany you, and give you any attention I possibly can, to make your trip pleasant. My position calls me to look after your personal comfort <u>here</u>, & why not when you are away?

Very truly & faithfully yours
B. B. French

French, who served as commissioner of Public Buildings during the Lincoln administration, apparently confused Mrs. Lincoln's plans with the president's. Mary headed for the White Mountains of Vermont the week French wrote this letter, but the president, evidently declining another invitation—this one from his wife—did not accompany her. Lincoln scribbled the following response to French's inquiry.

[To Benjamin Brown French]

I am grateful for your kind offer; but really I know nothing about a trip of mine away from here, except from your note, and the newspapers.

A. Lincoln

Aug. 3, 1863

1863

A Beleaguered Union Editor Asks Help for a Brother

Office of the Daily Times
Troy   August 14th 1863.

To His Excellency Abraham Lincoln:

I address you personally, because our Democratic system permits a citizen free access to the Chief Magistrate.

I am an editor of the leading Republican Administration organ of Northern and Eastern New York. I made more than one hundred and fifty speeches for you in 1860. I have done what I could in the recruitment of volunteers. Our office was lately sacked by a Copperhead mob and $10,000 worth of property destroyed. I myself had the honor of knowing that a rope was prepared for me.

Please do not lay this letter down here. I never asked for an office, and do not want one now.

I have a brother, the pet of aged parents, who left a comfortable home, enlisted as a private soldier, was wounded at Gettysburg, and suffered amputation at the thigh. His old father went down to nurse him and did so on the field, but when he was moved to a general hospital a red-tape Surgeon banished him. All he asks is permission a few hours a day, to sit beside his bed and cheer him. He will interfere with nothing—cost nothing. My brother languishes without him, and may die.

Three lines from you will set the matter right—accepting him and commissioning him as a nurse without pay.

I know this is not your business, but I have tried the outlets in vain and essay the fountain-head. You would rather write me thus much, I know, than expose the sinuosities of Copperhead sophisms.

Yours respectfully,
Geo. W. Demers
Editor Troy Times
My father's name is David H. Demers

A clerk wrote on the back: "Refer to the personal attention of the Surgeon General," then, "Ansd. permit sent Aug. 19. 1863".

Asking a Job with a Change in Climate

Berlin, N.Y., Sept. 15, 1863.

Hon. A. <u>Lincoln</u>, Pres't &c.—

<u>Excellent and Dear Sir:</u>—

Permit me now, if you please, a word personally, and <u>selfishly</u>!

By trade, I am a printer—have had some fifteen years' experience as editor of Temperance and Republican journals—and for about seven years have been pastor of the Baptist Church in this place, which relation I still maintain.

I am poor—"poor as poverty"—a kettle of it boiled down to a pint! Not much, to be sure, but of some moment to <u>me</u>! Well, what of it? <u>This</u>: I gave thought, and still think, that a change of climate and occupation might result beneficially, and replenish my purse. So, permit me to ask if there be not some position that you can bestow on me, either in Washington, or in the field, at home or abroad—perhaps as Paymaster in the Army?

I do not want a sinecure! One of the busy kind, I want something to do—am willing to labor, and labor hard, so that something can be saved for the benefit of my family—for I have a wife and three children. If it be not now the case, perhaps previous to January 1st there may be a suitable position within your bestowal. May I expect something?

If you wish to make inquiries concerning me, I refer you to Judge Underwood, late 5th Auditor, who has known me for years, even when an apprentice at Herkimer; also to Gov. Seward, with whom, in former years, and especially when an editor in Poughkeepsie, I was much in correspondence. My age is 36.

God bless you, my dear President, and enable you to hold a taut rein, until treason be dead and buried, and freed men, women and children, hymn its requiem.

Very truly and ever yours,
H. A. Guild

No reply is known to this compelling request by the churchmouse-poor editor and pastor from upstate New York.

1863

Asking Passage for Livestock

New York Sep. 17. 1863

To His Excellency Abraham Lincoln
Washington

Dear Sir—

We take the liberty to address you in regard to a recent order in relation to the Shipment of <u>Live Stock</u> to Foreign Countries, which bears particularly hard upon us at this time. For instance, we are the owners of a line of Steam ships running between this port and Havanna, and for several years past, we have taken the Horses purchased in New York by the Planters and Merchants of Havanna and the Island of Cuba generally; these Horses are purchased exclusively for their own use, and are never offered in the market for sale. Formerly there were but few of the Planters visited our City, but the establishment by us of a splendid line of Ships, that now run regularly making the passage to Havanna in 4 ½ days, and the return voyage in less than 4 days; has induced a great number of families to spend the summer in this City and neighborhood and the number at Saratoga Springs the past season is a proof of our statement. During the stay of these parties, they purchase from our dealers, great numbers of fine Carriages, Harnesses &c—and also Horses, and up to the present time, have enjoyed the priviledge of taking home with them in the fall, the articles so purchased; but as the order from the Department now stands, the Collector cannot grant the permission. Some time since we applied to the Secretary of the Treasury for permission to ship the horses as before described, and he referred us to Your Excellency in relation to the same; and we would most respectfully Now make the request, assuring you that no improper use shall be made of your kindness, the required facility be given us.

With great consideration and respect we remain most faithfully
Your ob. Svts.
S. Gifford Tileston Co.

No reply to this request has been found. That it was directed to the president of the United States, and at the suggestion of the secretary of the treasury, no less, suggests precisely how attentive the chief magistrate was then expected to be to the complaints of ordinary citizens, even during wartime.

1863

The President's Secretary Reports Poetically

Columbus, Ohio,
October 4, 1863

Dear President:

An accident detained me in Columbus today and gave me an opportunity of seeing [John] Brough [governor of Ohio—Ed.]

He requests me to apologize for his seeming rudeness in not answering your letter, and hopes that the verbal reply sent by Govr. [William] Dennison [Lincoln's future postmaster-general—Ed.] was entirely satisfactory.

He says they will carry Ohio by at least 25,000 votes, independent of the soldiers who will indefinitely increase it. The Vallandigam [*sic*] men have given up the fight here.

Brough is much more anxious about [Andrew] Curtin [Pennsylvania governor running for re-election—Ed.] than about himself.

> Brough thinks that as yet in the Keystone State
> The prospect is rather uncertain;
> The fifth act is near, and we only wait,
> Impatient, the rise of the Curtin.

A hazy joke, with which I close.

Yours respectfully,
John Hay.

No reply was sent to this epistle about politics and forthcoming state elections. Lincoln occasionally sent Nicolay or Hay on political or military missions to gather information for him from around the country. Andrew Curtin went on to win reelection in Pennsylvania.

1863

Requesting—and Winning—a Unique Donation

Chicago Sanitary Commission,
Branch of U.S. Sanitary Commission
Rooms No. 66 Madison Street
Chicago, Oct. 11th, 1863.

Abraham Lincoln, Pres. U. S. A.,

Dear Sir:

The patriotic women of the Northwestern States will hold a grand fair in Chicago on the last week of Oct., and the first of Nov. to raise funds for the Sanitary Commission of the Northwest whose head quarters are in Chicago. The Commission labors especially for the sick and wounded soldiers of the South western States, of whose bravery, and persistent endurance, we are all justly proud. I enclose you circulars, which will explain to you our entire plan, and show you the magnitude of the enterprise, by which we confidently hope to realize from $25,000 to $50,000.

The greatest enthusiasm prevails in reference to this Fair, which is now only two weeks distant. There are very few towns in Northern Illinois, Wisconsin, Michigan, and Iowa that are not laboring for it. Artists are painting pictures for it, manufacturers are making elegant specimens of their handiwork for the occasion, tradesmen are donating the choicest of their wares, while women are surpassing their ordinary ingenuity and taste in devising beautiful articles for sale, or decorations for the walls of the four spacious halls we are to occupy.

The Executive Committee have been urgently requested to solicit from Mrs. Lincoln and yourself some donation to this great Fair—not so much for the value of the gift, as for the eclat which this circumstance would give to the Fair. It has been suggested to us from various quarters that the most acceptable donation you could possibly make, would be the original manuscript of the proclamation of emancipation, and I have been instructed to ask for this, if it is at all consistent with what is proper, for you to donate it. There would be great competition among buyers to obtain possession of it, and to say nothing of the interest that would attach to such a gift, it would prove pecuniarily [sic] of great value. We should take pains to have such an arrangement made as would place the document permanently in either the State or the Chicago Historical Society.

There would seem great appropriateness in this gift to Chicago or

<hr>

1863

Illinois, for the benefit of our Western Soldiers, coming as it would from a Western President. We hope it may be possible for you to donate it to us.

But if it be not possible, then allow us to ask for some other simple gift, from Mrs. Lincoln and yourself—sufficient to show that you are cognizant of out efforts and are interested in them. Our Fair opens on Tuesday, Oct. 27th, in little more than two weeks.

Yours very respectfully,
Mrs. D. P. Livermore.

Lincoln did not immediately reply to this request, prompting Chicago Congressman Isaac N. Arnold to telegraph on October 21: "I am desired by the ladies having charge of the North western fair to remind of it & beg you will send the original of proclamation of Freedom if possible." Finally, on the eve of the opening of the ambitious charity fair, Lincoln complied with the request with the following reply. (Lincoln's reply, *Coll. Works*: VI: 539)

Executive Mansion.
Washington, Oct. 26. 1863

Ladies having in charge of the North Western Fair
For the Sanitary Commission
Chicago, Illinois.

According to the request made in your behalf, the original draft of the Emancipation proclamation is herewith enclosed. The formal words at the top, and the conclusion, except the signature, you perceive, are not in my hand-writing. They were written at the State Department by whom I know not. The printed part was cut from a copy of the preliminary proclamation, and pasted on merely to save writing.

I had some desire to retain the paper; but if it shall contribute to the relief or comfort of the soldiers that will be better

Your obt. Servt.
A. Lincoln

The Proclamation was sold at the Fair for $3,000, earning Lincoln a gold watch for being "the largest contributor to the Fair" (Mrs. Livermore and Mrs. A. H. Hoge to Lincoln, November 26, 1863, Lincoln Papers). Just as the organizers had promised, the Proclamation was deposited in the Chicago Historical Society. But the document, together with Lincoln's cover letter, were destroyed in the Great Fire of 1871. (Ed. note, *Coll. Works* VII: 75; Alvin Robert Kantor

---

1863

and Marjorie Sered Kantor, *Sanitary Fairs: A Philatelic and Historical Study of Civil War Benevolence* [Glencoe, IL: SF Publishing, 1992], 172–74)

Tennesseans Plead for Protection

[Telegraph]
Knoxville October 15 1863.

To the President of the US

In the name of Christianity & humanity, in the name of God and Liberty, for the sake of their wives and children & everything they hold sacred & dear on earth the loyal people of Tennessee appeal to you & implore you not to abandon them against the merciless dominion of the Rebels by a withdrawal of the U.S. forces from upper East Tenn

John Williams
and N. G. Taylor
Ex-M. C.

Lincoln wrote to the former Congressmen two days later.

John Williams & N.G. Taylor.   Washington, D.C.,
Knoxville, Tenn.   Oct. 17 1863

You do not estimate the holding of East Tennessee more highly than I do. There is no <u>absolute</u> purpose of withdrawing our forces from it; and only a <u>contingent</u> one to withdraw them <u>temporarily</u>, for the purpose of not losing the position <u>permanently</u>. I am in great hope of not finding it necessary to withdraw them at all—particularly if you raise new troops rapidly for us there.

A. Lincoln

The same day as he wrote this letter, Lincoln issued a proclamation calling for 300,000 volunteers. On October 18, General George H. Thomas declared from Chattanooga: "We will hold this town till we starve." The Chattanooga campaign ended a success. (Ed. note, Patricia L. Faust, <u>Historical Times Illustrated Encyclopedia of the Civil War</u> [New York: Harper & Row, 1986], 135; Lincoln's reply, *Coll. Works* VI: 523, 525)

1863

A Salute from New York Orphans

Five Points House of Industry
New York, October 16, 1863

To His Excellency Abraham Lincoln,
President of the United States:

Sir:

The undersigned, poor boys of the Charity School in the Five Points House of Industry, New York, remember with pleasure your visit to our School on a Sunday afternoon, in the month of March, 1860. We also remember that you then said the way was open to every boy present, if honest, industrious, and perserv[er]ing, to the attainment of a high and honorable position.

We take the liberty herein to congratulate you, sir, that your own life history illustrates the truth of the words you then addressed to us; and that so soon thereafter your own countrymen should have set their seal to your honesty and trustworthiness by conferring upon you the highest honors in the gift of a free people.

We pray God, the All-Wise Governor of the universe to have you in His care and guidance, to enlighten you by His wisdom, and to further honor you as His instrument in liberating a race, and in leading your countrymen through present troubles, to righteousness, peace, and prosperity, May He ever own and bless you and yours.

With true respect, we are, sir
your humble servants

Patrick McCarty	Walter Bushnell	James Higgins
John Donague	Robert McDowell	Robert Carey
Louis Clarke	William Looker	James Keating
Charles Lockwood	William Ryan	Christopher Oltraggs
Henry Duncan	Henry Clay Van Winkle	John O'Niel
George White	William Ayres	Robert Maxwell
		and 100 others

Lincoln had visited the school, located in New York City's notorious Five Points slum, on March 11, 1860, following a church service in Brooklyn. (Ed. note, Earl Schenck Miers, *Lincoln Day by Day: A Chronology, 1809–1865*, 3 vols. [Washington, D.C.: Lincoln Sesquicentennial Commission, 1960], II: 275; hereafter cited as *Lincoln Day by Day*)

1863

A Book on the Gettysburg Victory

Gettysburg Pa. October 24/1863

To His Excellency Abraham Lincoln

Dr. sir;

Two days ago, I mailed to your address a small volume, "Notes on the Rebel Invasion of Maryland & Pennsylvania, accompanied by a Map of the Battlefield." The notes were at first prepared for the private use of myself & family, but published at the earnest solicitation of many of my friends. The Map was constructed from actual measurements made by myself & son.

Please accept the volume as a token of the high regard I entertain towards you personally & officially.

Your obedient servant
M. Jacobs

No reply is known, but it is quite conceivable that Lincoln referred to the volume when he began preparing his Gettysburg Address the following month.

Introducing a Future President

New York Oct 31. 1863

Sir

It gives me pleasure to introduce my friend General Chester A. Arthur late Qr. M Genl of this state   Genl Arthur was an efficient and capable officer, and he is one of our truest political friends. If it is not taxing you too much I hope you may be able to see him a few moments

With high consideration I am

Your ob svt.

The President   E. D. Morgan
Washington

Lincoln probably did Governor Morgan the favor of meeting his eventual successor.

1863

Urging Equal Pay for "Colored" Troops

Office of Supervisory Committee
for Recruiting Colored Regiments
Philadelphia, November 5th 1863.
To his Excellency the President of the United States,

This memorial on behalf of the Supervisory Committee for recruiting Colored Regiments in the State of Pennsylvania respectfully represent

That notwithstanding the inequality of pay and bounty, the Colored people of the free states have heretofore responded to the call for volunteers with an alacrity and to an extent which clearly provide that they are not deficient in military spirit and patriotism. And it is believed by those who have the best opportunity for forming correct opinions on the subject, that the national forces would be very largely increased from this portion of our population, if the same protection and encouragement were extended to them as to others.

The courage, discipline and general good behaviour of the colored troops, as already displayed, have enlisted in their behalf a favorable sentiment throughout the country; and justice, as well as mere policy, would seem to require that, in the matter of pay and bounty they should be placed on a more equal footing.

It is believed that there is no insuperable objections to such a course, in existing laws, liberally construed, and your memorialists cannot doubt the disposition of the Government to extend to this class of its brave defenders every proper measure of protection and reward.

By the terms of your Proclamation of the Seventeenth day of October 1863 calling for three hundred thousand more volunteers to serve for three years, it appears to be doubtful whether colored troops are to be included in its provisions. Your memorialists would therefore respectfully bring this subject to your attention, and request such a further order in regard to the acceptance and compensation of colored volunteers, as their willingness and ability to aid in the suppression of a wicked rebellion, renders just and proper.

It is not doubted that under suitable encouragement, many regiments of colored troops can be raised in this and adjoining States. And your Excellency may rest assured of the readiness of the people of this community to cooperate in this and all other measures the Government may adopt for the purposes of reinforcing our armies now in the field, bring-

---
1863
---

ing their needful operations to a prosperous end, and thus closing forever the fountains of sedition and civil war.

On behalf of the Committee
Thomas Webster

The issue of unequal pay for colored troops remained a problem for the Lincoln
administration for many more months, until the president gave in to pressure
like that brought by Webster and his committee and increased wages for African
Americans in the military.

A Plan for Compensated Emancipation

Washington, D.C.
Nov: 10th 1863

Mr. President

Dear Sir

I take leave to suggest that there are persons in Maryland who are
willing to part with their slaves provided they can get compensation in
some way for them. I think that emancipation in the other states can be
promoted, and many slaveholders, be induced to favor it if the following
plan be adopted. Let Congress make an appropriation of—millions of
dollars, and let a board of commissioners be appointed to pay for each
slave that shall be brought before the Commissioners, such sum as may
be proper. Such slave or slaves of course to be freed. The master to take
an oath to support the government of the United States, and to forever
oppose secession. It would be useful to fix a time in which all who may
be willing then to dispose of their slaves shall appear before the commission. This course would not conflict with any state laws, or state
rights, and would not require <u>state legislation</u>, which may be difficult to
obtain in Maryland until a large number of slave holders can be induced
to part with their slaves. The plan can be applied also to the other border
states.

It would in my judgment make the plan more effective if Congress
would abolish all "fugitive slave" laws. This can be done as the Constitution does not <u>recognize</u> such laws as to be passed or to exist. While it
would show the slaveholder that he could get no aid from such laws to
recover his slave, and might add to the inducements, to part with him,

---

1863

it would reconcile thousands to the law appropriating money to secure his freedom.

> I am Dear Sir Respectfully &x &c
> E. P. Phelps

Phelps was a Methodist minister from Baltimore. There is no record of a reply to his suggestions for hastening emancipation in Maryland.

His Most Priceless Gift, Acknowledged

> Chicago Sanitary Commission
> Chicago, Nov 11th 1863 —

President Lincoln

Sir

We profoundly thank you for your gift to our North Western Fair of the original draft of the "Proclamation of Emancipation." It came to us in the midst of a wonderful outpouring of loyalty & liberality from the great throbbing hearts of the North West, nay, almost of the Nation; for all seemed ready to respond and give. Your proclamation is the star of hope, the rainbow of promise, that has risen above the din and carnage of this unholy rebellion, and will fill the brightest page in the history of our struggle for national existence; while it has become the anchor of hope, the rainbow of promise, to the oppressed of every land, at home and abroad. In the midst of so many varied and valuable donations, it has been reserved to you, Abraham Lincoln, the People's President, to bestow the most noble and valuable gift, for the sick and suffering soldiers. The treasure shall be carefully guarded & skilfully managed, so as to produce a revenue that shall make your heart glad, and soothe the woes of hundreds in hospitals. May God bless you, and preserve you, to rule over us another term in peace, with the same ability, uprightness and wisdom which He has given you to guide us through the storms of war at home, and threatening dangers from abroad.

With profound respect & gratitude
> Mrs. A. H. Hoge
> Mrs. D. P. Livermore

Lady Managers of the N. Western Fair

1863

Lincoln's "noble and valuable" donation to Chicago's Great Northwestern Sanitary Fair, his handwritten copy of the final Emancipation Proclamation, was sold for $3,000, winning for the president a gold watch for having been the "largest contributor" to the charity event. The manuscript was destroyed in the Chicago fire of 1871. Jane Hoge had written often to Lincoln—usually in an effort to win government appointments for her son. (Ed. note, Kantor and Kantor, *Sanitary Fairs*, 172–74; for Lincoln's additional correspondence about and with Mrs. Hoge see *Coll. Works* VI: 40–41, 96; V: 512; VII: 75; see also Mrs. A. H. Hoge and Mrs. D. P. Livermore to Lincoln, November 26, 1863, Lincoln Papers, Library of Congress)

Presenting "Jeb" Stuart's Eagle-Quill Pen

Washington Nov 17, 1863

To President Lincoln

My Dear Sir:

To day you were kind enough to give me an elastic pen-holder, which pleased me well, as fitting my rough hand, exactly. And now Sir, allow me to present to you in return, a quil of the Great Bald Eagle, of the Rocky Mountains. I hope you may find occasion to use it, during your present term, on signing your name to some great historic document— such, for instance, as a proclamation that the Union is restored and the law reigns—which may go down to posterity, for your own honor and your country's good.

This quil has a history. It was obtained in the Rocky Mountains, and and [*sic*], in the fall of 1860, sent to me, some two thousand miles, by my <u>then</u> young friend, Lieutenant Stuart, of Sumner's Regiment, of U.S. Dragoons (now General Stuart of the Rebel Army [no doubt "Jeb" Stuart—Ed.]).

I will not undertake to interpret the sign, nor to draw prophetic conclusions from the fact, that the brave young soldier, before deserting the flag under which he was reared, and joining hands with the enemies of her country, first stripped himself of the Eagle's plumage.

Let those who will, write out the mellancholy moral.

I have the honor to be most respectfully

Your friend &obt servt
Edw Bates

1863

The so-called "elastic pen holder" which Lincoln had sent to his attorney general, Edward Bates, has never been identified. Conceivably it was one of the many bizarre and impractical inventions sent to the White House each week. But the president may have hoped it would improve Bates's handwriting; his letters are among the most illegible to be found in the Lincoln Papers. No one knows whether Lincoln ever used the pen sent originally by Confederate hero J. E. B. Stuart to sign any historic documents.

A Request for the Gettysburg Address

Gettysburg Nov. 23/63

His Excellency A. Lincoln
President of U.S.

Sir:

On behalf of the States interested in the National Cemetery here, I request of you the original manuscript of the Dedicatory Remarks delivered by you here last Thursday.

We desire them to be placed with the correspondence and other papers connected with the project. (Please append your certificate to them). I am with great Respect

Your Excellency's obdt Servant,
David Wills

Judge Wills had written the invitation that brought Lincoln to the site of the war's greatest battle to deliver what became his greatest speech. No reply to this request is known, but in 1991, collector-historian Lloyd Ostendorf unearthed what he claimed was the handwritten second page of the lost "reading" copy of Lincoln's Gettysburg Address, endorsed to Wills. The document's authenticity has since been called into question by some experts, and no final consensus on it has been reached. Surely Lincoln obliged Wills, although whatever letter he may have addressed to him is lost. This request from Wills was endorsed on the reverse: "David Wills/Gettysburg Nov. 23, 1863,/On behalf of the States interested in the National Cemetery, requests the original manuscript of the Dedicatory remarks delivered by the President." (Ed. note, Lloyd Ostendorf, "Lost Copy of The Gettysburg Address Comes to Light," *Lincoln Herald* 94 [Spring 1992]: 24–27)

1863

Lincoln Becomes an Honorary Missionary

Cincinnati, Ohio November 25th, 1863

His Excellency/Abraham Lincoln/President of the United States
Washington/D.C.

Sir:

At a missionary anniversary held on the 16th August last, by the Third Methodist German Congregation in their Church on Buck Eye Street in this City it was unanimously resolved that you should be made a Life Member of the Cincinnati Conference Missionary Society, auxiliary to the Missionary Society of the Methodist Episcopal Church, by the payment of ten Dollars, which amount was immediately made up by the said Congregation, by whose direction I have this day forwarded to you, per Adams Express Company, free of charge, a certificate of said Missionary Society, by which you are constituted one of its life members.

You are herewith respectfully requested to accept the said certificate as a slight token of respect from said Congregation.

I have the honor, Sir, to subscribe myself most respectfully

Your Excellency's very obedient servant
Theodore Baur
Recording Secretary
3d Meth. German Church
Lock Box No. 57

No reply to this letter is known. Perhaps Lincoln was perplexed about why Baur had waited more than three months to notify him of this honor.

Loyal Missouri Woman Wants Slaves Returned

[ca. December 1863]

To the President of the U. States.

I dont know what to do in present troubles but apply to your excellency for assistance,   all the property I held consisted of seven negroes,

---

1863

---

who living with me, we were able to make comfortable support. My two men went with the soldiers, one with an Iowa regiment & the other is at Camp Edwards near the city—He say an Iowa Col. gave him free papers & told him to stay within the lines of the camp. My two women & girls have left & gone to Chicago because they say that as the husband of one was in the army a year waiting on officers they are entitled to their freedom. I am now 50 years old & this takes from me & my two daughters our all, which we sadly need—The Provost Marshall here will attest my loyalty at any time, as he knows me well & his wife is a relation of mine—I hope you will in your goodness Do something for our relief, either, have their value given to us or let us have them returned. They were well cared for & seemed perfectly happy, until the soldiers persuaded them off.

> Yrs repy.
> Mrs E. Stewart.

care of the Provost Marshal St Louis

There is no record of a reply. The White House forwarded this letter to the War Department, where it was placed in the records of the Colored Troops Division and endorsed: "file." (Letter, Colored Troops Division Files, National Archives)

Asked to a Boston Charity Fair

Dec. 8 1863.

To His Excellency Abraham Lincoln. President of the U.S.

Respected Sir,

The Committee of Arrangements for the New England Sanitary Fair to be held in Boston Dec. Fourteenth respectfully invite you to be present, with Mrs. Lincoln, and that you will be our guests on that occasion.

We can assure you of the warmest welcome from all our citizens, and your visit would cause an out-pouring of loyalty, which would cheer your heart, and confound the enemies of our Government.

I hope, this will find you in good health, and allow me to express my confidence that the wisdom, which has heretofore directed your counsels, will continue to guide you, and that in the future, as in the past,

Providence will watch over the destinies of our nation. An answer will greatly oblige.

> Yours very Truly & Respectfully
> Thomas Russell
> Chairman of the Committee

If Lincoln in fact obliged Russell with a formal letter declining this compelling invitation to a region where he was extremely popular, the letter has never come to light. On December 14, the day proposed for the charity fair in Boston, Lincoln remained at work in Washington. (Ed. note, *Lincoln Day by Day*, III: 226–27)

A Distant Relative Recommended

> The Pines near Quincy Ills.
> Dec 12th 63

To Abraham Lincoln President. U.S. A Washington D.C.

Your Excellency

J. T. Hanks son of your uncle Joseph Hanks lives four miles south east of this city A more worthy, honest upright and truly loyal man does not live. He is capable and in every way worthy of the favor of your excellency. Amid all your mighty cares will you not give him some reasonable appointment. "Good old Jake Hanks" as we call him does not know I have written this nor do I think he has ever dreamed of asking an office

> Respectfully
> K. K. Jones

The letter apparently referred to a relative other than John T. Hanks, son of Lincoln's cousin Dennis Hanks, who was at this time living in Oregon. Nothing else is known of this request—or of the job-seeker "Jake Hanks."

1863

An Oath of Allegiance from a Rebel's Widow

[December 14, 1863]
District of Columbia
Washington County

I, Emily T. Helm, do solemnly swear in presence of Almighty God that I will henceorth faithfully support, protect and defend the Constitution of the United States, and the union of the States thereunder; and that I will, in like manner, abide by, and faithfully support all acts of Congress passed during the existing rebellion with reference to slaves, so long and so far as not repealed, modified, or held void by Congress, or by decision of the Supreme Court; and that I will, in like manner, abide by, and faithfully support all proclamations of the President, made during the existing rebellion, having reference to slaves so long and so far as not modified, or declared void by the Supreme Court. So help me God.

In return for signing this affadavit—which Lincoln wrote out himself, and then rewrote in order to keep a copy in his files—his sister-in-law, Emily (or Emilie) Todd Helm, the widow of Confederate General Ben Hardin Helm, was given the following presidential pass: "It is my wish that Mrs. Emily T. Helm, (widow of the late Gen. B. H. Helm, who fell in the Confederate service) now returning to Kentucky, may have protection of person and property, except as to slaves, of which I say nothing. A. Lincoln." (*Coll. Works* VII: 64). Lincoln then drafted yet another document for Emily to sign. In it she vowed, "I will take absolutely nothing into the insurgent lines, which could be of value to them." This marked the first and only time Lincoln himself authored a relative's correspondence to him. "Little Sister," as Mary called Emily, was actually the daughter of her father's second marriage—the fifteenth of his sixteen children—and like other Todds supported secession and the Confederacy. After her husband fell at Chickamauga, she visited the Executive Mansion, prompting a firestorm of criticism. Emily apparently abused Lincoln's kindness; he eventually revoked her pass, saying it was never intended "to protect her against the consequence of disloyal words or acts." (Ed. note, Katherine Helm, *The True Story of Mary, Wife of Lincoln* [New York: Harper Brothers, 1928], 108–9, 221, 224, 231–32; Theodore Calvin Pease and James G. Randall, eds., *The Diary of Orville Hickman Browning*, 2 vols. [Springfield, IL: Illinois State Historical Library, 1925–33], I: 651)

1863

Another Request from "Little Sister"

Lexington Ky.
Dec. 20th. 1863.

Mr. Lincoln

Dear Sir.

We arrived here safely and I trust I am not intruding too much in again throwing myself upon your kindness. I brought some means from the South sent for the benefit of some prisoners at Camp Douglas—but I am told that they are not allowed to receive anything at all. Some of them I think need articles of clothing, and if it is possible I would be under many obligations if you would allow me the privilege of [indecipherable] the value of the money in clothes &c to them. I hope I am not intruding too much upon your kindness and will try not to <u>overstep</u> the limits that I should keep. Love to Sister Mary & kind regards to yourself and Tad.

Affectionately,
Emily Helm

Whether or not Lincoln felt that the Todd sisters were beginning to "overstep" is not known, but no record exists of a reply to this request from Emily. Three days earlier, yet another sister, Martha Todd White, had written from Washington with a plea for "permission to replenish my wardrobe" with articles "not now to be obtained in the south" before returning to Kentucky with Emily. He is not known to have replied to this request either, although the thought may well have occured to him—recalling his own wife's penchant for overspending—that extravagance on clothing was a Todd family affliction.

1863

1864

One of the least-known portraits from the best-known photographic sitting of Lincoln's presidency: the session that produced the models for engravings on the five-dollar bill and copper penny. It is the work of Anthony Berger at Mathew Brady's studio, Feb. 9, 1864. Courtesy Library of Congress.

On His Brother-in-Law's Disloyalty

Moline, Ill. Jan. 3, 1864.

To President Lincoln:

Dear Sir:

During the political campaign that resulted in your election to the Presidency, I happened to be sitting under the balcony of the Geneseo House in Geneseo, Ill. when an elderly gentleman remarked to three or four of us present, that he was in doubt who he ought to vote for for President. The tavern keeper replied that he thought he ought to vote for Mr. Lincoln, to which he replied that he understood that Mr. Lincoln's own brother-in-law asserted that he (Mr. L.) was not capable of the office. I then remarked, or rather inquired, is he an influential judge? At that, a tall lank man dressed in black broad cloth with a cane in his hand who stood within, nearing replied, "I never said Mr. Lincoln was not capable, he is a capable man, but I am opposed to him on principle.["] I then asked "wherein on principle"? To which he answered, I never talk politics on the street. This was my first introduction to "Ninian." I had heard of him before, however, for he had made speeches at "democratic" meetings, the substance of which some of my boys who were present rehearsed to me, which I thought at the time to be very tame as well as bitter, and it was generally understood that he had asserted that you were not capable of filling the office of president. The day after the fact was happily ascertained that you were elected, I met him on the street, and he was in a very talkative mood. Said he had always been almost a Republican, always opposed to the extension of slavery," &c. I did not then understand the origins of his newly born zeal, but a few weeks perfectly unfolded the riddle, when the papers announced that Ninian Edwards, Mr. Lincoln's brother-in-law, had obtained a lucrative office under the new administration. In this Ninian was quite sharp. Suppose Mr. D[ouglas]. had been elected, Ninian could have plead with great plausibility, "I opposed my own brother-in-law, and did all I could for your election, and of course am entitled to," &c. But in the event of your election, why he has married a Todd, and,—of course you know the rest. Now, as the yankees say, "was not this cute." But, I would not bother you with the matter, but that I am suspicious there is something a little "rotten in Denmark." I was over on the Island at the Barracks on the National Thanksgiving day, and went into the commissary's office, and

---

1864

seeing a Chicago daily, the <u>Times</u> [an anti-Lincoln journal—Ed.], <u>being</u> on the table near where I sat down to warm, I took it up and my eye soon fell upon a passage charging you with having perjured yourself, with trampling on the constitution, and other wicked misdemeanors. I then asked the commissary if that was his paper, he said, "yes." If he coincided with its sentiments? He said, "yes." I then asked him if he agreed with the passage alluded to, when he answered gruffly that he "was not under inquisition.["] I was afterwards informed by a friend, in office there (appointed by Mr. Edwards, and well acquainted with him) that Mr E. himself is a reader of the <u>Chicago Times</u>. Now I say it with all the authority of a man of no consequence, that any man who does not repudiate and loathe the <u>Times</u> is a villainous traitor at least. I presume you have a little idea of the venom of that paper, and of the baleful influence exerted by it wherever it is read. All loyal men through these parts rejoiced when it was suppressed, and mourned when the hand was drawn back that would have crushed the reptile.

Of course I have no means of knowing the political complexion of Mr. E's appointments, but I fear from the 3 only I do know, they are "shaky," two only of the three being as I think the genuine metal. The "democrats," I suppose you know, Mr. Lincoln, charge any possible amount of "corruption" upon your administration. The Saviour said, "it is impossible but that offences come," and while your knowledge is not infinite, and you cannot be omnipresent, it is unavoidable that some men be trusted that prove themselves to be mean dishonest whelps. How many of these are your political enemies, and secret friends of Jeff's kingdom [The Confederacy—Ed.] in office cannot now be known, but some think their name is "legion." All the Union men I know about here, are hoping you will be the next "nominee," and say, if you are you will be elected by an "overwhelming" majority, for while they admit you may have committed errors, been a "little too slow" in some cases, yet that our imperiled Republic is safer in your hands, than any other man in the nation.

[H. Van Order]

No reply is known to this severe rebuke of Lincoln's brother-in-law, Ninian W. Edwards. Edwards was eventually transferred from his sensitive military post in Lincoln's old home town of Springfield, Illinois.

1864

A Portrait of Grant

No. 104 Wall st. Row
York City, Jan. 4th, 1864

Most Honored Sir:—

I trust you will excuse the liberty I take in addressing you on a mainly private matter, knowing as I do, that you are already horribly bored, not only by visitors, but through the medium of the mails also. I trust, however, that you will read this letter with your usual patience.

When I had the excessive pleasure of calling upon you last spring and presenting you with a copy of the first volume of "The Military Souvenir," you expressed a great wish to see a correct portrait of the great General of the Republic, General Grant; as I informed you that the portrait in the above-mentioned work did not much resemble him. Some few weeks ago, General Grant sent me a very recent photograph (pronounced by his staff to be the best of him ever taken) of himself, which I have had finely engraved, on steel by one of our best artists. I am now enabled, therefore, to place before you, the only correct portrait of this great military chieftain, which I do with the sincerest pleasure.

I will take this occasion to refer, but briefly to your official course. Of course it matters not to you what my opinions are, but it is at least some satisfaction to me to repeat them. I cannot here say all I could wish, but suffice it to say, that it meets with my entire and unqualified approval, and I must say, that not since the days of Jackson have such patriotism, energy, ability, and honesty marked the Presidential chair as during the past three years.

I have the honor to be, with high respect and esteem
Most Truly Yours,
Frank J. Bramhall

His excellency, Abraham Lincoln,
President of the United States.

Although no reply is known, Lincoln was undoubtedly glad to receive the portrait. He had still not cast eyes on General Grant, and would not meet him for the first time for another two months. (Ed. note, Ulysses S. Grant, *Personal Memoirs*, 2 vols. [New York: Charles L. Webster & Co., 1892], II: 121)

1864

Presenting Emancipation Lithographs

Chicago, Ill. Jan. 7th 1864

His Excellency Abraham Lincoln

Dr. Sir,

I mail herewith for your acceptance the two <u>first</u> copies of the lithographed Fac-Similes of your Proclamation of Freedom.—Have the kindness to inform me if the copy impress you favorably as an exact Fac-Simile which it purports to be.— It may interest you to know that the Original Manuscript, which you had "some desire to retain," will be held by our Soldiers Home in trust for the benefit of the sick & disabled soldiers of the Union Army.—Although I purpose [sic] donating a share of the avails of my copyright to the Home, as mentioned in the certificate on the face of the print, yet at the voluntary suggestion of Dr. [Henry W.] Bellows of New York, all copies sold in the East will yield a fund for the U.S. Sanitary Commission, of which he is Prest., and he writes most cordially, pledging the hearty cooperation of the Commission.— The caption will therefore be changed, my desire being to donate the net proceeds to the soldiers.

Very Truly Yours,
Thos. B. Bryan

The display print that Bryan sent to Lincoln was a proof copy of Edward Mendel's lithograph of the president's final Emancipation Proclamation. It included a facsimile of Lincoln's letter to the chairwomen of the Chicago Sanitary Fair conveying the original document as a donation to raise funds for wounded soldiers. The print also featured a portrait of Lincoln based on a current Wenderoth & Taylor photograph and a figure representing the goddess of liberty clutching an American flag. True to Bryan's promise, copies of the final print carried a special notation indicating that under "an arrangement with Hon. T. B. Bryan, the U.S. Sanitary Commission derives a liberal share of the profits from the sale of each of this [sic] facsimile." Lincoln replied to the gift a few days after its receipt, failing either to register his appreciation of Bryan's generosity or to conceal his usual indifference about artworks that depicted him. This was not the first time Bryan had been involved in such a project. Back in 1860, he had exhibited G. P. A. Healy's life portrait of Lincoln at his "Bryan Hall" gallery in Chicago, but Lincoln had declined his invitation to visit. (Ed. note, Charles Eberstadt, *Lincoln's Emancipation Proclamation* [New York:

1864

Duschnes Crawford, 1950], 39–40, 45; *Coll. Works* IV: 144; Lincoln's reply, *Coll. Works* VII: 135)

Executive Mansion
My Dear Sir.   Washington, January 18th, 1864.
   I have received the two copies of the lithographed fac-simile of the original draft of the Emancipation Proclamation, which you have had the kindness to send me, and in answer to your question, I have to say that although I have not examined it in detail, yet it impresses me favorably as being a faithful and correct copy.
                                     Yours truly,
                                     A. Lincoln.

Thos B Bryan Esq
Chicago, Illinois.

Messenger of God Demands a Meeting

[Washington, D.C.]
Thursday Evening January 14th 1864
President Lincoln—

   I understood from your Servant that your "Reception" was held this evening—my carriage waits at the door will you see me or not? if you have <u>no reception</u>. I leave for the Potomac Army to-morrow, where I go by the express command of God to distribute 1000 copies of the Tracts, a copy of which I sent you some time since. <u>God</u> now desires that it should be known to many that "<u>He</u> is Jesus" before the great "<u>Tribulation</u>" falls upon the Nation.
   I have procured a "<u>Pass</u>" also letters to General [John] Sedgwick, [Fitz-Henry] Warren and Hayes [perhaps future president Rutherford B. Hayes—Ed], Mrs. Hayes, being an old acquaintance of mine. What God has for me to say to you <u>now</u>, I know <u>not</u> yet, it will be made known to you, if you will see me. If you cannot see me to-night the "Voice" said "Try to to [*sic*] see him on Tuesday.["] Can you not condescend to say "yes or no" Jesus once said when on Earth "He that rejecteth <u>you</u>, rejecteth Me["]—you disbelieve; because the Prophecies are not yet fulfilled, "<u>Revelations</u>" were given <u>1800</u> years ago and are not fulfilled

---

yet—I feel no anger at your silence, it is quite natural, but for your own sake again say "Receive me"—

Mrs. Haight

I would not have taken this long, tiresome, cold journey except to obey my God who is Jesus.

There is no record to indicate that Lincoln received the mysterious, heaven-sent Mrs. Haight, or replied in any way to this vaguely threatening letter.

Invitation from Future Political Enemy

Washington D.C.
Jan.14th [1864]
273 Vet. Ave.

Hon A. Lincoln
President of the U.S.

Sir.

I have the honor to present the request of the Committee of the "<u>Ladies Sanitary Fair</u>," that the President of the United States would honor the occasion of their opening ceremonies by being present at their new building on the evening of the 21st Inst. (Corner of 7th St. & Pa. Ave—)

I can assure you that it will add much to the interests & receipts of the occasion.

Very Truly
S[amuel]. C. Pomeroy

Although Lincoln would travel longer distances to attend sanitary fairs in Baltimore on April 18 and Philadelphia on June 16, there is no record that he attended the opening of the fair scheduled to occur, according to this letter, just nine blocks from the White House. Perhaps Lincoln was wary of the man who wrote to invite him. The next month, Senator Pomeroy of Kansas would sign and distribute to some one hundred influential Republicans a "private" letter calling on the party to replace Lincoln with Secretary of the Treasury Salmon P. Chase on the 1864 national ticket. Ironically, the "Pomeroy Circular," as it came to be known, served to improve, rather than injure, Lincoln's chances for renomination. Lincoln did appear at the fair's closing day, March 18, and he delivered the following remarks, as reported by the *Washington Evening Star*.

1864

(Ed. note, *Lincoln Day by Day* III: 235, 253, 265; J. G. Randall and Richard N. Current, *Lincoln the President: Last Full Measure* [New York: Dodd Mead, 1955], 98–108; Lincoln's reply, *Coll. Works* VII: 253–54)

Ladies and Gentlemen: I appear to say but a word. This extraordinary war in which we are engaged falls heavily upon all classes of people, but the most heavily upon the soldier. For it has been said, all that a man hath will he give for his life; and while all contribute of their substance the soldier puts his life at stake, and often yields it up in his country's cause. The highest merit, then, is due to the soldier. [Cheers.]

In this extraordinary war extraordinary developments have manifested themselves, such as have not been seen in former wars; and amongst these manifestations nothing has been more remarkable than these fairs for the relief of suffering soldiers and their families. And the chief agents in these fairs are the women of America. [Cheers.]

I am not accustomed to the use of language of eulogy; I have never studied the art of paying compliments to women; but I must say that if all that has been said by orators and poets since the creation of the world in praise of woman were applied to the women of America, it would not do them justice for their conduct during this war. I will close by saying God bless the women of America! [Great applause.]

A Hymn Uniting Religion with Patriotism

Elland P[ost]. Office Ohio
January 14 1864

Abraham Lincoln
President of the United States

Dear Sir

It would seem to be desirable to unite religious fervor with patriotism, as an aid for the advancement of the cause of our Country, and which I doubt not are the objects of the great measures of your administration

With that view I send you a copy of an Hymn slightly altered as sung by the musical union at the Great Western Sanitary fair at Cincinnati with good effect. The sentiments, you will agree with me are good, but arranged in such an old fashioned style, that it may be an objection, but

---

1864

if for want of a better, you see fit to introduce it to popular favor, please do it in any way you may choose.

Most respectfully Your Obt Servt.
G. Richards

I should mention that the 5th verse as printed was executed in singing by the musical Union as making it too long and as possibly objectionable to some. G.R.

National
Union Hymn.
Written by An Old Citizen of Ohio.
Tune—"<u>Old Hundred</u>."
For the Great Western Sanitary Fair

1

Great God,—Inspire the Patriot's heart,
    And nerve the Hero's arm with power;
Take Thou, we pray [changed to "Let them to take"] our Country's part,
    In every dark and trying hour.

2

Our patriot fathers, thou didst aid,
    Their counsels and their battles guide,
Until we were a nation made,
    By glorious <u>Union</u> sanctified.

3

A <u>Union</u>, founded in the right,
    The sacred, inborn rights of men;
Oh give us wisdom, grant us might,
    The priceless treasure to maintain.

4

Preserve in us, we ask with awe,
    The sense of Justice, Reason, Right,
Religion, <u>Liberty and Law</u>,
    Our constitution, <u>Union</u>, Might.

1864

5

<u>Father</u> of all, may we, we crave [changed to "pray"]
   Give all the races made by thee
Kind brotherhood, and in the slave [changed to "speed the day"],
   Protection, Aid and Liberty [changed to "of universal liberty"].

6

Thy Love, unceasing over flows
   To hearts receptive of its power,
For nations, and for human woes;
   A healing balm for saddest hour.

7

Christ,—"God with us," in mercy bring
   Thy blessed Peace,—In its pure reign,
Set up thy kingdom, be our King,
   The power and glory thine. Amen.

Elland, Butler & Co., Ohio

There is no record of a response from Lincoln to this "slightly altered" hymn. The Great Western Sanitary Fair in Cincinnati, at which this composition was apparently performed, had closed five days earlier, after raising more than $235,000 for soldiers' relief. (Ed. note, Kantor and Kantor, *Sanitary Fairs*, 174)

English Mutton for the President

New York Jany 14th/64

His Excellency Abraham Lincoln
President

Sir

   I send you by express this day, a saddle of English mutton received by the Scotch. I hope the disposition of the English may hereafter be as good as their mutton.

            Very Respectfully
            Rufus F. Andrews

1864

Lincoln may have eaten the English mutton, but he sent no known acknowledgment of its receipt.

Seeking an Autograph for Brooklyn

Brooklyn, N.Y.
January 15th 1864
His Excellency Abraham Lincoln,
President, <u>United</u> States

Dear Sir.

The people of our city have resolved on a general Fair,—men & women, heartily uniting, in aid of the U.S. Commission. The occasion is deemed so patriotic & benevolent, as to justify a small trespass on your time. I <u>ask no office</u>, but beg to solicit from you so many copies of your own <u>autograph</u>, for the purposes of the sale, as may be convenient & agreeable to yourself. Should you find time to add to some of the copies, a sentence or two as you think best, it will be regarded as rare favor. An answer any time this month will be in good time.

Relying on the known benevolence of your character, I feel assured I shall receive a favorable answer. Please direct to me. With sincere regard, I am,

your obt. servt.
D. O. Kellogg

The same day brought a similar request from the Soldiers' Aid Society of Waynesburgh, Ohio, asking, as correspondence secretary Edward Neill summarized it, for "a few lines from you over your autograph." The very next day he was solicited by correspondent Susan Sedgwick Butler "in the name of womanhood and for the sake of our enterprize" for "a short article from your honored hand," for publication in a commemorative newspaper for a fair in New York City. The day after that, Mary Lincoln was invited to attend yet another fair, this one in Lancaster, Pennsylvania. On the 18th, another Brooklyn official wrote to remind the president that his event needed Lincoln's autograph to enable it to compete successfully with other fairs. Another reminder came a few days later, and January 27 brought a plea from a Yonkers, New York, group for still another autograph to be auctioned off for charity. Never before in his presidency was Lincoln as besieged with such requests as he was during this one

1864

week in early 1864—which may help explain why no evidence exists that he complied with any of the pleas, although it is entirely possible that he did so. If he did, the results were probably sold for charity, as promised, and cannot easily be traced or linked to these January 1864 requests.

Proposing a Mysterious Invention

Washington, D.C. Jan 16 64

Hon. A. Lincoln

Mr. President:

More than a year since, the writer came from Saint Louis, at the urging of Jas. S. Lamb Esq of Springfield Ills. I was presented to your Excellency by the Attorney General, & laid before you a matter of which you were pleased to say: "I do not tell you that this is an important or a <u>very</u> important thing, but if one half of what you claim, it is <u>the</u> most important thing offered to the Union since the war began". I afterward obtained an <u>official demonstration</u> that it was <u>more</u> than I ever claimed, & no individual dares question that it would save millions & double the efficiency of the Cavalry and transportation—Yet, through many months have I tried hard and patiently waited, while <u>action</u> seems mysteriously witheld—the papers "<u>referred</u>" & that which your Excellency deemed of so vast importance in lieu of having been given to the service nearly a year ago, is still throttled nearly to death with <u>Red tape</u>.

In view of the above <u>facts</u>, (for the <u>truth</u> of which I am responsible) <u>Am</u> I wrong to ask you to name a <u>half hour</u> (at your convenience) that you can give to <u>so important</u> a matter as this is conceded to be.

You will be <u>interested</u> in my statements.

I am, truly Yours
J. H. Schenck
Rooms: 338 G. N.E. Cor. 12th
P.O. Box 792

This letter was endorsed by a secretary with "Wants an interview about his invention (?)"—the question mark suggesting that no one in the White House had the slightest idea what device Mr. Schenck had proposed that could possibly revolutionize cavalry and transportation to the degree claimed.

1864

On Behalf of "Decimated" Indians

To Abraham Lincoln President of the U. States

Honoured Friend

I sent thee lately a brief message of affectionate remembrance when taking tea with my kind friend Isaac Newton;—but this was far from doing justice to my feelings, of sympathetic interest on thy accounts;—permit me to say, that when S. A. Douglass [sic] and thyself canvassed the State of Illinois, with reference (perhaps) to the U.S. Senate,—I followed your course, as developed in "the National Era" of that day, and I very much approved of thine;—and when the Chicago Convention agreed upon thy name, for thy present high station,—I said to my wife "they have chosen the right man";—subsequent time, and events, have confirmed this opinion:— I have been much pleased to find in thy acts, and state papers, reference prominently made, to the Power, and Goodness of God,—and our accountability to him: "acknowledge the Lord in all thy ways, and he will direct thy paths, the steps of a good man are ordered of the Lord, & thou will keep him in perfect Peace, whose mind is stayed on thee, because he has trusteth in thee;"

The delegated Head of of [sic] any nation, or people, seems on the one hand, to be the agent, or instrument of the Lord, for that People;—and on the other hand, the leader, Governor, and so I believe thou feelest it to be, especially as all are required to "Judge righteous Judgement" in all this, thou hast the secret, and sincere sympathy of many prayerful Hearts. "Thou shalt guide me with thy counsel, and afterward receive me to Glory["] Psalm 73 vs 4

I feel constrained to make a plea on behalf of the original owners of our country, the poor, decimated and distressed Indians; their situation in many cases is very affecting to a feeling heart;—I heard last week from a sister of the wife of John Ross (Chief of Cherokees), some very sad trials, which that people have lately suffered;—very likely thou art already informed of it, as John Ross is I believe in Washington; his wife when young was a ward of mine, and I have known the chief for many years,—and esteem him, as a modest, and worthy man.

With sincere desires for thy comfort here,—and Peace hereafter I am very Respectfully

---

1864

Thy Friend
John W. Tatum

No record exists of a reply to this intriguing plea on behalf of Native Americans. In another letter written in November, Lincoln would describe Tatum as a friend. (Ed. note, *Coll. Works* VIII: 124)

Proposing a New Cabinet Department

Sarus Creek Md. 20th Jany 1864.

My dear Sir,

Having learned to read to a great extent by moonlight—and to write upon the lid of the rinsing trough of the barn, I have heretofore presumed to say a word of encouragement to a "rail splitter" as I did to Senator [Thomas H.] Hicks [of Maryland—Ed.]—to "stand still, and fear not," that the people were with you—and now I venture to make a suggestion, that you send a Message to Congress recommending the establishment of a "Department of Agriculture Manufactures and Commerce." I have always thought those great interests particularly Agriculture and Manufactures were fairly entitled to a position in the Cabinet—and now in view of the great responsibilities upon them and still greater in prospect, it would be a great gratification to them, to have long neglected justice done to them and greatly rebound to your own honor. I flatter myself Congress would willingly respond to the request under all the circumstances surrounding us and prospective.

I submitted a Preamble and Resolutions to the foregoing effect at Dec. Session 1860 in the Md. legislature but in that unaccountable body no opportunity was afforded to have them acted upon. House Journal page 613.

I will no further trespass upon your time.

I have the honor to be your friend and obedient servt.

D. W. Neill

See Washington's Message 1796.

Lincoln must have found this letter almost irresistible, written by a man who learned to read in much the way he himself had and who loathed the Maryland Legislature, which Lincoln was compelled to suppress in order to prevent the

1864

state's secession at the outset of the war. Nonetheless, Neill's suggestions for new cabinet posts devoted to agriculture and commerce were years ahead of their time.

Asking for a Lock of Presidential Hair

Friday January 22nd [1864]

To the President of the United States

Dear Sir:

My letter will be at once like, and unlike, many letters that you receive—<u>like</u> them because it asks a favor—<u>unlike</u> them because it shall be as brief as I can make it.

I doubt not that you have heard of the great "Metropolitan Fair" planned by the ladies of the city of New York, in aid of the U.S. Sanitary Commission, and I am sure that your sympathies are already enlisted in favor of such an enterprise, noble and needful as it is, and whatever you can do to aid it you will do most willingly.

I am desirous to obtain a lock of your <u>hair</u>, and also some from the heads of the various members of your Cabinet, and other prominent and distinguished men of the day.

With this hair it is my intention to embroider a device on velvet, and then to have it handsomely framed. The design and workmanship will be such as to make it very attractive, while the associations connected with the <u>hair</u>, will I am certain, render it a conspicuous and valuable, as well as salable, contribution to the Fair.

Will you be kind enough to send me the requisite lock of your hair, directed to my address, and believe me sir

Yours most respectfully
Miss M. Jennings
Care of Mrs. R. H. Corbett

118 West 42nd St. New York City.

There is no indication that Lincoln donated his hair for this unusual handicraft project. Instead Lincoln donated a handwritten copy of his Gettysburg Address, at the request of the orator who had preceded him on the platform on November 19, 1863—Edward Everett. (Ed. note, Kantor and Kantor, *Sanitary Fairs*, 107)

1864

Is the Colored Population to Suffer?

Washington D.C.
Jny 22 1864

Mr Abraham Lincoln

Dr Sir

Some Reckon and others guess   But what I wish to know is this.
what do you mean to do with us Col[ore]d. population are we to suffer
and our enemies reap or can we <u>Reap</u> now   I was brought up a farmer
and if I can have a hut in my own native land and a little help that will
suffice me, then I have a family you <u>know</u> well do the best you can and
oblige yr obt Servant

Ed. D. Jennings

NB

My address near Warrenton Springs Flangr Co. Va. (Come up,[)]

If Lincoln replied to this plea, his response has never been found. But Jennings's
letter was, unusually, retained in the president's own files. Most letters from
African Americans were routinely forwarded to the War Department's Bureau
of Colored Troops.

An Acrostic for an Autograph

Cuttingsville, Rutland Co. Vt. Jan. 26, 1864.

Hon. Abraham Lincoln—

My Dear Sir—

Perhaps I ought to beg your pardon for taxing a moment of your precious time, and also for the freedom I have taken with your name; but
please be so kind as to accept the enclosed acrostic from a humble individual as a faint expression of high personal esteem, and an index to the
interest felt in the high trusts with which you are charged.

To give you a clue to the source from which it comes perhaps I ought
to say that for more than twenty-five years I have passed for a Minister
in the Methodist Episcopal Church.

Please pardon the liberty of my thus addressing you. Probably I shall

---

1864

135

never have the pleasure of meeting you personally, but should you have a moment's time to favor me with your autograph it would be to me a matter of high personal gratification.

Most Respectfully Yours—
H. Eastman

To Hon. Abraham Lincoln
Washington, D.C.

(Written for the Vermont Record)

An Acrostic.

A be, the Honest's at helm, while the Old Ship of State,
B ravely breasts the rude storm with her all-precious freight;
R eeling, restless, and rocked on the rough-rolling tide,
A s his wisdom directs, shall the tempest outride.
H o! the haven of rest is now heaving in view,
A nd a calm shall succeed where the winds fiercely blow.
M ay her canvas be swelled with the breath of our might.

L et her anchor be fast in the strength of the right;
I n the midst of the blast shall she gallantly ride;
N or be lost the rich lading whatever betide;
C atch the breezes of Freedom now blowing so strong,
O n the perilous deep of Oppression and Wrong:—
L et the crew all be fearless, no wave shall o'erwhelm,
N ot so long as true Freedom and Abe are at helm.

E.

If Lincoln favored Reverend Eastman with his autograph—and surely he had earned it with this composition—it has never come to light.

1864

Compliments and a Job Request

Poughkeepsie New York
Jan. 28th 1864

Hon. Abraham Lincoln
President of the United States:

Honored Sir:

Will you permit me an humble individual to address a few words to you the Chief Magistrate of this Great Republic. I address you with the greatest confidence knowing that you were once like me a young Attorney depending upon your own unaided exertions to establish for yourself a name place and position among men and the course you have pursued, the integrity you have displayed and the success you have achieved will make you a model for young men in all coming time. I am glad to see that the American people recognize your fitness for the position of Chief Magistrate and are expressing the desire to renominate you for the same position. The same feeling prevails here as elsewhere in that respect and at the meeting of the Union League of this City on Wednesday evening of last week a resolution of mine that the best interests of the country would be promoted by your renomination & reelection was adopted after some discussion without a dissenting vote.

I had the pleasure, when you passed through this city on your way to Washington to assume the duties of the Presidency, to receive an introduction to you. With the ardor of youth and the zeal of a disciple I grasped your hand as in a vice and I never shall forget the look of pain and anguish you gave or the regret & sorrow it caused me to think how stupidly thoughtless I I [sic] had been. (I don't know as I ought to have written this for fear you will never forgive me)

Well You have been President near three years and I have sometimes wished that I had you by the hand that I might squeeze it again, but I have got over all that now and though there are some things I can't understand—as for instance the Missouri question & some others—still I have learned to have great confidence in your ability to understand and your wisdom to decide the most difficult problems. And now I'm going to ask a favor—which is that if you are renominated and reelected as I trust you will be—that you appoint me Postmaster of this city, & as briefly as possible I will offer a few suggestions relative to the matter.

1864

137

The appointment in this section under Whig & Republican rule have always been from the old school of Weed & Seward—men who have been workers for them in times past. The present incumbent is a hatter—a gentleman about 60 years of age & wealthy.—who went to the Chicago convention as a delegate and came home in the "swearing train" [disappointed that Seward was bested by Lincoln—Ed.]. Plate the Provost Marshall is another of the same school. A younger class of men are springing up of whom Allard Anthony, District Attorney & myself—late Clerk of Supervisors are the representatives in this part of the County and Col Ketcham of the 50th New York, & John B. Dutcher State Senator are the representatives of the same class from the Eastern part of the County. In time I can prove to you that I am worthy of the appointment, that I am competent—that it would not be unpopular—and can furnish a respectable list of petitioners in favor thereof. Besides I am poor—and there is a very estimable young lady, the daughter of one of our first citizens waiting for me to improve my circumstances so that we can marry. The office is worth not less than $2000 a year net (I think) and you can make us happy at once. Will you do it?

No one but myself knows of the existence of this letter—or shall know of it. Hoping that you will take the trouble to read it—that you will consider it favorably—that you will indicate to me your determination in the matter which shall be kept profoundly secret—I subscribe myself

Your obdt. Servant
Walter C. Allen

There is no record that Lincoln replied to this disarmingly straightforward letter, but the fact that it was endorsed by a secretary and passed along to the president suggests that he read it personally. If he did, he was doubtless reminded of his own youth, and his early life as both a struggling attorney and a village postmaster.

Invitation To An Organ Concert

119 Smith's Wharf
Balt. Jany 28/64.

To His Excellency Abraham Lincoln
Prest U.S. Washington

Sir,

I am aware you like brevity, & shall tax yr. valuable time as little as possible in this.— I propose giving a concert in yr city about Easter for my own benefit having never askd the Public aid before during my life, & shall feel most proud & happy that you would permit the use of yr honored name, & that of yr. most estimable wife, as consenting to be present by invitation.— I combine a Mercantile business here with a musical one, & am Organist at St. Peter's church in yr. city, the Pastor of which, Revd. F. E. Boyle holds a chaplaincy thro yr. kind appointment some 2 years since. Our Senator Johnson is acquainted with my Father.—I got up & directed a concert in Washington 2 years since, without <u>charge</u>, which realized some 700$ for the Poor of yr. city & now needing aid myself, beg a reciprocation from the Public there. I intend offering to my Washington Friends, a combination of talent, such as has not been heard before in yr. city.

Hoping to have a favorable reply to the within, & anxiously awaiting same, I remain honored Sir, Very respectfully

Yr. obedt St.

Geo. W. Walter

I have been visiting Washington every saturday & returning here on Tuesdays for past 3 years & still do so, on musical business—

There is no surviving evidence that Lincoln endorsed or attended Mr. Walter's proposed concert, or even answered this request for both.

1864

Asked to a Christian Commission Anniversary

[Telegraph]
Philadelphia Jan 29 1864.

His Excellency A Lincoln Prest U.S.

The anniversary of the U.S. Christian Commission was one of the largest & most enthusiastic meetings ever held in this city. The meeting manifested the most unbound Enthusiasm for the Country its President its Cabinet & its noble defenders in the field. We hope to have a meeting of Equal interest in the Hall of the House of Reps on Tuesday Evening next. We trust you will find it convenient to honor us with your presence

George H. Stuart

President and Mrs. Lincoln together attended the Christian Commission anniversary gathering on February 2—one of the few public events which Lincoln graced with his presence during his term of office. (Ed. note, *Lincoln Day by Day* III: 237)

Inquiries into the Family Tree

Marshfield Mo. 8th Feb/64

Hon. Sir

Your Exlncy.

I hope you will pardon the present transgression upon your already engaged Time?

Did you have a sister Mary Ann, who married about the year 1821 one J. T. Wyrick—or had you Bros. named Mordecai & Jesse Lincoln?

I have the honor to be Ever Respfly.

M. Lincoln Wyrick

Address me at Marshfield Webster Co. Mo.

This letter was endorsed and filed by the White House staff, but there is no evidence that Lincoln ever answered the inquiries of Mr. Wyrick, who was a "druggist and apothecary," according to the business card he enclosed with his note. The president seldom discussed his family, so it is conceivable that Wyrick

---

1864

never learned that Lincoln had neither a sister named Mary Ann nor brothers named Mordecai or Jesse.

A New "Pen Wiper"

Erie Penna
February 16 1864

To His Excellency, Abraham Lincoln
President of the United States:

Sir:

Accompanying this find enclosed a "Washington Pen Wiper," which you will please accept as a token of regard from a warm friend of your course as our "Chief Executive" an ardent admirer of your honesty as a politician, and, your worth as a statesman.

The design, it is confidently hoped, will, as you make use of the wiper day after day, preserve in fresh remembrance, the christian purity, and nobleness of purpose of that life which yours is proving so striking a counterpart, and the reward of which, a grateful people will determine the same as that of your illustrious model.

Very Respectfully & Truly
Your well wisher
Laura Culbertson
Box 84, Erie City Pa.

No acknowledgment is known for this Washington pen wiper, which probably arrived at the White House sometime between Lincoln's own birthday and that of his great predecessor.

1864

From the Inventor of the Gatling Gun

Indianapolis Ind
Feby 18th 1864

To His Excellency A. Lincoln
President of U.S.

Sir

Pardon me for the liberty I have taken in addressing you this letter.

I enclose herewith a circular giving a description of the "Gatling Gun" of which I am inventor and patentee. The arm in question is an invention of no ordinary character. It is regarded, by all who have seen it operate, as the most effective implement of warfare invented during the war, and <u>it is just the thing needed to aid in crushing the present rebellion</u>.

The gun is very simple in its construction, strong and durable and can be used effectively by <u>men of ordinary intelligence</u>.

The gun, was, months ago, tested at the Washington Navy Yard and gave entire satisfaction to the officers who attended the trial, and it was adopted by the Naval Bureau with the understanding that any requisitions for the guns made by Naval officers would be allowed, since which time a number of requisitions have been sent in for the guns by different Naval officers, but none of said requisitions have been granted to my knowledge.

Genl. [Nathaniel] Banks, commanding at New Orleans, has also made requisitions for a number of the guns to be placed on transport vessels in his Department, where they would be found, no doubt, very serviceable. Many other army officers are very anxious to obtain the guns.

Messrs McWhinney & Rindge,—partners of mine in the manufacture & sale of the gun—are now in Washington with a sample gun and I hope ere long to hear of its adoption by the War Department. Its use, will, undoubtedly, be of great service to our armies now in the field.

May I ask your kindly aid and assistance in getting the gun in use? I know of a truth that it will do good & effective service.

Such an invention at a time like the present, seems to be providential, to be used as a means in crushing the rebellion.

                    With great consideration

1864

I am your obt servt
Richard Gatling

P.S. I have seen an inferior arm known as the "Coffee Mill Gun" which I am informed has not given satisfaction in practical tests on the battle field. I assure you my invention is no "Coffee Mill Gun"—but is entirely a different arm, and is entirely free from the accidents and objections raised against that arm.

RJG

No direct reply from Lincoln is known, but the Gatling gun—the first reliable machine gun ever introduced—was used in the Petersburg campaign late in 1864 with mixed results. The gun was eventually improved and sold throughout the world, ushering in the age of the machine gun in war. (Letter, Ordnance Files, National Archives)

Tickets to See Edwin Booth on Stage

Feb 20—1864

Your Excellency

I have the honor to offer for your acceptance a double Private Box for Friday night next. The occasion being the performance of Shylock and Don Caesar de Bazin [sic] by Mr. Edwin Booth.

Your favorable answer will be taken as a great Compliment to the artist, as well as an additional honor to

Yours loyally
Leonard Grover

Grovers Theater   Thursday morning

Lincoln had seen the great Booth, the most celebrated actor of his day, perform in *Richard III* the very night before its proprietor sent this letter. Nonetheless, the president not only accepted Grover's invitation to see Booth play two roles, Shylock and Don Coeur de Bazan, in *Merchant of Venice* on February 26, but he also attended Booth's performance as Julius Caesar the evening before. Then, in early March, he returned to Grover's Theater repeatedly to watch Booth in *Hamlet* on the 2nd, in *The Fool's Revenge* on the 7th, and in yet another performance of *Richard III* on the 10th. Thirteen months later, Lincoln would be murdered by the star's brother, John Wilkes Booth. (Ed. note, *Lincoln Day by Day* III: 241–44)

1864

Offering Unusually Decorated Currency

Rochester N.Y. Feb 22—1864

President Lincoln

Dear Sir.

Please excuse one for taking the liberty of writing to our most worthy President.

I have executed a peace [sic] of work with a paint Brush (that is I have painted a United States Treasury Note so perfect that it troubles those who have seen it to tell which is the original). And I have been advised by some of our most prominent men to send the same to Washington and dedicate it to our President—I have laboured some time on this peace of work, and should it be accepted and the President should deem it worthy of a recompence it would I assure you make me a Happy Man. I wish to know if you please how I shall to send the curiosity or come with it myself, and I remain your

Most Obedient Servant
H. J. Kellogg
Rochester N.Y.
P.O. Box 2057

If Lincoln sent Kellogg an invitation to bring his creation to Washington, or an offer of "recompence," the letter has been lost.

A Pair of Slippers "for an Office"

Cedar Hill [Pa.] March 4th 1864

Respected President

Having sent you by Adams Express from Mount Joy 10 days ago a pr of slippers with stars and stripes & the American Eagle as I give them myself to the Agent directed to you & got the receipt which I put in the post office the same day not having heard you had received them, as the Agent for the Express is a regular Copper head the term given to all Politicians who are opposed to your Administration. I concluded the Box had not been sent nor the receipt from the post office as the Post

Master's wife took it & said it would not go unless I put the 3 cent Stamp on it   I told her I would not insult the President of the United States by prepaying it as all correspondence went to you free. I hope if you are reelected this day twelvemonth & you have my daily prayers & good wishes for it although the 3 years you have been President you have had trials troubles & abuses from the Copper heads North as well as South   We are surrounded by them in Mount Joy   May you by your good & just Administration be able to rout out all the evils belonging to the so called Copper heads. Gods promises never fail   If we put our trust in him & lean upon him <u>as our support all things will in the end work for our good</u>. That has been my experience   I hope the Post Master will be exchanged in Mount Joy for a better one if you are reelected although he calls himself a Republican   He is a poor <u>specimen of</u> a true one <u>Interest for an Office is what he craves</u>.

Yrs Truly
Mrs Mary A. Frazier Near Mount Joy
Lancaster Co Pennsylvania

Lincoln never acknowledged receipt of the patriotically decorated slippers, possibly because a secretary interpreted this letter as a plea for an appointment, endorsing it: "Mrs Mary A. Frazier . . . sent by express a pair of slippers for the President <u>Probably</u> for an office."

Requesting Lincoln's Old Invention

Union Steam Works
22d St Cor of 2d Ave
New York March 10 1864

To His Excellency, Abraham Lincoln
President of the United States

Sir

As a member of the committee on "Machinery" of the metropolitan fair—for the benefit of the Sanitary Commission I would respectfully solicit your consent to reproduce a model of an invention of yours for raising sunken vessels—which is in the Patent office at Washington; knowing that its high associations would make it an object of great attraction.

1864

We have already secured as a donation from Mr Jerome the Engines and Boilers of his steam Yacht "Clara Clarita" to which vessel they were adapted by Mr. E. N. Dickerson who prophesied great speed for the boat. On her trial trip she accomplished one mile in two and a half hours they were removed; and thanks to Mr Jeromes generosity and Mr Dickerson's talents they are now the property of the Sanitary Commission & will be used to drive the machinery department.

We have no excuse to offer for addressing you on this subject. We are appealing Everywhere for contributions—and in making this request of the Chief ruler of the United States of America we sincerely hope to have it faborably considered and remain

Yours with sincerest respect
Adam S. Cameron

Fifteen years earlier, Lincoln had applied for a patent for "a device for lifting boats over sand bars." Using a jackknife, he carved a red cedar model and submitted it with his application. There is no record of Lincoln's response to this intriguing request that he resuscitate this long-forgotten device. (Ed. note, Louis A. Warren, ed., "Congressman Lincoln's Patent," *Lincoln Lore*, no. 843 [June 4, 1945])

An Appeal to the President as a Husband

April 10 1864

To His Excellency the President of the United States

Honored Sir

I can only apologise for presuming to thus address you by stating that having read that at the time of your nomination or election (I know not which) when first hearing of the great honor conferred upon you by our people,—You said "excuse me gentleman [*sic*] but there is a little woman up at my house that would like to hear of this."—Sir when I remembered you were a husband I summoned courage to pen that, which I have deferred for many weeks—trusting that the man who turned to his wife his first thoughts in the happiest moment of his life; would at least listen to a woman who has enshrined in her heart one that will prove the subject of this epistle. My husband Charles Murphy recd. from you last April an appointment as Commissioner of the first

District in the Provost Marshal's office Philada. in which he faithfully performed his duty (although sick from Bronchitis continually there) up to the 22nd of December, when he recd. a revocation of that appointment, stating no cause whatever.

After going twice to Washington, & making every effort to find a cause for this, he recd. from Mr [John B.] Fry [Quartermaster General—Ed.] a paper exonerating him from any wrong by "<u>word act</u> or <u>deed</u>" but refusing to reinstate him, then when I asked him why he had not the courage to trouble you, having written with his friend John M. Butler a statement of the facts at the time unsuccessfully, felt quite disheartened & submitted to what I felt a grievous wrong.

Sir Mr Murphy has been a Republican from its infancy, working always for the party & the first office ever held by him was that to which you appointed him—he is poor (a lawyer by profession) with a family of four children & when acting a commissioner was obliged to lay by his legal business, which as a matter of course is now almost gone from him. He does not know of this writing nor do I wish him to, except you should feel enough interest to look into the unjustness of his case & learn from knowing ones [sic] his true worth.

This to you our President—whose greater cares have not been retailed to wives & husbands as singly may seem a small matter—but as the rain drop appeals to the great ocean for a place on her bosom so my <u>honored</u> sir do I <u>appeal</u> to you as the great head & front holding the keys of Justice. If you would learn further from other sources you can do so by addressing

Robt. P. King Pres. Nat. Union Club Sansom St. above Sixth Philada.

John M. Butler 700 south 11th St.

Hon Chas. P. Beill member house Washington D.C. Hoping to be pardoned for my boldness, & every kind wish for your welfare

I am with the highest respect for your Obedient Servant
                                Margaret E. Murphy
                                620 Sansom St.
                                Phila.

To His Excellency The President of the United States

No reply has been unearthed to this request, extraordinary for its reference to a very personal Lincoln story that has since evolved into the realm of legend—his insistence on rushing home to report his presidential victory to his wife. Apparently the story was in currency in Lincoln's own time.

1864

A Scarf to Keep Him Warm "Sometime"

Meriden [Connecticut] April 16. 1864.

Dear Uncle Abraham.

My mother Mrs. Hiram Foster sends you this very patriotic scarf, which she hopes may comfort you by keeping you warm sometime, and proving the affection of your nephews and nieces. Yours truly

Mrs. Hiram's little daughter

Abraham Lincoln
President of the U.S.

No reply is known.

Returning a Long-Lost, Undelivered Letter to Mary

P.O. LeRoy Genesee County N. York
April 25th 1864

To His Excellency Abraham Lincoln Prest

Dear Sir:

When in the Army of the Potomac a few weeks ago, I met a young man; who in the course of conversation remarked that he had an original letter of the President. Expressing a desire to see it, he complied & produced the enclosed. On a further request that he would allow me to retain it, he assented. And what under other circumstances I should have greatly prized (an original letter of the Prest), a <u>private</u> and <u>domestic</u> one like this, all the "proprieties" seemed to forbid that I should retain. On my return through Washington I thought to have returned it, but being presented by my father in law Mr Gordon at one of your public receptions (the only occasion of seeing you), the opportunity was not favorable. I therefore now enclose it,—trusting that after so long & adventurous a journey, it may reach its original source. Had it been a <u>fragment</u> of the original Emancipation Proclamation, or the Syracuse letter [probably Lincoln's so-called "Albany Letter" to Erastus Corning and others

---

1864

on the subject of civil liberties—Ed.] it would not probably have <u>thus</u> found its way back to the author.

I will only remark that I know nothing of the circumstances by which it came into possession of the party who delivered it to me. His only answer to my inquiry on the subject was the vague one, "it was picked up in the Amy." It is evident from its <u>soiled</u> condition that it has had a "career."

Hoping that you will pardon this intrusion I remain with the highest considerations of esteem & regard

Very faithfully

Yr Obt Servt

D. P. Bacon

How an intimate letter from Abraham Lincoln to his vacationing wife in Vermont fell into the hands of an unidentified Union soldier in the field remains an unsolved mystery. Lincoln had written the note nearly eight months before Bacon, a village postmaster from upstate New York, took possession of it and finally sent it on to the president. By then it was long out-of-date; the news it brought of the loss of a family pet, a financial investment, and the latest political news from Kentucky was no longer current. So Lincoln filed it away, endorsing it: "Letter about 'Nanny-goat.' " Perhaps embarrassed that such a personal communication had been read by a stranger, however, the president did not write to thank the good Samaritan—or, if he did, the letter was lost. Following is the undelivered letter that Lincoln wrote to Mary, reprinted from the still-soiled copy that remains to this day in the Lincoln Papers in the Library of Congress. (Lincoln's letter, *Coll. Works* VI: 371–72)

Executive Mansion, Washington,
My dear Wife.   August 8, 1863.

All as well as usual, and no particular trouble any way. I put the money into the Treasury at five per cent, with the previlege of withdrawing it any time upon thirty days' notice. I suppose you are glad to learn this. Tell dear Tad, poor "Nanny Goat," is lost; and Mrs. Cuthbert & I are in distress about it. The day you left Nanny was found resting herself, and chewing her little cud, on the middle of Tad's bed. But now she's gone! The gardener kept complaining that she destroyed the flowers, till it was concluded to bring her down to the White House. This was done, and the second day she had disappeared, and has not been heard of since. This is the last we know of poor "Nanny"

The weather continues dry, and excessively warm here.

1864

Nothing very important occurring. The election in Kentucky has gone very strongly right. Old Mr. [Charles A.] Wickliffe got ugly, as you know, ran for Governor, and is terribly beaten. Upon Mr. [John J.] Crittendens death [the veteran senator was best known for offering a compromise to conciliate between North and South in 1860—Ed.], Brutus Clay, Cassius' brother, was put on the track for Congress, and is largely elected. Mr. [John W.] Menzies, who, as we thought, behaved very badly last session of Congress, is largely beaten in the District opposite Cincinnati, by Green Clay Smith, Cassius Clay's nephew. But enough.

Affectionately
A. Lincoln

Will the President Endorse a Book?

Walker, Wise, & Company
Publishers, Booksellers, and Stationers,
245, Washington Street, Boston, Apl. 27 1864

Dear Sir:

We send by this mail, a copy of our Prospectus of "Martin's History of France," wh. we have in press:— We feel sure the enterprise will meet yr. approval, & shall be happy to add yr. name to the list of subscribers, wh. Hon. Edward Everett has headed.

You need not return the Prospectus, but clip off the lower part of the last page with your signature, if you kindly accede to our solicitation,— & mail it us

Very respectfully Yours
Walker, Wise, & Co.

Hon. A. Lincoln

The Prospectus was not found in the Lincoln Papers. Lincoln may have signed and returned the coupon or, perhaps, turned the question over to his wife, who had a broader knowledge of French history.

1864

Engraver Proposes New Portrait

New York May 6th. 1864

His Excellency President Lincoln

Dear Sir:

I desire Engraving in best style & large size <u>your Portrait</u> on steel— and wishing a reliable Photograph to copy from—I have taken the liberty to address you for the purpose of obtaining one pleasing to yourself and family.

Will you please favor me with the same—together with your autograph to engrave on the Plate—by Mail or otherwise.

& very much oblige

Very Respectfully Yours &c.
Geo. E. Perine

Although there is no surviving direct evidence that Lincoln responded to this request, printmaker Perine did issue several engraved portraits of Lincoln for the campaign year of 1864. All were based on flattering photographs, and most featured a facsimile signature evidently based on a genuine autograph. Perine was a prolific portrait engraver in New York City who produced most of his work for book illustrations.

Frontier Cousins Ask Favors

Charleston, Ills. May 9th 1864

To His Excellency A. Lincoln

Dear Sir

As I am now out of business I write to you for the purpose of making application for a permit to trade within the lines of the Western Army in all kinds of merchandise, Liquors excepted. I would of course expect to be governed by the rules of Trade as established by the <u>Treasure</u> department. If you will grant me this request you will confer a favor that will not be soon forgotten.

Yours very Truly
Allison C. Poorman

1864

Allison Poorman was married to Amanda Hanks, the daughter of Lincoln's cousin, Dennis Hanks. Lincoln wrote the following endorsement on this letter, which he had first transcribed in his own hand, or perhaps wrote himself on behalf of his semi-literate relative.

May 15, 1864

Indorsed

The writer of the within is a family connection of mine, & a worthy man; and I shall be obliged if he be allowed what he requests, so far as the rules and exigencies of the public service will permit.

A. Lincoln
May 15. 1864

The same day, Lincoln transcribed and again "indorsed" the following "letter" from yet another of Dennis Hanks's sons-in law, again no doubt writing it himself when his visitor—apparently Dennis himself—was unable to do so. (Lincoln's endorsements, *Coll. Works* VII: 342)

Charleston, Ills. May 9th 1864

Hon. A. Lincoln

Dear Sir

This will be presented to you by Father Hanks who will now more fully lay before you my wants than I can explain. I will simply say that if consistent with your feelings, and not in any way conflicting with Army regulations I would like a permit to trade within the lines of the Army of the Cumberland, Mississippi and Arkansas in Cotton & Hides for shipment North. For reference I can only offer Father Hanks.

I am very truly your Obt. Servt.
W. F. Shriver

May 15, 1864

Indorsed

The writer of this is personally unknown to me, though married to a young relative of mine. I shall be obliged if he be allowed what he requests so far as the rules and exigencies of the public service will permit.

A. Lincoln
May 15. 1864

1864

A Forgotten Old Relative Writes

New London Henry County Iowa

11th May, 1864

Abraham Lincoln Esq
President of the United States

My dear Sir

You may not recollect an old man now tottering on the verge of the grave—then living in Macon County Illinois who wore the name of William Miller and married your cousin Nancy Hanks.

With the keenest remembrances of old times I will never forget your visits to my humble home which you will recollect although plain was free as the air to yourself. Providence has exceeded your expectations and mine in placing you in the great White House. Whilst age has made me feeble When in Illinois I was so well acquainted with you that I could venture to talk to you about everything and I hope your elevation to place has not changed your native kindness.

You will perhaps recollect Aunt Nancy's Sister, Celia Hanks. You will recollect she married John D. Wright who afterwards came to Des Moines Iowa—John was our County Surveyor was a member of the Legislature and of the State Convention which formed our Constitution and was withal a very honest clever man.

Poor Celia died about twenty years ago when her twin children, Elisha and Electa were one month old—I took them children and raised them. Elisha had a very good education and clerked in a Store until the way broke out and then he volunteered to go to the war to help Cousin Abe (as we call you) preserve the Country   Elisha is a good sensible honest trust worthy boy, and has been in many hard fights, and is a good soldier   I want him to get promotion after so much fighting and suffering   He is worthy of a place in the Regular Army as Lieutenant and will in such position never disgrace his kinsman who can easily give him the appointment he so richly deserves. He is a private in company K 19th Iowa Infantry

I need not add more which will tire you. I am now upwards of seventy and have to get a friend to write for me as I dictate as I am feeble.

I feel anxious before I die to do something for my dear relative Elisha and feel sure that you will do this for me.

1864

153

Aunt Nancy is feeble like myself. She joins in my love to you that God will help you in this great time of trouble

> I am your cousin affectionately
> William Miller

No response has been located, but a month after this letter was received the name Elisha M. Wright of Iowa appeared in Lincoln's hand on a list of applicants for the post of secretary of Montana. Lincoln endorsed the envelope in which his cousin's letter arrived twice: first, with a formal entry, "William Miller"; then, perhaps thinking back to his days on the frontier, he added, "Bill Miller."

Pineapples from His Chiropodist

> 760 Broadway
> New York May 13th 1864

To His Excellcy A. Lincoln.

Dear Friend.

I sent you some days ago a Box of fine <u>Pine apples</u>, which I hope you received, kind regards to Mrs. Lincoln. I remain

> Yours Truly
> I. Zacharie M.D.

Lincoln enjoyed a warm, if somewhat mysterious, relationship with Dr. Isachar Zacharie, a Jewish chiropodist. In September 1862, Lincoln wrote a testimonial in his behalf, asserting: "Dr. Zacharie has operated on my feet with great success, and considerable addition to my comfort" (*Coll. Works* V: 436). Zacharie in turn used the endorsement to promote his practice, inspiring the *New York Herald* to editorialize that they now understood why Lincoln was powerless to control the Radical Republicans: "How could the President put his foot down firmly," the newspaper teased, "when he was troubled with corns?" But Zacharie's involvement with Lincoln extended well beyond a doctor-patient relationship. The president sent the chiropodist on several secret missions during the war, once to New Orleans, which boasted a large Jewish population. These missions have never been fully explained. (Ed. note, Mark E. Neely Jr., *The Abraham Lincoln Encyclopedia* [New York: McGraw-Hill, 1982], 164)

1864

An Old Prairie Friend Appeals
for a Destitute Neighbor

Havana Mason Co Ills
May 19th 1864

To The Honble A. Lincoln
Washington

Honble Sir

I take this liberty to inform you that my son, William Duff has got home and is now married and doing well at this present time

Now Honerable Sir I have one more request to ask of you and I have hope through your good and kind feeling for the distressed you will grant it to me.

It is this there is here in my neighbourhood a daughter of Old Mr Jonathen Louge an old acquaintance of yours and she is in a very destitute condition on account of a long and protracted case if Sickness, and She having a large family of Small children she cannot now get along in any way without the assistance of her husband whose names is Louis Ishmel he is in Company C 85th Regiment Ills Infantry and has been in the service now nearly two years and has never had any leave of absence since he left home

And she is now in Such destitute circumstances that she is not able to maintain herself and family and he has always bourne an honourable character at home

I hope you now will grant my request by Discharging him from the Service and restoring him to his now destitute family and by so doing you will confer a favor on his poor Wife and me

I remain Honble Sir
Your obedient Servant
Hannah Armstrong

There is no record of a reply or any action by the president to grant "one more request" for Hannah Armstrong, a friend of thirty years' standing, whose family had played a part in two legendary episodes of Lincoln's life. It was Hannah's husband, Jack Armstrong, who challenged Lincoln to the famous wrestling match they fought in New Salem in 1831. Jack left Hannah a widow around 1857, but the following year, their son, Duff, became Lincoln's client in the most famous trial of his entire legal career. Lincoln successfully defended

---
1864
---

young Armstrong against a murder charge by dramatically producing an almanac that proved there was no moon on the night a witness swore he saw Armstrong kill his victim by bright moonlight—from 150 feet away. Lincoln did not charge the impoverished family a fee for winning Duff's acquittal. As president, he continued to act generously in their behalf. When told that Duff had taken ill while serving in the Union army, Lincoln ordered him discharged—a favor to which Hannah referred in her new plea for the daughter of "old Mr. Louge." It is conceivable that Lincoln never read this letter. When it arrived on his desk, refolded and summarized by a secretary, it bore the identification, "Hannah Taylor," rather than Hannah Armstrong. Failing to recognize the name, Lincoln may well have filed it without opening it. (Ed. note, *Journal of the Illinois State Historical Society* 14: 266; *Coll. Works* VI: 462)

Fruit Cake for the President

Corn Exchange Bank,
Philadelphia, 23d June 1864

His Excellency Abraham Lincoln

Prest. U.S.

I have the honor to forward to you to day by Express the splendid Fruit Cake, prepared for you by Mrs. Harkinson of Germantown, a widow lady who has now five sons in the Service of the U.S. four of them in the Army and one in the Navy— You will perhaps remember that this Cake was exhibited to you by the Ladies of the Corn Exchange Table, as you passed along "Union Avenue" on your late visit to the Fair [the Philadelphia Sanitary Fair a week earlier—Ed.]— With an earnest prayer that God's earnest blessings may ever attend you; Very Respectfully Your obt Servt

W. G. Cattell

No reply is known.

The Secretary of the Treasury Resigns

Treasury Department
June 29, 1864

My dear Sir,

I have just received your note and have read it with great attention [the President and his Treasury Secretary had been sparring over an appointment for Assistant U.S. Treasurer for New York City; Chase proposed Maunsel B. Field, and Lincoln replied that he did not think him "a very proper man for the place."—Ed.]. I was not aware of the extent of the embarrassment to which you refer [Lincoln had protested that he could not name Field, in the wake of New York Senator Morgan's opposition, "without much embarrassment."—Ed.]. In recommendations for office I have sincerely sought to get the best men for the places to be filled without reference to any other classification than supporters and opponents of your administration. Of the latter I have recommended none; among the former I have desired to know no distinction except degrees of fitness.

The withdrawal of Mr. Cisco's resignation [the current Assistant Treasurer for New York, who agreed to stay on—Ed.], which I enclose, relieves the present difficulty; but I cannot help feeling that my position here is not altogether agreeable to you; and it is certainly too full of embarrassment and difficulty and painful responsibility to allow in me the least desire to retain it.

I think it my duty therefore to enclose to you my resignation. I shall regard it as a real relief if you think proper to accept it; and will most cheerfully tender to my successor any aid he may find useful in entering upon his duties. With the greatest respect,

Yours truly
S. P. Chase

The President

Chase had offered his resignation before, but Lincoln had consistently rejected it. This time Chase's one-line official resignation, "I respectfully resign the office of Secretary of the Treasury which I have the honor to hold under your appointment," was endorsed by the president: "Secretary Chase, on occasion of his retiring." Lincoln then wrote the following letter of acceptance to the man who had hoped to replace the president as the 1864 Republican nominee.

1864

Hon. Salmon P. Chase   Executive Mansion
My dear Sir: Washington, June 30, 1864.

Your resignation of the office of Secretary of the Treasury, sent me yesterday, is accepted. Of all I have said in commendation of your ability and fidelity, I have nothing to unsay; and yet you and I have reached a point of mutual embarrassment in our official relation which it seems can not be overcome, or longer sustained, consistently with the public service. Your Obt. Servt.

A. Lincoln

"It is a big fish," Lincoln told private secretary John Hay about his decision to rid himself of Chase. "I thought I could not stand it any longer." Hay, who believed the president wrong to accept the resignation, confided in his diary that "Chase's leaving at this time is little less than a crime." (Ed. note, Dennett, *Lincoln and the Civil War* 198, 282, 291 (Lincoln's reply, *Coll. Works* VII: 419).

Make Peace Now!

Niagara [Falls, N.Y.], July 2d 1864

President Lincoln

Note within—Be wise & save yourself & your Country from destruction by declaring for an armistice & cutting loose from your entire Cabinet & party—relying solely on your God & right.
                                        Yours,
                                        Jewett

The writer, William Cornell "Colorado" Jewett, was a frequent critic of the Lincoln administration. This letter came with newspaper clippings describing his recent meetings with Southern representatives in Canada. But, like all of Jewett's missives, it failed to elicit a response from Lincoln.

1864

A Visitor Lost En Route

Willard's Hotel
Thursday pm [summer 1864]

President Lincoln

Dear Sir:

Man proposes, but God disposes. I left Willard's at 7-1/4 last night to meet your kind engagement with me at 8—

The driver, it seems, did not know the way [to the summer White House, the Soldiers Home—Ed.], or else was drunk. He brought up at Fort Stevens, & when the guard there showed us the need of retreating, his next move was on Fort Slocum!

It was now 10 at night, & of course, I could not intrude upon you after that hour.

If you can see me at any time to day, or at Soldiers Home at 8 this evening, I shall try again.

If not, I shall conclude that it is not best for me to see you at all, as I believe in Providence, & hope you do

Yours truly
John McClintock

A line of answer by the bearer will oblige me

Mary Lincoln had written that at the family's summer retreat at the Soldiers' Home, "we can be as secluded, as we please." Apparently, that seclusion made it difficult for visitors like McClintock to find the house, which was located two-and-a-half miles outside Washington. McClintok's belief in destiny was understandable; he was a Methodist minister, the onetime pastor of the American chapel in Paris.

Kentucky Woman Wants Her Slaves Back from Army

Fairview, Jefferson Co, Ky July [?] 1864

My Dear Sir:

I can assure you it is with great diffidence that a lady of my humble abilities presumes to address your Excellency; but the motives by which I am actuated must be my apology on the present occasion.

1864

I addressed a letter to your Excellency a week ago which was forwarded through the urbanity of Capt. P. H Smith Prov. Mar. of Ky; but fearing it may not have reached you in consequence of the recent rebel raids in the vicinity of Washington, I have determined to send a second letter containing the substance of the first, with some additional remarks. At the commencement of the rebellion my husband and self took a decided stand on the side of the government and have remained firmly fixed ever since; though we are entirely surrounded by bitter rebel sympathizers. I have earnestly advocated your views of gradual emancipation and ardently desired that Kentucky would accept your proposition of compensated emancipation; for I then thought, and still think, it was the best policy that she could adopt. I have been in favor of gradual emancipation from my earliest youth when I was a school-girl at the Capital of this state and listened to the earnest and eloquent appeals of Kentucky's great statesmen the immortal Clay in behalf of colonization.

Entertaining such views I have brought up from infancy and have been educating four servant boys—three of them, my own, and one belonging to my Mother—preparatory to sending to Liberia when I thought they were competent to take care of themselves. Two of those boys have enlisted in a coloured regiment being organized in this state, and it is for the purpose of obtaining their release that I now address your Excellency. I am fully persuaded that they were induced to enlist through the excitement of the times, and not of their own free-will; for up to the time of their leaveing home which was the day previous to their enlistment, they said that they never intended to go into the army unless compelled by the draft. I believe my case is an isolated one. In the Barracks where three thousand blacks are enlisted, I was told that not one of them had the promise of freedom by their masters. My servants being young and inexperienced, did not appreciate their high privileges but rushed into the army without any reflection, and solely as they have since confessed to me, because they saw others going with whom they associated.

The eldest one, twenty years of age, who enlisted by the name of James Minor, belongs to my Mother, and was manumitted by my Fathers will fourteen years ago to take effect at her death. He is her only means of support and she is a widow of seventy years of age, has been afflicted with Rheumatism for fifteen years, and has been entirely helpless as an infant for the last three years.

The youngest boy, Alex, eighteen years of age, belonging to myself has been her constant nurse for eight years. Her grief is so excessive in consequence of his loss, united with the loss of her own servant whom she regards with the affection of a son that she is almost deprived of reason and I fear it will eventually cause an entire derangement of mind. The eldest of my three servants left two months ago, when the drafting of the negroes commenced; and as we have received no intelligence of him, we suppose he has been taken in the army. Our servants have been our principal support, and we have but one left, a boy of twelve years of age. My husband is in the decline of life and has not sufficient health to labour for the support of his family. We have no children to fall back upon, my health very delicate and so affected with nervousness, that I am dependant on my husband to pen this letter.

In view of all these things I have resolved to throw myself on your mercy and appeal to you as a philanthropist and a christian, as I trust you are, to authorize the release of my servants if it is in your power; and if not, I beseech you to use your influence with the Secretary of War in my behalf; and not suffer all my domestic happiness to be impaired, and all my hopes to be blighted that I have cherished for so many years in regard to their present and future welfare. If you should be so merciful as to send an order for their release—which I hope and believe the feelings of your heart will prompt you to do—I want you, if you please, to have it so fixed that they cannot reenlist without our consent.

I feel assured that if you will comply with my earnest request. God will approve, and the prayers of a venerable and pious Mother, united with mine, will be daily offered at a throne of grace for your present and everlasting happiness. Yours with much respect

Elizabeth A. Minor

Lincoln or his staff referred this letter to the Bureau of Colored Troops, which on July 23, 1864 denied Mrs. Minor's request, asserting: "the reasons given in your request are considered insufficient, and to discharge them [the slaves] would establish a precedent injurious to the interests of the service." (Letter, Colored Troops Division Files, National Archives)

No Bodyguard Needed

(Hd Q Sr Guard) Camp Tod July 3rd/64
To His Excellency Abraham Lincoln.

I received orders from Maj Genl [Christopher Columbus] Augur [commander of the Department of Washington—Ed.] and Military Governor of the district of Washington to report ninety men to your excellency as an escort. I reported the same and received a verbal order that the men were not wanted and will report the same to you in the morning providing you wish it.

Yours Respectfully,
James D. Jameson
2nd Lieut C Co.

The guards may have been proposed in response to renewed Confederate threats to Washington, which would reach their climactic moment nine days later when General Jubal Early approached Fort Stevens on the outskirts of the city—skirmishing that was witnessed by Lincoln himself. During this period, as in previous summers, Lincoln was commuting daily between the White House and the Soldiers' Home outside the city. Nevertheless, he endorsed this letter as follows: "I believe I need no escort, and unless the Sec. of War directs, none need attend me." Eventually, Lincoln was assigned a regular military guard to travel with him to and from his summer residence. (Letter, courtesy of The Forbes Magazine Collection, New York)

Black Soldier's Wife Needs Husband's Pay

Mt Holly [New Jersey], July 11 1864

Abraham Lincoln
President

Sir,

my husband, who is in Co. K. 22nd Reg't U.S. Col'd. Troops, (and now in the Macon Hospital at Portsmouth with a wound in his arm) has not received any pay since last May and then only thirteen dollars. I write to you because I have been told you would see to it. I have four children to support and I find this a great struggle. A hard life this!

1864

I being a col'd woman do not get any State pay. Yet my husband is fighting for the country.

Very Resp'y yours
Rosanna Henson

Lincoln's staff forwarded this letter to the War Department, but there is no record in Mrs. Henson's file to indicate whether any action was taken. (Letter, Files of Letters Received for the President and Executive Departments, National Archives)

Black Soldiers Vow "Stringent Mesures" to Get Equal Pay

Folly island South Carolina
July 16th 18.64

The President of the United States

Sir

We The Members of Co D of the 55th Massachusetts vols Call the attention of your Excellency to our case

1st   First We wase enlisted under the act of Congress of July 18.61 Placing the officers non Commissioned officers & Privates of the volunteer forces in all Respects as to Pay on the footing of Similar Corps of the Regular Army   2nd   We Have Been in the Field now thirteen months & a Great many yet longer We Have Received no Pay & Have Been offered only seven Dollars Pr month Which the Paymaster Has said was all He Had ever Been authorized to Pay Colored Troops   this was not acording to our enlistment   Consequently We Refused the Money   the Commonwealth of Massachusetts then Passed an act to make up all Deficienceys which the general Government Refused to Pay But this We Could not Recieve as The Troops in the general service are not Paid Partly By Government & Partly By State   3rd   that to us money is no object   we came to fight For Liberty justice & Equality. These are gifts we Prise more Highly than Gold   For these We Left our Homes our Famileys Friends & Relatives most Dear to take as it ware our Lives in our Hands To Do Battle for God & Liberty

4th   after the elaps of over thirteen months spent cheerfully & will-

---

1864

ingly Doing our Duty most faithfuly in the Trenches Fatiegue Duty in camp and conspicious valor & endurance in Battle as our Past History will Show

P 5th therefore we Deem these sufficient Reasons for Demanding our Pay from the Date of our inlistment & our imediate Discharge Having Been enlisted under False Pretence as the Past History of the Company will Prove

6th Be it further Resolved that if imediate steps are not takened to Relieve us we will Resort to more stringent mesures

We have the Honor to Remin your Obedint Servants
The members of Co D

No record of a reply is known. The petition, signed by seventy-four members of the 55th Massachusetts Colored Infantry, was forwarded to the Bureau of Colored Troops of the War Department. For a year, both the 55th and 54th had refused to accept lower pay than white soldiers, refusing all compensation—even when the Massachusetts legislature voted to pay the difference—despite the hardship that resulted. On June 15, 1864, a month before this petition was forwarded to Lincoln, Congress had finally acted to equalize pay for all privates, black as well as white, at $13 per month. The raise was retroactive to the date of enlistment for freed blacks, and to January 1, 1864 for black soldiers who had been slaves. (Letter, Colored Troops Division Files, National Archives; Ed. note, Berlin, *Freedom: The Black Military Experience*, 401–2)

An Inventor's "Foolish" Notion

Manhattan Riley Co Kan July 18th 1864

President Lincoln,

Honored Sir,

Wishing to do good, I herewith submit what is, in all probability, a foolish thing. Yet it seems to me that these land Monitors would allow a storming party to approach a line of rifle pits with impunity. To be made of steel. As the soldier kneels upon one knee to deliver his fire, the monitor strikes the ground and he is relieved from the weight, and at liberty to use his gun to load and fire, as long as orders permit. In rising, his shoulders come up into the holders, and the waist support comes up to its place, with no adjustment necessary.

1864

Wishing you a long Life and a triumphant reelection, I am
respectfully Yours
S. P. Hurlbutt

Hurlbutt's "land monitor" invention, no doubt inspired by the introduction of ironclads into naval warfare, was a portable, two-sided piece of armor shaped like an open book, with a porthole for soldiers to see through as they marched carrying the shield. As early as 1861, would-be inventors began proposing portable armored shields to the president and the War Department (S. P. Davis to Lincoln, August 26, 1861, Lincoln Papers). Hurlbutt's suggestion was forwarded to the Ordnance Department without comment. "One universal idea" afflicting Lincoln's correspondents, White House secretary William O. Stoddard complained, was "that if any given gun, cannon, ship, armor or all-killing or all-saving apparatus chanced to take the eye of the President, it must thereupon speedily be adopted for army use and forced into a grand success by Executive authority. It was in vain that Mr. Lincoln systematically discouraged this notion," Stoddard contended, "and never went further, even with inventions that pleased him most, than to order an examination and trial by the proper professional authorities." (Ed. note, William O. Stoddard, *New York Citizen*, September 8, 1866)

Chain Mail for Union Soldiers

Adell, Sheboygan Co. Wis. July 25th 1864

To His Excellence Abraham Lincoln
President of the U. St. of America.

Dear Sir!

As I reflected to many a means in saving mens life in that terrible war, I came to that following coat of mail, called by myself, "Panzerhemd." Certainly, that invention is not a new one. Napoleon I had made himself one of it which could not perforate a ball fired at the distance of ten steps. But it was made very artfull and an Emperor only could pay for it. I deliver up to You a single and cheap construction of a "Panzerhemd." Please, examine the inclosed delineation and description, and you will find that it is practicable easy and cheap.

What a terror would get a rebell firing at ten steps distance against a northern man and the latter laughed at him! What trust (next that in

---

1864

God) should bring it in the army and how would approach the volunteers, as soon as they heard they get a "Panzerhemd" or could buy one. Be not tardy to accept my offer to buy that invention for the benefit of the government and exercise it as soon as possible. Indeed, that thing must be hold very secret against every southern men and neither description nor "Panzerhemd" ought to come to their ear or sight, because an imitation is very easy.

Send me a check of "hundred thousand Dollars" ($100,000) courancy, then the drawing and description of my Panzerhemd shall be the property of the government of the U. States.

Respectfully Your obedient servant
A. Brose

The self-proclaimed inventor enclosed drawings of his "Panzerhemd" (German for "armored shirt") together with a slogan he had devised for it: "Overwhelm the south before the first of Nov." Enclosed, too, was a one-page description that conceded, "The Panzerhemd is nothing else than a long waistcoat reaching over the hips, but not to hinder the marching . . . made of fine steel chains" not unlike the "chains of the 'Kearsarge'," the well-protected Union warship that had recently destroyed the Confederate commerce raider, *Alabama*. Not surprisingly, Lincoln did not send Brose the $100,000 he demanded. (Letter, Ordnance Files, National Archives)

Black Soldier Protests
"Weak and Starving Condition"

New Orleans Camp Parpit Louisiana
[August] 1864

My Dear Friend and x Pre

I thake up my Pen to Address you A fiew simpels And facts   We so called the 20th u.s. Colored troops we was got up in the state of New York so said By A grant of the President. we Dont think he know wether we are white or Black we have not Bin Organized yet And A grate meney Brought Away without Being Musterd in, and we are treated in a Different maner to what others Rigiments is Both Northern men or southern Raised Rigiment   Instead of the musket It is the spad and the Whelbarrow and the Axe cuting in one of the most horable swamps in

---

1864

Louisiana stinking and misery   Men are Call to go on thes fatiuges wen sum of them are scarc Able to get Along the Day Before on the sick List And Perhaps weeks to And By this treatment meney are thowen Back in sickness wich thay very seldom get over. we had when we Left New York over A thousand strong   now we scarce rise Nine hundred the total is said to Be   we lost 1.60 men who have Left thire homes friends and Relation And Come Down hear to Lose thire Lives in For the Country thy Dwll in or stayd in   the Colored man is like A lost sheep   Meney of them old and young was Brave And Active. But has Bin hurrided By and ignominious Death into Eternity. But I hope God will Presearve the Rest Now in existance to Get Justice and Rights   we have to Do our Duty or Die and no help for us   It is true the Country is in A hard strugle   But we All must Remember Mercy and Justice Grate and small. it is Devine. we All Listed for so much Bounty Clothing and Ration And 13 Dollars A month. And the most has fallen short in all thes Things   we havent Recived A cent of Pay Since we Bin in the field. Instead of them Coming to us Like men with our 13 Dollars thay come with only seven Dollars A month wich only A fiew tuck it   we stand in Need of Money very much indeed And think it is no more than Just an Right we should have it   And Another thing we are Cut short of our Ration in A most Shocking maner. I wont Relate All now But we Are Nerly Deprived of All Comforts of Life   Hardly have Anough Bread to Keep us From starving six or 8 ounces of it to Do A Soldier 24 hours on Gaurd or eney other Labor and About the Same in Meat and Coffee   sum times No meat for 2 Days   soup meat Licqour with very Little seazing the Boys calls hot water or meat tea for Diner   It is A hard thing to be Keept in such a state of misery Continuly   It is spoken Dont musel the ox that treads out the corn. Remember we are men standing in Readiness to face thous vile traitors an Rebeles who are trying to Bring your Peaceable homes to Destruction. And how can we stand them in A weak and starving Condition

---

The letter is unsigned, but was discovered in the Colored Troops Files of the National Archives in the same folder as another letter, in the same hand, by one Nimrod Rowley.

1864

Requesting Charity for "Homeless Little Ones"

Office Corresponding Secretary
Orphans' Home Society
Springfield, Mo. Aug 15 1864.

To His Excellency Abraham Lincoln
President of the United States

Honorable Sir.

I appeal to you in behalf of the destitute Orphans of this town and vicinity many of them children of Soldiers deprived of their fathers by this "Cruel War" others refugees who have fled to us for protection leaving all their worldly goods behind them many of them are living in tents and others are without shelter living as best they can   The ladies of Springfield have organised a society for the purpose of providing for these homeless little ones they propose to purchase a farm with as good buildings as can be had but in order to do this we must have money and there is very little of that in the Treasury not more than $700. We wish to get a shelter for these children before winter and are compelled to solicit subscriptions from abroad   Our citizens will do all they can but they have been heavily taxed during the war and are made to raise the whole amount—We need at least $4000. Our farm will cost us $5000. Will you not assist us? And influence others to lend a helping hand   I know that you will that it is only necessary to lay this case before you to have your ready aid and sympathy   May I hope to hear from you at your earliest convenience

Yours Very Respectfully
Mrs. Wade H. Burdin Cor Sec

There is no record of a reply, endorsement, or contribution from Lincoln, who was rather unresponsive to pleas for charity during the war.

1864

Proposing a Lincoln Club . . . On Condition

No 440 East 16th
New York City
August 24th 1864

At my own expense I am organizing a Club to support your re-election. The Club will be situated in a District (18th Ward) hitherto unapproachable by any but the rankest anti-administration kind. My popularity will, however enable me to make an impression and establish an opinion favorable to the Party.

I am aware that the planting of a <u>Union Flag</u> in the midst of Irish-Copperheadism will not be unattended by serious difficulties which I shall endeavor to overcome and do so with pleasure if I had your personal assurance that our Government will not prevent the readmission of the rebellious states under their former constitutions, provided it should come to pass (and I think it will) that they will lay down their arms on those conditions.

If your reply is favorable then my interpretation of your Emancipating Proclamation [*sic*] that such States can return as Slave States, is correct.

The people into whom I am about to infuse a sense of loyalty are plain and ignorant, hence my plain question.

A reply at your earliest convenience will greatly oblige.

> Your humble servant
> George Chopat
> formerly of Lousiana

To his Excellency Abraham Lincoln
President of the United States

Lincoln had no intention of reversing his Emancipation Proclamation. Presumably, the writer of this letter so discovered, and his Lincoln club was never organized.

1864

A Slave Wants "To Be Free"

Belair [Maryland] Aug 25th 1864

Mr president

It is my Desire to be free. to go to see my people on the eastern shore. my mistress wont let me   you will please let me know if we are free. and what i can do. I write to you for advice. please send me word this week. or as soon as possible and oblidge.

Annie Davis
Belair Thorfad Co[unty] MD.

Annie Davis was not free. The Emancipation Proclamation ordered the liberation only of slaves in the rebellious states, and Annie Davis lived in Maryland, a slave state that had remained loyal to the Union. The Republican platform for 1864, adopted in June, urged an "amendment to the Constitution . . . as shall terminate and forever prohibit the existence of slavery within the . . . jurisdiction of the United States." But it would be more than a year before the Thirteenth Amendment became law. For now, Annie Davis's letter remained unanswered and her hopes of freedom unfulfilled. (Letter, Colored Troops Division Files, National Archives; Ed. note, David Long, *The Jewel of Liberty: Abraham Lincoln's Re-Election and the End of Slavery* [Mechanicsburg, PA: Stackpole Books, 1994], 280)

Sister-in-Law Seeks Pardon for Prisoner of War

Lexington Ky Sept 5th 1864

My Dear Mr Lincoln

Please excuse me for addressing you in your private capacity, but my recollection of your former treatment of myself & family I hope shall warrant me in so doing. I wish to bring to your attention a case & will be as brief as possible knowing the pressure of business on your time. I visited Camp Chase [a prison outside Columbus, Ohio—Ed.] a few weeks ago to see a cousin (17 years old, captured at Atlanta & the only son of Uncle the late Dr. Humphreys of Louisiana) and minister to his destitute condition. On the occasion of this visit I was made somewhat acquainted with the case of Judge Van Dyke through Col Richardson commandant of that post. The Judge is held as a hostage and as I un-

---

derstand it his case is an unusually hard one. I had you enclosed a note secured from him a few days ago which will hardly explain the case. Judge Van Dyke has never held any but a judicial position & has never been particularly mixed up in the political affairs of the Country. He is a gentleman of high social and literary position, of advanced age, and too delicate in physique I think to go through with a <u>prison</u> life this <u>winter</u> His greatest complaint seems to be that he cannot have his case investigated. When Genl Sherman entered Athens Tenn his Head Quarters was at the house of the Judge. There is a strong personal friendship between them, Genl Sherman <u>repeatedly refused</u> to arrest or interfere with him at the suggestion of political opponents. The arrest was made by some subordinate after Genl Shermans advance & is yet no doubt unknown to him.

I take special interest in this case from the fact that Judge Van Dyke & family were kind friends to sister Emily [Todd Helm] before & after the death of Genl [Ben Hardin] Helm [Emily's husband and Lincoln's brother-in-law, killed at the Battle of Chickamauga in 1863 — Ed.]. Now you Mr Lincoln will bear me witness that my appeals for your favour have not been numerous. Efforts to reach <u>you</u> through <u>me</u> are made weekly & almost daily by reason of our family connection, but I think I have resisted them with prudence & due consideration for you. Do I beg of you to order this case to be examined & dispose of it as I know you will in accordance with the dictates of justice and humanity. I think the fullest reliance can be placed in any statement he may make.

I would be glad to come to Washington if I could be assured of a personal interview. May I hope for a response to this? While I remain, as ever, your sister

Margaret Kellogg

Margaret Todd Kellogg was Mary Lincoln's half sister, one of nine children of her father's second marriage, many of whom, most notably General Helm, pledged loyalty to the Confederacy. But Margaret remained close to the Lincolns; she visited the White House early in her brother-in-law's term and helped secure a government appointment for her husband, although Mary dismissed their original ambitions as "preposterous." Still, there is no record that Lincoln responded to this plea for the imprisoned Judge Van Dyke, and if the judge was known to General Sherman, there is no mention of him in his memoirs. (Ed. note, Harold Holzer and Mark E. Neely Jr., *The Lincoln Family Album* [New York: Doubleday, 1990], 57)

1864

Yet Another Sister-in-Law Makes a Plea

Lexington Kentucky
September 5 64.

To His Excellency the President of the United States

Mr Lincoln—

You will doubtless be surprised at receiving a letter from me but never the less I hope it will be welcome—I have written to you to ask if you will grant an especial Exchange of Brig Genl W. N. R. Beall of the Confederate States Army captured at Port Hudson Miss—last July 5th 1863. He is a prisoner now at Johnsons Island, Ohio. Genl Beall's family have always been old and warm friends of my father's and if you would grant my request We all would be under everlasting obligations   If you would parole him to go to Richmond Va. and affect the Exchange of an Officer of an equal rank in the United States Army, any one you might name, no doubt would be exchange [sic] for Genl Beall—Should you object to an exchange, would you parole him to New York, Missouri or Kentucky for a few weeks. Hoping you will be kind enough to grant me this request—With love to Sister Mary, and kind wishes for yourself in which Emilie [Todd Helm] joins me, trusting I may hear from you an answer to my letter

Believe me, affectionately Yours
Kittie Todd

No reply has been found to this request from one of Mary's more decidedly Confederate half sisters.

A Scheme to Guarantee His Reelection

Cincinnati Ohio September 9th 1864

To His Excellency Abraham Lincoln
President of the United States

Dr Sir

I had the honour of voting for you at the last Presidential Elections, and hope I may be spared to vote for you again, and as I am in my hearts centre a Union man, and anxious to see this unholy rebellion crushed,

---

1864

and sincerely believing you of all other men should be elected, to finish the great work which I believe you have been called in the Providence of God, that of saving our Country and freeing the slaves, I thought I would write you a few lines by way of making a suggestion which I believe would certainly secure your reelection. It is this. Get the National Union Committee to arrange with the Fremont committee to agree to have but one set of Electors voted for by the Friends of yourself & Mr Fremont. Have some of the tickets printed with your name on them & some with Mr Fremonts name on them. Let the electors be those who have been selected to cast their vote for you in the event of your Election. Then have it agreed between the two committees that whoever gets the largest vote for that one they shall cast their vote, and in this way not a vote would be lost and beyond all question you will be reelected. Should this Suggestion strike you favorably & it should be adopted, & thus secure your reelection it will be to one a pleasant recollection the rest of my life. With the most sincere wishes for your health & happiness, & my prayers that in the Providence of God you may be again Elected to your present position, & this wicked rebellion crushed and the Stars and Stripes may very soon wave over every State, Fort & Capital, I subscribe myself

Very truly yours &c.

D. H. Meers

Lincoln did not reply to this proposal to guarantee his reelection by making a deal with insurgent Republican John C. Fremont to share electors. The letter was filed and endorsed: "Political." Within two weeks, Fremont withdrew from the race anyway, probably in return for the resignation of Postmaster General Montgomery Blair from Lincoln's cabinet.

A Lost Invitation to Speak in Buffalo

Office U.S. Military Telegraph,
War Department.
Buffalo, Sept 9 1864.

His Excy A Lincoln Prest U.S.

Will you kindly answer our letter written in August of invitation to the national union mass ratification meeting to be held in this city on

---
1864
---

fifteenth Sept. We desire to have it read to the meeting which will be one of the most inspiring ever held in the Union.

> Isaac M. Schermerhorn
> Prest of Union League
> of S[tate of] N.Y.

Lincoln replied by telegraph to this urgent wire on the same day.

Isaac M. Schermerhorn   War Department
Buffalo, N.Y.   Washington City, Sep. 9, 1864.
    Yours of to-day received. I do not think the letter you mention has reached me. I have no recollection of it.

> A. Lincoln

Schermerhorn raced back to the military telegraph the next morning to respond to the president's message.

> Office U.S. Military Telegraph,
> War Department.
> Buffalo Sept 10 1864.

His Excy A Lincoln Prest US
    The letter referred to was an invitation to attend the National Union ratification meeting on fifteenth in this City the meeting will be one of the most imposing ever held in the country & we desire a letter from you in answer to an invitation.

> I. M. Schermerhorn
> Prest of State of N.Y..

Lincoln would seldom pass up the chance to send a public letter to be read aloud at an important pro-Union rally. When he received Schermerhorn's second wire, the president dutifully began composing such a document. He drafted three paragraphs in pencil, and then had second thoughts and abruptly abandoned the effort. Instead he wrote a private letter to Schermerhorn, explaining that he was simply too busy to undertake a formal statement. Besides, he added, it was too close to the presidential election to issue a policy paper. In Lincoln's era, such a document might have been considered an act of raw political campaigning—still considered unacceptable in presidential canvasses. Following is the draft Lincoln began but did not complete, along with the letter he ultimately dispatched to Schermerhorn to explain why he had decided to remain silent. This rich exchange is unique in the Lincoln canon: it embraces an invitation to

---

1864

speak which was never received, an urgent telegram asking why no reply was sent, followed by a half-hearted attempt at a speech and, ultimately, a letter of regret. (Lincoln's reply, *Coll. Works* VIII: 1–2)

Isaac M. Schemerhorn [*sic*] Executive Mansion,
My dear Sir. Washington, Sept 12. 1864.

Yours inviting me to attend a Union Mass Meeting at Buffalo is received. Much is being said about peace; and no man desires peace more ardently than I. Still I am yet unprepared to give up the Union for a peace which, so achieved, could not be of much duration. The preservation of our Union was <u>not</u> the sole avowed object for which the war was commenced. It was commenced for precisely the reverse object—<u>to destroy our</u> *Union*. The insurgents commenced it by firing upon the Star of the West, and on Fort Sumpter, and by other similar acts. It is true, however, that the administration accepted the war thus commenced, for the sole avowed object of preserving our Union; and it is not true that it has since been, or will be, prossecuted by this administration, for any other object. In declaring this, I only declare what I can know, and do know to be true, and what no other man can know to be false.

In taking the various steps which have led to my present position in relation to the war, the public interest and my private interest, have been perfectly paralel, because in no other way could I serve myself so well, as by truly serving the Union. The whole field has been open to me, where to choose. No place-hunting necessity has been upon me urging me to seek a position of antagonism to some other man, irrespective of whether such position might be favorable or unfavorable to the Union.

Of course I may err in judgment, but my present position in reference to the rebellion is the result of my best judgment, and according to that best judgment, it is the only position upon which any Executive can or could save the Union. Any substantial departure from it insures the success of the rebellion. An armistice—a cessation of hostilities—is the end of the struggle, and the insurgents would be in peaceable possession of all that has been struggled for. Any different policy in regard to the colored man, deprives us of his help, and this is more than we can bear. We can not spare the hundred and forty or fifty thousand now serving us as soldiers, seamen, and laborers. This is not a question of sentiment or taste, but one of physical force which may be measured and estimated as horse-power and Steam-power are measured and estimated. Keep it and you can save the Union. Throw it away, and the Union goes with it. Nor is it possible for any Administration to retain the service of these

1864

people with the express or implied understanding that upon the first convenient occasion, they are to be re-inslaved. It <u>can</u> not be; and it <u>ought</u> not to be.

<u>Private</u>.   Executive Mansion,
Isaac M. Schemerhorn, Pres't &c.   Washington,
Buffalo, N.Y.   September 12th. 1864.

My dear Sir:
    Your letter, mentioned in your two telegrams, has not reached me; so that I am without knowledge of its particulars. I beg you to pardon me for having concluded that it is not best for me now to write a general letter to a political meeting. First, I believe it is not customary for one holding the office, and being a candidate for re-election, to do so; and secondly, a public letter must be written with some care, and at some expense of time, so that having begun with your meeting, I could not well refuse others, and yet could not get through with all having equal claims. Please tender to those you represent my sincere thanks for the invitation, and my appeal to their indulgence for having declined their request.

                                            Yours very truly.
                                            A. LINCOLN.

An Election-Year Hoax on the Race Issue

                                            New York Sept. 29 1864

To his Excellency Abraham Lincoln
President of the United States;
    I herewith transmit a copy of my work on "Miscegenation," in the hope that after you have perused it, you will graciously permit me to dedicate to you another work on a kindred subject, viz: "Melaleukation."
    In the first work I discuss the mingling of all the races which go to form the human family; but my object in the new publication is to set forth the advantages of a blending of the white and black races on this continent. From the favor with which "Miscegenation" has been received—a great many thousand copies having been sold, and its leading ideas having been warmly endorsed by the progressive men of the

---

1864

country—I am led to believe that this new work will excite even greater interest. May I ask your permission to dedicate it to your excellency?

I am tempted to make the request from the various measures of your administration looking to the recognition of the great doctrine of human brotherhood, and from your speech to the New-York Working Men, in which you recognised the social and political equality of the white and colored laborer. I am aware that the subject creates prejudice among depraved and ignoble minds, but I am sure that you in common with the foremost men of our age and time can see no other solution of the negro problem than the gradual and certain blending of the two races.

In conclusion permit me to express the hope that, as the first four years of your administration have been distinguished by giving liberty to four millions of human beings, that the next four years may find these freedmen possessed of all the rights of citizenship and recognized as one of the elements that will enter into the emancipation of the future American race.

Very Respectfully
Author of "Miscegenation."

P.S.   Please address in reply
      Author of "Miscegenation"
      Care American News Company
      121 Nassau St. New York

This letter accompanied a new book entitled *Miscegenation: The Theory of the Blending of the Races, Applied to the American White Man and Negro*, which was published in New York by Dexter Hamilton & Co. in 1864 and sold for twenty-five cents. Its authors proposed new words for racial amalgamation: "miscegenation" (from the Latin *miscere*, to mix, and *genus*, meaning race) and "melaleukation" (from the Greek words *melas* and *leukas*, meaning white and black, respectively). Lincoln was not the only dignitary to receive the inflammatory tract. Complimentary copies were dispatched to a number of leading anti-slavery men along with similar letters asking for endorsements. But Lincoln, for one, did not acknowledge the gift. Unlike Lucretia Mott and the Grimke sisters, who did reply, Lincoln no doubt quickly perceived that the book was an election-year hoax designed to frighten nervous voters into believing that the administration favored race-mixing. Its pages contained such provocative declarations as, "The blending of the Irish in this country with the negro will be a positive gain to the former." *Miscegenation* was actually the work of David Goodman Croly and George Wakeman of the anti-Lincoln *New York World*, described by the *London Morning Herald* as "obstinate Democrats in

1864

politics." They no doubt collaborated in authoring the above letter to Lincoln as well, hoping that the president would reply with an encouraging thank-you note that Democrats could then circulate to prove that the Republicans indeed favored a bi-racial society. "This 'dodge' will hardly succeed," the *London Morning Herald* reported, "for Mr. Lincoln is shrewd enough to say nothing on the unsavory subject."

Lincoln's personal copy of *Miscegenation* survives in the Library of Congress, with the original Croly and Wakeman letter pasted into the inside front cover. Remarkably, this letter has never been reproduced in its entirety. A long excerpt published in the *Journal of Negro History* in 1949 was filled with errors in transcription. (Letter, Rare Books and Documents Collection, Library of Congress; Ed. note, Sidney Kaplan "The Miscegenation Issue in the Election of 1864," *Journal of Negro History* 34 [July 1949], 324; Long, *The Jewel of Liberty*, 153–66)

Court-Martialed Black Sergeant Protests Conviction

Fort Barrancas Florida Oct 7 1864

To. The. Honerable Abrham Lincon

I your Partishener Wm D Mayo 1st Sargt Co D. 86 cullard Infentry of L.A. will now state to you the condishons I am in being confined in the Provost Guard House under the sentanc of A Genl Cort Marshal held hear on the 8inst of Aug last   this centence being to serve a turm of one year and 9 months hard Labour without pay on Tortugas Island   the charges bein against me is 1st disobediants of Orders which I can prove I am not guilty of by over 25 of the same Regt   charge 2nd Breach of Arest which I plead guilty to under those surmstances, thare was a Private John Vier suffering punishment in the way of Riding a Wooden Horse [a particularly brutal form of soldier punishment in which the victim was forced to straddle a wooden rail for hours— Ed.]   the word came to me that he had fallen from the horse dead   I was excited and Humanity hurid me to his asistince at once not remembering that I was under arest until My Capt ordred me back to my quarters which I returned to amediatly   charge 3d Mutinus conduct in that I Wm D Mayo gathered some 6 or 8 men and said I would not serve under Capt Miller any longer which they faild to prove and which I can say before God and Man I never utterd   one thing more I will draw

---

1864

your attention to is I was denyed the privaleges of having some 25 wites-
ness who I could of Prooved my entire inocences by and alowed but 2
only   thare being two comishend Officers against me I was suposed of
course to be guilty. under this unlawfull and unjust punishment I can.
but Apeal to your Honner for Justice in this case   in a pucenarury point
of view I say nothing however I will say one thing. I am getting towards
50 years of age and my Wife is over fifty and Goverment will hav to
suport while I am reely willing and able to as enny good Loyal Souldier
should and concequencely I want Justice don me in return by hir   when
I was sent to the Guard house I was deprived of My own private property   I had the Army Regulations that I bought and paid for with my
own money, and charged me with reading that which a Nigar had no
buisness to know. now Dear Sir I Apeal to a Greate Man a man that is
governing this Nation to govern the Justice and punishment that is delt
out to one of its Faithfull subjects   I Remain
                              Your Obediant Servent
                              Wm. D. Mayo

Lincoln or his staff referred this appeal to the Judge Advocate General's office,
which replied on May 13, 1865—a month after Lincoln's death—that they had
found "no grounds to justify the exercise of Executive clemency in your behalf." Mayo's court-martial papers charged that he "did parade some eight or
ten privates . . . telling them that he loved his men and would live by them and
die by them . . . and would never go into a fight with Capt. Miller." But not
surprisingly, they made no mention of his being told by white officers that a
"Nigar" had no business familiarizing himself with army regulations. (Letter,
Colored Troops Division Files, National Archives; Ed. note, Berlin, *Freedom:
The Black Military Experience*, 453)

For Chase for Chief Justice

                                        Pomeroy Ohio Oct 13 1864

His Excellency A. Lincoln
President

Sir

    I sent a Dispatch today stating that the appointment of Mr. S. P. Chase
as Chief Justice U.S. Supreme Court would give much satisfaction to the

---
1864
---

people generally of this portion of the Country. I desire now to express to you the same opinion. Your personal acquaintance with Mr Chase renders it unnecessary for me to say anything as to his special qualifications for the office.

I am yours very trily
V. B. Horton

Former Secretary of the Treasury Chase had opposed Lincoln for the 1860 Presidential nomination and had harbored a desire to challenge him again in the midst of war in 1864. Although a constant thorn in Lincoln's side, he ultimately won appointment as Chief Justice, just as this correspondent had hoped.

A Threat to His Life from West Virginia

Wheeling West Va Nov 2/64

Mr Linkin Sir

Permit me to Relate to you the Conversation which I heard between two men and the Circumstance Connected with the same, I am at work in a new flouring mill which is now being Built in this plaise & Some time in September or the furst of October a man Came to the mill and wanted Work as a millright he Said he had deserted from the Rebel armey—the owner of the mill Let him to work. I notised him often going to the post office an got letters one I saw Came from Canady after we had him hear about two weaks than Came another man to See him tha had Some twenty minuts private Conversation and tha parted two days after that he Came back at twelve o clock when all hands was gone to Dinner and tha had another talk these visits war Repeated for four or five days   I Concluded that thare was Somthing Rong So one day as the men all went to Dinner I Conceald My Self in a bin of wheat near whare these two men used to have thar talk and Soon the other man Came in and tha had the following talk he told to the man that workt in the mill that he ad Receivd his mail from Richmond and also from Canada and it was all Right that the plan was all made that if old Abe was Realected we are agointo kill him and I am the man that is agoin to do it with your help now keep dark the plan is all Said then he handed the other a letter Said he Read that after he Read it He Said to the other that will do it   then one Said to the other Ben will be hear on Saturday and we

---

1864

will get to gether on the river bank whare no one can hear us and we will avenge the the [sic] mail busness. The one that workt in the mill Said to the other when Bill Comes here with the Richmond mail for Canada I will take it and go to St Catherine and get the mail thare and we will all meat in Washington this is the Conversation that I heard I also Saw the[m] together the following Sunday I markt them well for I went up and talkt to the one that workt in the mill

I omited to State on the other Side that a weak or ten days after the Election tha ware all to meat in Washington

Now Mr Linclon [sic] these are facts now god knows that the nations life depends all together on your life So I warn you as a friend to be Carful and watch

I may have done rong for writing this to you but I could not Rest untill I did &c I hope you will forgive me if it is Rong I have not mentiond it to no living Soll

Yours Sincerley
Seymour Ketchum

As if to punctuate this heartfelt alert, the man who had hidden himself in a bin of wheat in order to eavesdrop on the suspicious behavior of his co-workers scrawled across the top of his letter: "I have not written half—the man that workt in the mill left 26, October." No one knows whether the White House ordered this report investigated. But the letter remained in the Lincoln Papers— unusual for material of such sensational nature—endorsed benignly by a secretary: "Letter of warning."

"Put the President on His Guard"

St Paul [Minnesota] Nov. 6, 1864

My dear N[eill].

The weather to this date is of the finest character, not a particle of ice has yet been seen on the river & I hope to leave on Wednesday, after the election, by boat.

Our party is well organized in the state & especially so in this city, and we shall improve over former elections—we will carry everything; but of all this you will learn by telegraph before this reaches you.

A respectable gentleman of this city, a democrat by association, but

---

1864

not much of a politician, but withall a patri[ot] Sought an interview with me some time since through the agency of John Nichols, whom you know, our State Senator, and communicated to me confidentially these facts.

Shortly after the Nom. of McClellan a gentleman, an old acquaintance of his, temporarily at St Paul and a "Knight templar" in the order of Masons, said to him that Mr Lincoln would be assassinated if elected—to the inquiry "who would do it" he replied "the Knights" My informant is a "Knight templar" himself, and at the time and for a season after supposed the "Knights of the Golden Circle" were meant, but upon reflection he fears his informant meant the "Knight Templars" & if so he fears their detection will be more difficult & begged me to put the Prest. on his guard.

I supposed there was so much to induce the Prest. to be on his guard that even if there was anything in this its introduction was scarcely needed, if however it is otherwise you may exhibit this letter to the Prest.

I will be in Washington for a few days in the course of a week.

Very truly
Your friend
Alex. Ramsey

Revd. E. D. Neill
Executive Mansion
Washington D.C.

This letter to Lincoln's correspondence secretary, Edward Duffield Neill, was not retained in the Lincoln Papers, so we cannot be sure that he discussed the alleged assassination threat with the president. It is included here because Neill wrote later of the many such warnings that crossed his desk while he worked at the White House, though he preserved no example but this one. After Lincoln's assassination in 1865, some suspicion did fall for a time on the Knights of the Golden Circle—a secret pro-slavery, pro-Confederate organization boasting chapters, or "Castles," throughout the North—but not on the Society of Freemasons. (Letter, Edward D. Neill and Family Papers, Minnesota Historical Society)

1864

A Tribute in Verse

ENCLOSING A CAMPAIGN POEM

New York, Nov. 7/64

Dear <u>President</u>

Please honor the author of the enclosed, by your autograph—& Address of your humble Servant

H. O. Newman
care L. B. Chittenden & Co.
350 Broadway NY

NOVEMBER EIGHT, 1864
By the author of "Sumter"

Ho, FREEMEN to the rescue!—your injured country calls
In tones of deepening thunder; up, gird you for the POLLS!
Let sire and son of Freemen with loyal ardor burn,
To crush the head of TREASON, at FREEDOM's holy urn.

Ho, Freemen to the rescue!—like our Niagara's roar,
Whose deep and troubled waters resistless roll before,
From Maine to Rocky Mountain, sweep down to ocean tide—
The mighty voice of FREEMEN, majestic in its pride!

Ho, Freemen to the rescue!—let traitors learn to fear;
While rolls the tide of battle, guard well the Soldier-rear!
On many fields, all gory, our martyr hosts lie slain!
Say, shall their blood to Heaven cry from the earth in vain?

Ho, Freemen to the rescue!—heardst not their slogan sound?
Secession hosts are rallying their traitor chiefs around;
Arrayed in stolen panoply, and foul device of war,
Their skillful ones are marshalling, their toscin sounds afar.

Ho, Freemen to the rescue!—rouse, rouse ye in your might!
This is no border warfare—God favor now the right!
Stand for your homes and altars; stand for your loved ones near;
Strike for your FLAG dishonored; strike for your country dear!

1864

Ho, Freemen to the rescue!—now be your courage strong,
The only e'er should falter, who battle for the wrong.—
Now for the right to be valiant! be not your heart dismayed!
Go, in the name of Heaven—and Heaven shall be your aid!

Ho, Freeman to the rescue!—high on the roll of fame,
By hand of seraph graven, shall be each loyal name!
Bloodless though the victory—our <u>Northern</u> foes subdued—
So greener bays await ye, than <u>garments rolled in blood</u>!

Ho, Freemen to the rescue!—our LINCOLN leads the van—
A patriot true, and statesman—a tried and honest man!
When treacherous sands and ice-bergs the Ship of State surround,
<u>His</u> trumpet from the quarter-deck gives no uncertain sound.

Ho, Freemen to the rescue!—GRANT, SHERMAN, in the field!
ATLANTA shouts to VICKSBURG, "<u>Our heroes never yield</u>!"
O'er hurried tramp of foemen, like echo through the night,
The far-off voice of SHERIDAN comes booming, "<u>All is right</u>!"

Ho, Freemen to the rescue!—lo! 'mid metoric storm,
Grim FARRAGUT and PORTER turn in terrific form!
Their heel upon the gory deck, with lightning in their eye,
Demand of you, in thunder tones, to <u>purge the record high</u>!

Ho, Freemen to the rescue!—a whirlwind sweeps along,
That stirs the heart of millions, to love of country strong,
To guard our gallant heroes, by whom great deeds are done,
As we revere and honor th'immortal WASHINGTON!

Ho, Freemen to the rescue!—but meet the foe once more;
Break through their serried phalanx—your fathers did of yore!
And scattered shall their legions be, as when some mighty wind
Sweeps o'er the autumn forest, and leaves its wreck behind!

This ambitious poem, one of several such tributes still in the Lincoln Papers, was endorsed, "Ack Nov 10, 64"; but the president's thank-you letter has never surfaced.

1864

How He Learned He Was Reelected

Election day, November 8, 1864, began with routine work at the Lincoln White House. The president saw a Wisconsin woman named Mary E. Collins about arranging an exchange for her father, a captain in the 10th Wisconsin Infantry. Hearing her plea, a sympathetic Lincoln wrote to General Ethan A. Hitchcock: "Please see & hear this lady about a special exchange." Then Lincoln officially recognized Teodoro Manara as the new consul from Guatemala to New York. The momentous event of the day—the most important election in American history according to historian David E. Long—finally intruded when Lincoln's young son, Tad, burst in to tell the president that he had just seen soldiers on the White House lawn casting their votes for the Lincoln-Johnson ticket. At Tad's urging, Lincoln walked to the window to watch the troops casting ballots. It would be many more hours before Lincoln learned that Union soldiers throughout the country—their ballots counted separately if they could not obtain passes to return home to vote—had chosen Lincoln overwhelmingly.

That evening at 7 P.M., as a gentle rain fell over Washington, Lincoln and his assistant private secretary, John M. Hay, walked to the War Department to wait for the official returns. There, after hours of vote-counting, he learned of the full extent of his triumph: Lincoln amassed 55% of the vote to Democratic candidate George B. McClellan's 45%, with 2,213,665 raw votes to 1,802,237. The electoral vote count was even more lopsided. Lincoln won 22 of the 25 states participating in the election (the Confederate states, of course, did not), for a total of 212 electoral votes to McClellan's 21. The soldiers' vote favored Lincoln by 78%-22%, with 116,887 raw votes to 33,748.

Reveling in his triumph, Lincoln happily shoveled out fried oysters at the War Department, John Hay recorded, and then returned to the White House for a celebratory serenade. Thus did Lincoln become the first president since Andrew Jackson to win a second term. More important, as he told a crowd of well-wishers on November 10, the election had answered a crucial question about the young American republic: "whether any government, not too strong for the liberties of its people, can be strong enough to maintain its own existence, in great emergencies." As Lincoln put it, "We can not have free government without elections" (*Coll. Works* VIII: 100-101). Following are some of the telegrams that poured into the War Department from friends on election night, among them many Washington officials who had returned to their home states to vote. (Ed. note, *Lincoln Day By Day*, III: 294)

1864

A. Lincoln—Prest U.S.
  Returns from all parts of Penna. show very large Union gains—I will send you more news before returning.
                              Simon Cameron [former secretary of
                              war]

A Lincoln
  Considerable gains Every where—all returns throughout the state favorable.
                              Wayne McVeagh

His Excellency A Lincoln—
  Connecticut will give about three thousand union majority
                              N. D. Sperry
                              Secy of Nat'l Union Committee

Abraham Lincoln Prest. U.S.
  New Hampshire subscribes herself yours truly
                              Daniel Clark

Abraham Lincoln
  St Louis County gives you about five thousand (5000) majority The state will give you about ten thousand (10,000)
                              McKee & Fishback
                              Missouri Democrat

1864

Head Quarters Balt. Nov 8 1864

President Lincoln

Voting proceeding quietly. The vote polled up to one oclock is fully one half (½) larger than cast at the constitutional election Our majority in the city will be in the neighborhood of fifteen thousand (15.000) which secures the State by a majority of from five (5) to ten-thousand (10000)

Henry W. Hoffman

[Telegraph]
Indianapolis Nov 8 1864.

Hon Abraham Lincoln

Your majority in this City over Eight thousand (8000) Fifteen hundred more than Mortons [the governor, Oliver P. Morton, who was reelected, some believed, by arranging to furlough 9,000 Indiana soldiers in time to vote—Ed.].

A. H. Conner

[Telegraph]
Springfield [Ill.], Nov 8 1864.

The President—

Springfield township gives 20 maj. for Lincoln.

Jno. G. Nicolay

Mother of Black Soldier Asks for His Release

Carlisles [Pennsylvania] nov 21 1864

Mr abarham lincon

I wont to knw sir if you please wether I can have my son relest from the arme   he is all the subport I have now   his father is Dead and his brother that wase all the help that I had he has bean wonded twise   he has not had nothing to send me yet   now I am old and my head is blossaming for the grave and if you dou I hope the lord will bless you and

---

1864

---

me   if you please answer as soon as you can if you please   tha say that
you will simpethise withe the poor   thear wase awhite jentel man told
me to write to you   Mrs jane Welcom if you please answer it to

   he be long to the eight rigmat co a u st colard troops   mart welcom
is his name   he is a sarjent

It was not Lincoln's custom to respond personally to letters from African
Americans. He sent Mrs Welcom's plea on to the War Department's Bureau of
Colored Troops. The surviving file includes a draft reply, dated December 2,
1864, that indicates that the impoverished mother's plea was denied. The draft
explained that "the interests of the service will not permit that your request be
granted." (Letter, National Archives Colored Troops Division Files)

Election Congratulations
from Karl Marx and Colleagues

[Between November 23 and 29, 1864)

To Abraham Lincoln
President of the United States of America

Sir,

   We congratulate the American people upon your re-election by a large
majority.

   If resistance to the Slave Power was the reserved watchword of your
first election, the triumphant warcry of your re-election is, Death to Slavery.

   From the commencement of the Titanic-American strife the working
men of Europe felt instinctively that the star-spangled banner carried the
destiny of their class. The contest for the territories which opened the
dire epopee [an epic poem—Ed.], was it not to decide whether the virgin
soil of immense tracts should be wedded to the labour of the emigrant,
or prostituted by the tramp of the slave-driver?

   When an oligarchy of 300,000 slave drivers dared to inscribe, for the
first time in the annals of the world, "slavery" on the banner of Armed
Revolt; when on the very spots where hardly a century ago the idea of
one great Democratic Republic had first sprung up, whence the first Dec-
laration of the Rights of Man was issued, and the first impulse given to

---

1864

the European revolution of the 18th century; when on those very spots counter-revolution, with systematic thoroughness, glories in rescinding "the ideas entertained at the time of the formation of the old Constitution", and maintained "slavery to be a beneficent institution", indeed the only solution of the great problem of "the relation of labour to capital", and cynically proclaimed property in man "the comer-stone of the new edifice" [quotations from a speech by Confederate Vice President Alexander H. Stephens in Savannah, Georgia, on March 21, 1861— Ed.], then the working classes of Europe understood at once, even before the fanatic partisanship of the upper classes for the Confederate gentry had given its dismal warning, that the slave-holders' rebellion was to sound the tocsin for a general holy crusade of property against labour, and that for the men of labour, with their hopes for the future, even their past conquests were at stake in that tremendous conflict on the other side of the Atlantic. Everywhere they bore therefore patiently the hardships imposed upon them by the cotton crisis [the shortages of 1861, deeply felt in Europe—Ed.], opposed enthusiastically the pro-slavery intervention, importunities of their betters—and, from most parts of Europe, contributed their quota of blood to the good cause.

While the working men, the true political power of the North, allowed slavery to defile their own republic; while before the Negro, mastered and sold without his concurrence, they boasted it the highest prerogative of the white-skinned labourer to sell himself and choose his own master; they were unable to attain the true freedom of labour or to support their European brethren in their struggle for emancipation, but this barrier to progress has been swept off by the red sea of civil war.

The working men of Europe feel sure that, as the American War of Independence initiated a new era of ascendancy for the middle class, so the American Anti-Slavery War will do for the working classes. They consider it an earnest of the epoch to come that it fell to the lot of Abraham Lincoln, the single-minded son of the working class, to lead his country through the matchless struggle for the rescue of an enchained race and the reconstruction of a social world.

Signed on behalf of the International Working Men's Association
The Central Council

Le Lubez, Corresponding Secretary for France
F. Rybczinski (Pole)
Emile Holtorp (Pole)

<hr>

1864

J. B. Bocquet
H. Jung, Corresponding Secretary for Switzerland
Morisot
Georgy W. Wheeler
J. Denoual
P. Bordage
Leroux
Talandier
Jourdain
Dupont
R. Gray
D. Lama
Setacci
F. Solustri
P. Aldovrandi
D. G. Bagnagatti
G. P. Fontana, Corresponding Secretary for Italy
G. Lake
J. Buckley
G. Howell
J. Osborne
J. D. Stainsby
J. Grossmith
G. Eccarius
Friedrick Lessner
L. Wolff
K. Kaub
Henry Bolleter
Ludwig Otto
N. P. Hansen (Dane)
Karl Pfander
Georg Lochner
Peter Petersen
Karl Marx, Corresponding Secretary for Germany
A. Dick
J. Wolff
J. Whitlock
J. Carter
W. Morgan
William Dell

1864

John Weston
Peter Fox
Robert Shaw
John H. Longmaid
Robert Henry Side
William C. Worley
Blackmoor W.
R. Hartwell
W. Pidgeon
B. Lucraft

> G. Odger, President of Council
> William R. Cremer, Honorary General
> Secretary

Although authorship of this letter has never been definitively established, on December 2, 1864, signatory Karl Marx wrote to Frederick Engels about the "Address, this time to Lincoln," noting: "I had to write the stuff . . . in order that the phraseology to which this sort of scribbling is restricted should at least be distinguished from the democratic, vulgar phraseology." The letter was first published in a European newspaper on December 23, 1864, and then appeared in *The Bee-Hive Newspaper*, which described itself as "a journal of general intelligence advocating industrial interests." The version printed here is adapted from the English-language translation in volume 20 of the *Collected Works* of Karl Marx and Frederick Engels (Moscow: Progress Publishers, 1985), which was checked against the original manuscript. The editors of the Marx-Engels Papers attribute the letter to Marx, and a copy is kept on permanent display at tire Karl-Marx-Haus in Germany. The text was transmitted to Lincoln by the American ambassador to Great Britain, Charles Francis Adams. On January 9, 1865, Secretary of State Seward replied to Adams: "These interesting papers have been submitted to the President." Seward carefully added, "So far as the sentiments expressed by the council are personal, they are accepted by the President with a sincere and anxious desire that he may be able to prove himself not unworthy of the confidence which has been recently extended to him by . . . so many friends of humanity and progress through out the world. . . . You will please communicate these sentiments to the council of workingmen." Marx, in turn, had Seward's reply published in several English newspapers, and then wrote to Engels to boast: "The fact that Lincoln has replied to us so courteously . . . has made such a stir here that the 'Clubs' in the West End are shaking their heads over it. You can understand how much good this does our people." (Ed. note, A. Seddelmeyer, "Lincoln's 'Red Letter' Day," *Lincoln Herald* 95 [Summer 1993]: 60–65)

1864

Black Soldier Wishes Reunion with Enslaved Family

Taylors Barrecks [Louisville, Kentucky) December 4th 1864
Mr Abrham Lincoln

I have one recest to make to you that is I ask you to dis Charge me for I have a wife and she has four Children   thay have a hard master one that loves the South hangs with it   he dos not giv tham a rage nor havnot for too yars   I have found all   he says let old Abe Give them Close   if I had them I raise them up but I am here and if you will free me and hir and heir Children with me I Can take Cair of them

She lives with David Sparks in Oldham Co Ky

My Woman is named Malindia Jann my daughter Adline Clyte and Malindia Eler and Cleman Tine and Natthaniel Washington and my name is George Washington heir in Taylors Barrecks and my famaly suffering I have sent forty dollars worth to them cence I have bin heir and that is all I have and I have not drawn any thing cence I have bin heir   I am forty eight years   my woman thirty three   I ask this to your oner to a blige

yours &c
your un Grateful Servent
George Washington

Washington's letter pointed out the bitter irony facing black soldiers from the loyal border states. While they fought in the ranks, their families remained in slavery, unaffected by the Emancipation Proclamation. But like all such letters to Lincoln from non-whites, this one was merely forwarded to the Bureau of Colored Troops at the War Department. The surviving file indicates that no response was sent. Lincoln probably never saw the correspondence. (Letter, Colored Troops Division Files, National Archives)

1864

Emancipation Memento
from "Colored People" of New Orleans

New Orleans, 8 December 1864

To His Excellency Abraham Lincoln,
President of the United States

Respected Sir,

On the evening of Tuesday, the sixth of this month, a meeting was held at the St James Church on Roman St, composed of the Pastors, officers and Members of the different Benevolent Societies of the citizens of African descent, for the purpose of presenting a gold and Silver mounted volume to the President of the United States, and the undersigned was present by invitation, in order to receive and transmit to you the volume, which then came into his hands from the following named gentlemen, composing the committee of presentation: viz.

Henry Raymond, chairman;	A. L. Young
Francois Boisdoré	Henry Chermine
John Smith	Laurence Quanders
Peter Hillard	Rev. Geo. W. Steptoe
Robert Smith	Rev. R. H. Steptoe

Rev. S. W. Rogers

In completing the honorable trust which these respectable persons have conferred upon him, by making him the organ of their communication with the Chief Magistrate of the Country, the undersigned begs leave to assure the President that the donors represent a most worthy, loyal and patriotic portion of our population, and as such as have testified to their devotion to the Government by sacrifice of the highest character, and that the spirit who their offering is made, is one of the most heartfelt devotion and gratitude to the country.

The volume itself will be found to be an elegant specimen of good taste and skill, while the subject of its contents—the celebration of the emancipation ordinance of the Louisiana Convention—is one of the most interesting character.

The undersigned begs leave in conclusion to assure you of the heartfelt respect and affection entertained by those whom the donors repre-

1864

sent, for the Government and Chief Magistrate of our country; and begs
to be permitted to subscribe himself,

With great respect, Sir,
Your most obdt. Servant,
Thomas J. Durant.

This expression of gratitude for Lincoln's leadership in ending slavery accompanied the gift of a magnificent silver, gold, and red morocco copy of a thirty-two-page volume entitled, *Grand Celebration in Honor of the Passage of the Ordinance of Emancipation, by the Free State Convention.* The publication commemorated passage of an ordinance of emancipation freeing all slaves still held Louisiana, a prerequisite for that state's readmission to the Union. Enacted by a Constitutional Convention on May 11, it passed with an overwhelming 80% of the popular vote (although pro-Confederate voters likely did not participate) on September 5. Louisiana was thereafter duly readmitted to the Union, and Lincoln told the state's first post-secession governor that he believed the time had come to entertain the idea of granting suffrage to some newly freed blacks. The elaborate book, and the speeches it contains, offer strong evidence that African Americans of his time held Lincoln largely responsible for the end of slavery. A gilt-silver plaque on the book reads: "To His Excellency A. Lincoln, President, U.S. By the Colored People New Orleans La." But emancipation had not yet opened the door to correspondence between people of color and the president; the author of this transmission letter, local politician Thomas Jefferson Durant, was white. The volume itself, together with Durant's note, now reposes in the Frank and Virginia Williams Collection of Lincolniana, by whose permission the transmission letter is here reprinted.

An Artist's Letter of Introduction

North Shore Staten Island
9 December 1864.

To the President:

My dear Sir:

I have great pleasure in presenting to you my friend, the artist, Mr. Thomas Nast, whose designs in Harper's Weekly have been scattered all over the land, and have especially penetrated the lines of the army, showing the country what it is fighting for and in what spirit—and all with a power & felicity the wide good results of which are known to me. You

---

1864

and the country have no more faithful friend than Mr. Nast. Very respectfully, Sir,

Your friend & servant
George William Curtis

At the urging of Curtis, political editor of *Harper's Weekly*, and a delegate to the National Union Convention that had nominated the president for reelection, Lincoln welcomed Nast to the White House on December 10. The illustrator would achieve his greatest fame years later exposing the notorious "Tweed Ring" in a series of cartoons, but he may have sketched Lincoln during his White House visit. In 1865 he produced a painting of Lincoln's triumphant entry into Richmond. (Ed. note, *Day by Day* III, 301; Albert Bigelow Paine, *Th. Nast: His Period and His Pictures* [New York: Macmillan, 1904], 104

A Trusted Old Friend Warns of Would-Be Assassins

Washington, D.C.
. Dec, 10, 1864, 1.30 o'clock, A.M.

Hon. A. Lincoln:

Sir,

I regret that you do not appreciate what I have repeatedly said to you in regard to the proper police arrangements connected with your household and your own personal safety. <u>You are in danger</u>. I have nothing to ask, and I flatter myself that you will at least believe that I am honest. If, however, you have been impressed differently, do me and the country the justice to dispose at once of all suspected officers, and accept my resignation of the marshalship, which is hereby tendered. I will give you further reasons which have impelled me to this course. To-night, as you have done on several previous occasions, you went unattended to the theatre. When I say unattended, I mean that you went alone with [Senator] Charles Sumner [of Massachusetts] and a foreign minister, neither of whom could defend himself against an assault from any able-bodied woman in this city. And you know, or ought to know, that your life is sought after, and will be taken unless you and your friends are cautious for you have many enemies within our lines. You certainly know that I have provided men at your mansion to perform all necessary police duty,

---
1864

195

and I am always ready myself to perform any duty that will properly conduce to your interest or your safety.

God knows that I am unselfish in this matter; and I do think that I have played low comedy long enough, and at my time of life I think I ought at least to attempt to play star engagements.

I have the honor to be

Your obedient servant,
Ward H. Lamon

Ward Hill Lamon, an old friend and law associate of Lincoln's from Danville, Illiniois, had come west with the president-elect in 1861, serving as both companion (he told ribald jokes and sang beautifully) and unofficial bodyguard during the dangerous trip to Washington. Lincoln kept him on, rewarding him with the post of U.S. Marshall for the District of Columbia. Thereafter, Lamon made the president's safety a priority, occasionally sleeping the night, heavily armed, on the floor outside of his bedroom door. After the assassination he boasted to the new president, Andrew Johnson, that Lincoln would have been killed even earlier had it not been for his vigilance. Lamon insisted that the president had said of him in 1865, "This boy is a monomaniac on the subject of my safety," promising to "do the best I can" to exercise more caution. But the next day, Lincoln sent Lamon on a special assignment to the conquered Confederate capital of Richmond; ironically, he was there, far from his chief's side, when Lincoln was fatally shot on April 14, 1865.

Lamon later wrote a controversial book about his early days with Lincoln that was heavily reliant on a ghostwriter, injuring his credibility with contemporaries and historians alike. Following his death in 1893, his daughter, Dorothy Lamon Teillard, assembled old newspaper clips together with Lamon's surviving notes and reminiscences and patched together another memoir, where this hitherto-unknown letter was first published. The original does not survive in the Lincoln Papers, and some scholars have cited its self-serving tone to suggest that it was invented after the fact. But all warnings about Lincoln's safety were apparently expunged from the papers after the assassination, and this one would have been discarded as well. Besides, five days later, Lamon wrote another letter concerning the president's safety to John Nicolay, Lincoln's secretary, and the original survives. (Ed. note, Dorothy Lamon Teillard, ed., *Recollections of Abraham Lincoln*, 1911; reprint, Lincoln, NE: University of Nebraska Press, 1994], 274–75; see also pp. 280–81; for doubts about Lamon's reliability, see Don E. Fehrenbacher and Virginia Fehrenbacher, eds., *Recollected Words of Lincoln* [Stanford, CA: Stanford University Press, 1996], 281, 293; see also Lamon's letter to John G. Nicolay, December 16, 1864, Lincoln Papers)

1864

1865

"The latest photograph of President Lincoln," in the words of its caption, turned out also to be the last. It was taken on the White House balcony by Henry F. Warren on Mar. 6, 1865, just two days after Lincoln's second inaugural. Six weeks later Lincoln was dead. Photograph courtesy of author.

A "Last Warning" — in Verse

Declare O Lord what is the due
Of Lincoln and his bloody crew
The laural [sic] crown and golden rod
He hopes to gain but what says God
No murderer of Human Kind
In heaven a place will ever find
The highest power Creation Knows
Accords sweet mercy to its foes
While Justice guards the Throne above
It's always mixed with peace and Love
And man advanced to place and Power
Should in the dark avenging hour
Never Humanity discard
In executing Justice hard
Justice and Mercy both disdain
To own a place in Lincolns reign
Tis Savage malice Hellish pride
And lust of Conquest that divide
The heart of Lincoln worst of Men
This world ever saw or will again
The sounds of grief and woe he hears
Are musick in the Tyrant's ears
Insatiable he still remains
a Million slain on hostile plains
Fleets to Oceans bottom sunk
With blood have made the Tyrant drunk
And still he rages in his ire
Cities consigned to sword and fire
The people driven from their Homes
And desert wastes are forces to roam
The canopy of Heaven "what woe"
Is all the Tent these wretches know

Those plains of late rich harvests crowned
And every comfort there were found
The plains so rich, and in the Shade
Content a paradice [sic] had made

1865

199

Like Eden's garden late they were
A Wilderness they now appear
But can this state of things endure
Has God ordained the humble poor
Should still groan neath the Tyrans [sic] power
No. there's a limit, there's an hour
In his Inscrutible decree
When we'll be asked—what, weak as we
Art thou decended [sic] to the grave
Could power and wealth from Death not save
O what can power and wealth then do
Since Death has seized even you
Rejoice O Land since Lincoln's dead
His sword they have buried with his head
A monument may mark the spot
In which his hated bones do Rot
Or with the funeral of an ass
From City drawn his corps[e] may pass
Thrown on the moore in Open day
To vultures and to dogs, a prey
With curses on whose guilty shade
A paradise a desert made
We leave the carcass now to rot
Be it in grave or be it not
Suffice the bloody dog no more
Can glut his lust in human gore
His bow now broke from his left hand
His avows too at God's command
Are broken useless on the land
His progress brought to a full stand

His name is no more a terror found
To those who live upon the ground
His sin upon his bones shall lie
Till the Arch Angel from the Sky
Shall summon all the dead to appear
Before the Judge's Face severe—

The Lord has said thou shalt not Kill
And also that thou shalt not steal
But Lincoln's slain a million men
A fallen Dynasty, to sustain

1865

And that he might his ends attain
To plunder He did not disdain
Divine and Human laws by him
Were set aside; this Tyrant grim
Has seized on Railroads all do know
To pour his Legions on the Foe
All private property; the whole
O'er which the State had no controul [*sic*]
Houses machinery and Lands
Are grasped by his rapacious hands
The hope of Families, whose tears
And cries alike the Tyrant Hears
With Heart more hard than any Stone
And ears like the deaf adder grown
Nor did the Tyrants rage stop here
Many were forces [*sic*] to shed the tear
Wives deprived of their chief Stay
Husbands and Fathers torn away
Sons torn from weeping mothers side
Are led to swell the Crimson tide
Their life blood shed upon the plain
Or else a prisoner to remain

Doomed to wear the foeman's chain
Few few will whole return again
At first the Tyrant's Legions drilled
And led by men in war well Skilled
In numbers they did far exceed
Those Beauregard against them led
Numbers dont always win the strife
Freedom is far more dear than life
And so it happened on that day
The Tyrants Legions ran away
And when the Yankees grow so bold
Again to boast, it shall be told
Long as the Sun shall rule the day
That at Bull Run They ran away
I don't attempt to blame the men
Who from the battlefield run then
But that they ever came again
To Swell the Catalogue of Slain
The Tyrant and his savage crew

1865

Themselves should have the work to do
If they for war are so inclined
Why then not satisfy their mind
Why dont they arm and bravely try
To crush rebellion or to die
Like curs they bark but cannot bite
No courage have they for the fight
Great burdens they on others laid
A finger they've not reached to aid
The people of the states should rise
And take these barkers by surprise
Their blood should flow in every state
Union would be then complete
Long as these monsters tread the ground
Peace in the states can ne'er be found

The reeking flesh torn from the bone
To hungry dogs should then be thrown
Collect the bones into a pile
And leave them for to bleach awhile
This lesson would be learned then
Here's the reward of wicked men
The mainroad that connects the States
For these destroyers bones no waits
Let them from North to South be spread
That peaceful men may on them tread
Peace then would like a river flow
Each one who walked trod on a foe
To Justice and Humanity
An abhorring to all flesh they be

Thus in anticipation I
Predict the spot your bones should lie
I do not say that this just doom
Shall surely surely on you come
Perhaps you'll be permitted Still
To Ravage plunder and to Kill
The dogs may have some time to wait
Before they get their promised treat
And while they look with longing eye
And wonder why dont Abe die
The Rebels yet may yield to you

1865

For what wont Fraud and Lying do
Suppose them brought 'neath your control
Is this the value of your soul;
Suppose your power would yet extend
Even further than you now intend
Yet after all die, die you must
And dying be fore ever cursed,

Atlantic would soon change its hue
To Sanguine red from purple blue
If all the blood your orders shed
Were poured into the Ocean's bed
The greatest Tyrants that of Yore
Had drenched this earth with Human gore
And Slaughtered all within their power
Throughout their limited "one hour"
If but permitted once again
To walk this earth 'mongst living men
And view the desolated waste
O'er which your Miraudors [sic] have past [sic]
The cities smoking on the plain
The heaps upon heaps of mangled slain
And hear the cries of wounded men
Which festering in their blood remain
Between both Armies on the plain
So eager were you for the Strife
The famished wounded yields his life
Many perished in the flame
Whom History does not even name
Your Cities fill'd with maimed men
Which but a Burden must remain
On whom, but for your hated Reign
'Twas their own duty to Sustain
Your wealth all lavished and destroyed
Your pleasant places made a void
Of blooming wives you've widows made
And Orphans by your Waring [sic] trade
A debt remaining on your State
There's no man knows how very great
They must confess when this they see
In wickedness they yield to thee
And for each man whose blood they shed

1865

You can produce a dozen dead
In savage fury all allow
Mere children they; a Giant thou

But Giant as thou art beware!
To meet thy God, I say, prepare
I mean with thee to try my might
'Tis in the name of Christ I fight
I nail my gauntlet to your gate
And for the strife impatient wait
But as the rules of Chivalry
Demand that you should know of me
What is my State and Pedigree
I'm far more highly born than thee
And that I've plainly let you see
You, Ruler of the Northern States
Legions of Angels round me wait
You move an army at your nod
My life his hid with Christ in God
You've riches, pleasures, wealth and pride
I know for me, my Saviour died
Destruction still attends your dart
The peace of God rules in my heart
A sinner you move on the earth
I have experienced second birth
You're doomed to hell whene'er you die
I have a mansion in the sky
You on the arm of flesh rely
My strength is in the Lord most High
This earth is all the heaven you'll see
Heaven was prepared for such as me
And now I have explained to you
That I'm a noble Night [sic] and true
And also that I'm Faithful too
Giant! I hope to prove on you

As you approach stalking along
The ground shakes that you tread upon
You look like Leviathan great
Whose solid coat of mail complete
Resists whatever darts are thrown
At thee by mortal man alone

1865

Remember Monster He who made
Thee, also made a two edged blade
With that I mean this fight to try
By either edge of which you die
This sword is sharp and pointed too
Piercing both soul and body through
And brings all secret things to view

I see that thou art armed complete
A coat of mail from head to feet
A motto on thy limbs which shine
In armour bright, to eye like mine
Reads thus "we into evil Run"
And as in Mottos I've begun
I'll try to read them one, by one
The iron shoes that on your feet
You wear your armour to Complete
Are not without their motto meet
Destruction is in all their ways
And misery follows with like pace
I lift my eyes now to your face
And even there is Motto trace
Their eyes are for their Covetousness
Thy forehead bears a stamp no less
Than I care not what I do amiss
And to my eyes appear beside
Wrote over all thy features wide
"King over all the Children of Pride"
Thy teeth like those of lions are
Made for to ravage and to tear
Despair attending on thy frown
Speaks thus; my enemies cast down
Destroy them all with fire and sword
Go, do your work, you have my word
But who would think on such as thee
For thus to read "Hypocracy"
Yes thou hast dared a Fast to call
To gain the aid of God withal!
To further thy ambitious aims
And realise thy wakeing dreams
Of conquest till thine empire spread
O'er Land and Sea and Crowned head

1865

Your conduct but deserves that I
Myself a Motto would supply
You wish for universal rule
I give a motto you're a Fool
The plate of brass which on your breast
You wear has "motto" thus imprest
I've gone so far I'll go the rest—
The spear which in your hand you hold
With head of brass as bright as gold
Speaks thus I have for Empire sold
My soul and I am grown so bold
I will not have my faults be told
But Lincoln you are growing old
Those men to whom we Debtors be
If left alone to Grant and me

A girdle round your loins I see
With motto which speaks thus to me
Support me friends and you will see
If you but give me your regards
Observe how well I'll play my cards
I hate a debt upon the State
As much as I long to be great
Those debtors left to Grant and me [this line crossed out—Ed.]
Trust me your eyes will never see
We've learned a way to pay old debts
Which most the Constitution frets
But on this point I say no more
I do not wish to strike too sore
But I think Lincoln and his pet
Will prove wise financiers yet
A sword I see hangs by your side
Becoming well such man of pride
And on the Scabbard is descried
A motto Lincoln cannot Hide
I never will the States divide
But o'er all Liberty I'll ride
My Cannons roar on land and Sea
I shall cease but when Confederacy
A thing that's past shall ever be
A garment compasses about
Your lofty figure strong and stout

1865

This moved by every fleeting breeze
Each man of Wisdom clearly sees
A motto in such lines as these
Pride as a garment compasses
And violence no peace declares
Your armour bearer I behold
Gleaming bright with plundered Gold
Before you bears an ample Shield
Which only you can lightly wield
You hope, by this to win the field
This is its motto—"never yield"
Your Servant has a motto too
Which now comes fully to my view
And as he comes before my eye
These letters plainly I descry
This is the man in whom I trust
He represents the Federal Host

Now I have described the man
Which in my fancy now I scan
And while I read God's book within
I find thee called the man of Sin
And as I have described thee true
I wish thyself to take a view
Of this same image that I drew
And say if it resembles you
And do not let those eyes so proud
Which look down on the cringing crowd
Through self love view it through a cloud
Let conscience speak and that full loud
And let them analyse each part
And compare them with your life and heart
And Abe Lincoln ere we part
Thou will say that thou man thou art
And since I have convinced you
That you're the man that thus I drew
Abe Lincoln repent and pray
Or else upon a future day
You'll think on all the words I say
And on this true similitude
Which I have drawn to do you good
But if you view it with an eye

1865

207

Of careless infidelity
And think there's something wrong with me
And perhaps think that mad I be
I say hereafter you will see
That you've been far more mad than me
And though you'd eyes yet they to you
Could never bring the truth to view
And though you'd ears you could not hear
A heart you had but yet no fear
Of God before your eyes appear
Tremble Lincoln! Shake with Fear!
It is God's True Sayings that you Hear
For These Same Words that Now I Write!
God's Holy Spirit does indite [sic]!
And this Should fill thy soul with Fright!
Although thou art a Giant quite!
And pray that God with heavenly light
Would illume your dark eyeballs quite
And from your heart would draw the Veil
And give a heart of flesh to feel
And place his Love your heart within
And root out all in dwelling Sin
And that, than on your most Guilty Head
He would his gracious Mercy shed
And for the sake of his dear Son
Forgive you all the Ill you've done
And make you an Adopted one
Of his own family become
And Make you Like His Own Dear Son

In Meekness and Humility
Till Like a Little Child You Be
This is The State We Must Come to
No matter What We've got To do
A poor man I. A great one You
The difficulties must be Great
To One Who's Called to Rule a State
Temptations Love must Him Await
With business, Cares, and Pleasures too
And Wealth to boot What can He do
His Friends are Many and not Few
His Enemies are Many too
I Tell Thee Lincoln What Thou'll do

1865

208

Although Thou be a Statesman Great
Of Whom I would Somewhat Relate
He pities men in Every State
And Loves from Snares However Great
The Greatest Sinner of Or Race
Will Find in Christ Abundent [*sic*] Grace
When He will All His Sins Forsake
And God's Salvation Truly Take
If God Had Not Given Up His Son
To die for us there is not one
Of All that Lived Beneath the Sun
To Whom This Offer Could Be Made
Or to Whom it ever Could be Said
Would
Salvation is Free Indeed
But God Himself has Become Man
And Bourne our Sin and Guilt and Shame
That We from Guilt being Fully Freed
From Sin We Might be Free Indeed
Take heed O Lincoln what you read
And do not trust in any thing
Short of Salvation which I sing
That you with God be Reconciled
That You be His Adopted Child
That You become a Creature New
That You do Know Him That Is True
That He Will You the Victory Give
O'er the Evil World in which We Live
That Satan Be Subdued by You
Your Evil Lusts and Passions too
All in you must be made Anew
The Holy Spirit in Thy Heart
Must Assure Thee That Thou Hast a Part
In Christ who is gone up On High
And Reigns Triumphant in the Sky
Your earthly Glories All Must Fade
Before Salvation Thus Displayed
Your Worldly Honors all Forego—
Or They Will Prove Your Greatest Foe
Your Pleasures Must Be Thrown Aside
Yourself in All Things Be Denied
With Christ You Must Be Crucified
You Must Confess Your Lord Whom You

1865

Have Found to Be The Saviour True
All Your Powers of Body And Soul
Must Submit to Christ's Control
Must by Your Life this Truth Be Told
Wisdom Is better Far than Gold
All the Power Committed Thee
This must Remember is from Me
All Must be for Me Employed
Nothing Wasted or Destroyed
All Must for My Glory Be
Carrying On My Victory
These Command Christ Lendeth Thee

Now Lincoln When This Message Greets Your Ears
Receive It On Your Knees With Tears
Let It Excite Tears
Let It Excite Thy Tears and Terrors Too
And I Tell Thee Lincoln What You Will Do,
Call on The Lord With All Thy Might
And Absolve Thee From Thy Sins Outright
And Not Remember All Thy Guilt
And All The Blood That Thou Hast Spilt
And Thy Course of Evil Run
Beneath the Circle of the Sun
For Tears Thy Life May Soon Be Done
And Eternity Begun
But That He Would Pardon Thee
And Make Thee From Thy Sins Quite Free
And That Thou Mightest His Favour Gain
And Eternal Life Obtain
With Jesus Christ In Heaven To Reign
Throughout Eternity Amen

If This Warning Thus From Heaven
By Jesus Christ Himself Thus Given
Shall Fail to Move Thy Stubborn Heart
And Force Thee From Thy Sins To Part
And Make Thee Bend Thy Stubborn Knee
And Yield Submission Unto Me
This is Thy Last Warning Unto Thee
Lincoln!!! That Ever You Will Have from Me
Your Blood on your own Head Shal [sic] Be
And All Your Crimes and All Your Guilt

1865

And All Your Sin and Villiany [*sic*]
And All the Blood that Has Been Spilt
All that Were By Your Orders Slain
All That Prisoners Do Remain
All The Wounded, Did Endure
All The Sufferers Of The Poor,
And All The Pains and Misery
And All the Evils That Shal [*sic*] Be
Lincoln!! On Thy Own Head Shall Lie
Throughout All Eternity

This extraordinarily lengthy diatribe in verse—so long that it had to be written by two different people (the handwriting changes with the verse that begins, "Tremble Lincoln!")—was, understandably, not preserved in the Lincoln Papers. Correspondence secretary Edward Duffield Neill retained the abusive tome, seventeen foolscap pages long, and it was discovered by historian Theodore C. Blegen nearly a century later in the Neill Papers at the Minnesota Historical Society. This is the first time the poem has been reproduced in full. Although the date assigned to the composition (1865) is somewhat vague, it certainly dates to the last year of Lincoln's life, the period when Neill saw White House service. According to Neill's own reminiscences (see Introduction), this "denunciatory and hortatory religious poem" from a "messenger of the King of Kings and Lord of Lords" came from New Zealand. Neill included an excerpt in his story, but either he or the editor who supervised its publication in 1964 added punctuation and capitalization that the original poet had failed to provide. (Poem, courtesy Edward Duffield Neill Papers, Minnesota Historical Society; Ed. note, Theodore C. Blegen, ed., *Abraham Lincoln and His Mailbag: Two Documents by Edward D. Neill, One of Lincoln's Secretaries* ([St. Paul]: Minnesota Historical Society, 1964], 48–49)

A Kentucky Relative Asks a Pardon

Hardin County Ky Jan 7 1865

To his Excellency the president of the
United States of America

Your petitioner would Submit for your consideration a request which comes from one of your relations my name is Lucretia Allstun a daughter of William Brumfield who marriade Nancy Lincoln

Sir I have a Suninlaw in prison at Camp Douglas by the name of

Henry Harbolt and has been there since fuly 1863 he has a wife and three Small children dependent upon me for Support and I am a Widow and have a family of my own

Dear Sir my object in writing is to ask you to release him if consistent with your feelings one of my neighbors got him to follow John Morgan [a Confederate cavalry general captured in 1863 — Ed.] to try to get some horses that was taken by Morgans men and he was persuaded by them to gow with them his release would be regarded as a very great favor by your friend and relation as he has requested me to do Something for him

These few lines leaves me and family in good health and hope when they come to hand they may find you in the enjoyment of the Same blessing please answer this as Soon as convenient my adress is Red Hill Hardin County Kentucky

Lucretia Allstun

So far as it is known, Lincoln never answered this letter from his Kentucky birthplace of Hardin County. His assistant private secretary, John Hay, endorsed the request: "The President dont see it."

New Vice President Proposes Skipping Inauguration

[U.S. Military Telegraph]
Nashville Tenn. 5 P.M. Jan. 17th 1865

Private
His Excellency A. Lincoln

President:

The ordinance abolishing slavery will be adopted by the people [in Tennessee — Ed.] on the 22nd of February. Legislature and the Governor will be elected on the 4th of March, and will meet on the first Monday in April when the State will be organized & resume all the functions of a state in the Union. I would prefer remaining where I am until that time, and then hand it all over to the people in their representative character.

I would rather have the pleasure and honor of turning over the State organized, to the people properly constituted, than be Vice President of the United States. — At some convenient time after the first Monday in

1865

April, I could be qualified, &c. There are precedents for qualifying Vice Presidents after the fourth of March.—Give me your opinion on the subject. I think it would have a good effect and set the right precedent in restoring the State authority, whose people have been in rebellion.

Andrew Johnson

Lincoln had reportedly looked favorably on his party's decision to nominate Andrew Johnson as his running mate in 1864 precisely because of his pro-Union record as military governor of Tennessee. But Lincoln probably did not like the idea of allowing Johnson to remain home and miss the inaugural ceremonies in Washington. No formal reply to this telegram has come to light, but Johnson reported to the capital in time for his inauguration as vice president on March 4. After it was over, Lincoln doubtless wished he had encouraged Johnson to remain in Nashville. His drunken behavior at his swearing-in mortified the entire audience, the president included. (Ed. note, Hans L. Trefousse, *Andrew Johnson: A Biography* [New York: W. W. Norton, 1989], 189–90.)

Accepting Lincoln's Son in the Army

Annapolis Junction Md.
Jan.y 21st 1865

A. Lincoln, President,

Sir;

Your favor of this date in relation to your son serving in some Military capacity is received. I will be most happy to have him in my Military family in the manner you propose. The nominal rank given him is immaterial, but I would suggest that of Capt. as I have three Staff officers now, of considerable service, in no higher grade. Indeed I have one officer with only the rank of Lieut. who has been in the service from the beginning of the war. This however will make no difference and I would still say give the rank of Capt.—Please excuse my writing on a half sheet. I had no resource but to take the blank half of your letter.

Very respectfully your obt. svt,
U.S. Grant Lt. Gen

Robert T. Lincoln became captain and assistant adjutant general of Volunteers on February 11, 1865, and served four months, witnessing Robert E. Lee's surrender to Grant at Appomattox Court House, Virginia, in April. Lincoln's eldest son had hoped to join the service after his graduation from Harvard in 1864, but his mother pleaded with the president to prevent it, arguing: "I am so frightened he may never come back to us." Lincoln replied that "many a poor mother . . . has had to make this sacrifice," and in January 1865 finally secured Robert's enlistment with the following letter to his commanding general—an irresistible plea, as he surely knew, for special treatment for his son. Robert served in the army for some two months beginning February 11, 1865. (Ed. note, Helm, *Mary Lincoln*, 227; Simon, ed., *Papers of Ulysses S. Grant* XIII: 281–82; Lincoln's reply, *Coll. Works* VIII: 223.)

Executive Mansion, Washington,
Lieut. General Grant: Jan. 19, 1865.

Please read and answer this letter as though I was not President, but only a friend. My son, now in his twenty second year, having graduated at Harvard, wishes to see something of the war before it ends. I do not wish to put him in the ranks, nor yet to give him a commission, to which those who have already served long, are better entitled, and better qualified to hold. Could he, without embarrassment to you, or detriment to the service, go into your Military family with some nominal rank, I, and not the public, furnishing his necessary means? If no, say so without the least hesitation, because I am as anxious, and as deeply interested, that you shall not be encumbered as you can be yourself.

Yours truly
A. Lincoln

Imprisoned Black Soldier
Wants New Hearing for Comrade

Fort Jefferson Tortugas Fla.
January 24th 1864 [1865]
Sir

I have the honor to respectfully call your attention to a few remarks which I hope may receive your libral consideration.

I am a prisener here at fort Jefferson turtugas fla. I was sentence here for the short period of six months   I will not mention the injustice I received at the discretion of my court martrial. for I have but such short

period to remain here that I deem it hardly nessessary to enter into the
merits of the case. but I shall speek inbehalf of a great number of poor
but patriocic colored soldirees who have become victoms to a cruel ponishment for little arror. I will attemp to state in bref the circumstences
connected with the case of Jack Morris of Co. "F" 73th U.S. Colored
Infy. who enterd the U.S. servise on the 27th day Sept 1862 and was
errested on the 27th day of June 1864. and sentencd. on about the 20th
day October 1864 at Morganza. having served some two years allmost
fathfully without even as much as being once ponish in the lease. He
was trie and held to answer the charge of leveing his post   he had often
been told by his officers he said not to leve his post the consequence of
which he know not   he having call siveral times for the corporal of
the guard but without responce   with respects to you sir It being case
of necesity he thought that it would not be a killing circumstance as
much as he did not go out sight and hearing of his post   he was absent
but five minits and when he returned the corpral ask him where he had
been   he told him after which he was poot immediately under arrest.
and received a sentence of two years hard labor at this post   he is a man
of famely and has not had no pay sinc he has been in servise but once
and then he received but few months pay at seven dollars per month
which of course couldnot efford his famely much releaf. I am well awere
that every breach of military regulations which officers or soldiers are
guilty of is ponishable at the discretion of a propper court martial but
I do say and appeal to your honor that there aut to be a liberal consideration and allowance made for ignorence   the person refered to en-
fect most all of the colored troop recruted in this department with few
excepttion are egnorent men who know nothing more then the duties
of hard labor and as slaves was held for that perpose and where not
permtted to even as much as hendle there masters book. much less having the privelage of reading or even allow the use of a small elementry
speling book and of corse are as total egnorent of the regulations as a
poor while efrican is of gramer or elgebra. I appeal to your honor and
most respectfuly request in the name of him who has at his command
the destination of all nations that his sentence may be repreved. he says
he dont mind the ponishment that he is receiving here but he would like
to be where his serviseses may be of some use to the contry and the
proceeds of which may be used for the support of his famely which is in
great need of it   in this department it is different from the most of the
military post   the famely of the (colored) soldiers perticulary the poor
who are depending upon there husband for support   the most of the

---

1865

inhabitince perticular the welthey portion are so prejudice against the famely of colored soldiers in the US servise that thay wont even give them employment for no prise to sustain if posible the old hipocrittical idea that free colored people wont work and of cours the soldiers families have to suffer   in other states infact in most of the northern states there is releaf fonds but here there is none, and if the only support are taken away by death or any other cause thay must suffer and that severely. for I have been and eye witness to a grate many cases not only deprved of there homes on the a/sc^t of little means to pay there house rent but laught at abused by passes by insulting words such as (now you see what the yenkees will do for you had you not better stay with your masters.) the soldier seeing his famely subject to such crual ponishment and ill treetment does feel some what discuraged when he is ill treeted by thoes who is his only relience is for justice and his present existence for I have never have saw a more solom lot a priseners then I saw here from like circumstances (all thay have to say that the yankes treat me more woser then the rabs)   for my part I cant complane I have had evry respect shown me since I have been in the servise with but few exceptions   I even was allowed while under arrest as a freehold cittizon of the state of New York to cast my vote on a ritten form for that perpose for the first time for the candidate of my choise and as we hale the election of the fondor of the proclamation of emencipation we as poor priseners with undanted patriocism to the cause of our contry look foward towards washing[ton] to here something in behalf of poor priseners   we know that your four years of administration has been as berdensome as it has victorious and no dought you have but lettle time to listen to the grate many pleas that comes through such scorce   we do feal as union soldiers that we may ask with that positive assureanc that we will be herd   all we can say that we are sory that we have become victoms to a millitary crime and do senserely repent and ask to be forgiven   we cant do no more   where we to remain here 5 years we should be know less sory then we are know. Very respectfully your humble & obt servt
                                 Samuel Roosa

This extraordinary letter—an appeal from one imprisoned African American soldier on behalf of another—was referred by Lincoln to Judge Advocate General Joseph Holt, who reported himself unmoved by Roosa's impassioned plea. Private Morris had admitted stealing fruit from his company sutler, but pleaded "not guilty" to deserting his post as a sentinel, insisting that he had "a necessary purpose" for doing so and had tried in vain to call a superior "to his relief."

1865

The corporal of the guard had contradicted this assertion. On February 28, 1865, Holt reported back to the president, indignant over the notion that "special leniency should be exercised in punishment inflicted upon Colored recruits from Southern States, on account of their ignorance, and the fact that their families are entirely dependent on them for support." Holt's review of the Morris case concluded: "He was sentenced to two years confinement, with forfeiture of pay during that time—a sentence that was warranted by the circumstances, and should be fully executed." There is no evidence in Morris's surviving file that Lincoln attempted to overrule this review. (Letter and endorsement, Judge Holt, Colored Troops Division Files, National Archives)

A "Wild Youth" Pardoned

Washington, D.C., January 28th, 1865.

To His Excellency The President:

Sir:—

My son, James Callan, a private in Company E, Second Regiment District of Columbia Volunteers, volunteered for <u>three months</u> at the outbreak of the Rebellion. At the end of that period, he re-enlisted for <u>three years</u>, which second term expired on the eighth day of the present month;—but, about a year ago, he again re-enlisted for <u>three years</u> more, thus giving an example of loyalty and devotion to the cause of the Union that cannot fail to command him to your Excellency.—He was a young boy, and careless and wild as youth is generally, and was consequently unfortunate enough to get into trouble on the 26th day of August, 1864, when he was tried at Alexandria, Va., by a Court Martial, in pursuance of Gen. Order No. 40, and found "guilty": of "conduct prejudicial to good order and military discipline," and of "absence without leave." He was sentenced "to be dishonorably discharged [from] the military service of the United States with the loss of all pay and allowances now due, or that may become due, and be confined at hard labor in Fort Delaware, or such other place as the Commanding General may direct, for the period of three years."

He has now been undergoing punishment for more than five months, and has already suffered sufficiently for his imprudence. In a conversation with his Colonel, (Alexander) that officer declared that my son

1865

"was a good man, and that if he had been wild, the punishment he had already undergone would make him a good soldier and that he would cheerfully receive him again in his Regiment, if the President would grant his pardon."

I have another son in the Navy, from whom I have been unable to hear for a long time; James is a prisoner for a thoughtless act of folly, while those who have done nothing for the cause are free. He was one of the earliest to volunteer in defence of his country; he served her in the darkest hour of her need; and it would be his, and my own proudest desire that he should be one of the strong arms to strike the death blow of the Rebellion, or if need be, to die in defence of the Union.

Hoping Mr. President, that you will pardon my son, and order him to return to his Regiment, for duty, I am

Your Excellency's Obt Servant,
Mrs. Mary Buckley

Lincoln's response to this plea was prompt and sympathetic. On February 7, he wrote the following notation on the letter: "If his Colonel will say in writing on this sheet that he is willing to receive this man back to the regiment, I will pardon & send him. A. Lincoln." The next day, Callan's commander obliged with an endorsement from the headquarters of the 2nd D.C. Volunteers in Alexandria, Virginia: "I would be most happy to receive this man back as a member of this Rgt. as I believe him to be a good soldier." As promised, Lincoln followed, earnestly if ungrammatically, with yet another notation on the letter on February 10: "Let this man go to his regiment and upon faithfully serving out his time in which he is fully pardoned. A Lincoln." Double-endorsed letters to Lincoln are extremely rare. (Letter, Military Service Record Files, National Archives)

A Death Sentence Commuted

[Telegraph]
Frankfort Ky. January 29th 1865

A. Lincoln, President

In behalf of loyal parents & friends I ask the release of an inexperienced boy named W. E. Walker recently ordered to be shot without any chance of trial this boy will take the Amnesty oath & adhere to every

---

1865

requirement of the same to the fulfillment of the promise. I together with his friends pledge our lives.

P. B. Hawkins late Colonel 11th Ky

Lincoln telegraphed General Stephen G. Burbridge, the officer in command at Frankfort, on February 2: "Suspend execution of death sentence of W. E. Walker until further orders, and forward record of trial for examination. A. Lincoln" (*Coll. Works* VIII: 256). Two days later, General Burbridge answered: "Execution of death sentence in case of W. E. Walker, guerrilla, has been suspended. He was ordered to be shot in retaliation for the murder of union citizens." Extenuating circumstances must have been presented to Lincoln, for on February 11 he wired Hawkins: "Gen. Burbridge may discharge W. E. Waller, [*sic*] if he thinks fit. A. Lincoln" (*Coll. Works* VIII: 289). But Burbridge did not think it fit. Colonel Hawkins again telegraphed Lincoln the very same day: "Genl Burbridge says he would release W E Waller if he had the power Aching hearts ask it of you. he ought to be." But if Lincoln wrote again in Walker's behalf, no record of his instructions have been located. The disposition of the Walker case remains unknown.

Announcing His Presence
Outside the White House Window

January 31st 1865

My dear friend Abraham Lincoln and Lady, peace be upon you, and do not be offended with me if I appear this day before the Executive Mansion, with my cart which I draw through the country, and lodge in it, a faithful high way preacher and peace maker, without money scrip rations or pay, and always on duty.

I am truly your sincere friend

Walter of Greenburg [N.Y.]

from Westchester County New York State.
the mottos upon the cart I send you

Front

My motto is to forgive each other to hold each other innocent and practice it, therefore, what ever human kind may do to me I am determined to be peaceful merciful and forgiving to them.

1865

My preaching and practice is peace, by abolishing money, hired slavery, property, and trade, the causes of war, which if human kind will not do then what can they do but dispute deceive quarel and fight continually.

on the two sides

I believe in no government but truth, and in no duty but to obey the truth, which are only such principles as harmonize, and upon which no two individuals can disagree or dispute.

I know of no rebels but those who rebel against the truth, and they are equally the same both north and south, neither one has yet volunteered out of the speechles womb of ignorance into the new birth of such wisdom and peace.

If Lincoln glanced out of his window to examine "Walter's" curious, slogan-festooned cart, it was not recorded. (Letter, The Lincoln Museum, Fort Wayne, IN)

Salmon Trout after a Failed Peace Conference

House of Representatives
Washington City, Feb 1st 1865

To His Excellency President of the U.S.

Sir:

I have the honor to present you with a fair specimen of our Mackinaw Salmon Trout. The fish was sent to me by Express, and came from Mr. Harvey Williams, one of my constituents who is eighty years of age, and who has followed fishing on Lake Huron for thirty of forty years. He has been a life long Democrat, but in the last Election made a trip of forty miles in one of his fishing boats to vote for you and the Union candidates. May I beg of you an autograph receipt to send to the old gentleman which I know he will highly prize.

Very truly yours
J. F. Driggs

Lincoln, no doubt exhausted and disappointed by the recent, fruitless Hampton Roads peace conference, returned to the White House to find waiting for him both the salmon trout and the following reply to Michigan Congressman

---

1865

Driggs. The letter is in the handwriting of assistant secretary John M. Hay, but bears Lincoln's signature. Although the letter is dated February 3, Lincoln likely did not sign it before February 4, the day he arrived back in Washington from Hampton Roads. (Ed. note, *Lincoln Day by Day* III: 311; Lincoln's reply, *Coll. Works* VIII: 257)

Executive Mansion, Washington,
My Dear Sir: 3rd February, 1865.
    I have received at your hands a very fine specimen of the Mackinaw Salmon Trout and I beg that you will convey to Mr. Williams my cordial thanks for his kind thoughtfulness; and accept my acknowledgments for your courtesy in the transmission of this present.
                             I am sir, very truly yours
                             A. Lincoln.
Hon. J. F. Driggs &c. &c.

Black Soldier Wants a Leave

                                        [City Point, Virginia,] Feb the 2 1865
Mr Abebrem Lenken the Presdent of the U. S. stats

    I will rite you A few Lins to let you now that I am not Well and i Can not rite to Day for i am sick but i am in Good hops that you will rede this   i have ben sick Evy since i Come her and i think it is hard to make A man go and fite and Wont let him vote and wont let him go home when he is sick   We had Boys her that Died that Wood gout well if thy Could go home   thy Can Come back as Well as A whit man   i hope you will give us some pleser of our life   give us A chenc of A man   i Will rite no more this time   i Dont wont you to get mad with what i say for i Dont mene any harme   rite soon if you pleze and let me no how you feel   so No More this time
    my wife is left A long and no helf and thy wont let me go home   Derect you letter to City Point 8 Reg U.S.C.T. 25 Corps 2n Briggad 2nd Divsion Com. B re Derict to
                             Zack Burden

This letter was, not surprisingly, forwarded to the Bureau of Colored Troops, and no record of a reply is known. (Letter, Colored Troops Division Files, National Archives)

1865

Suggesting That the President Pray

Wilmington 2/5th 1865

Much Esteemed & Honoured Friend
Abraham Lincoln President U.S.

My <u>heart</u> has so gone <u>with</u> and <u>into</u> this whole effort for <u>Peace, espe-</u><u>cially</u> to thy self sacrificing journey to "<u>The James</u>" [for a conference with Confederate leaders—Ed.];—that now as it beats fearfully, and slowly, under an apprehension, <u>perhaps</u>, this momentous matter, still hangs trembling in the balance, I cannot refrain from imploring thee (my dear friend) to turn it over, and over again, in thy prayerful approaches to our dear, and merciful Lord, that so his gracious purpose may be made known <u>to thee</u>,—<u>His Holy Will be done</u>—and his Glory be promoted.

Very Respectfully, Thy Sincere Friend
<u>John W. Tatum</u>

P.S. Thy prompt and confiding kindness, in the liberation of those 3 friends from "Point-look-out", was touching to my heart, and I hope, has made a lasting impression of gratitude thereon.

The previous November, Tatum had urged that Lincoln pardon three friends "pressed into the confederate army against their will." On November 30, 1864, Lincoln had ordered: "Let the men . . . be discharged on affirming according to the oath of Dec. 8. 1863, and that they will remain North" *Coll. Works* VIII: 124. But Tatum's hopes for a heaven-sent peace were premature. Lincoln's conference with Confederate representatives at Hampton Roads did not produce an agreement to end the war.

Her 300th Pair of Socks

Salem, Mass. Feb. 7th. 1865.

To His Excellency, Abraham Lincoln,
President of the United States:

A year or two since, a pair of socks was sent to you by Mrs. Abner Bartlett of Medford, Mass. which you kindly acknowledged. She was 87 years old on the 24th of Dec. 1864 and has knit more than three hundred pairs of socks for the soldiers since Sept. 1861. She has consented to have me send the 300th pair to you as a birth-day gift.

Mrs. Bartlett is the only surviving sister of Tristram Barnes, formerly in Congress from Rhode Island; and although so advanced in years, no one is more alive to the great issues of the hour, or more inspired to a true love of liberty, and no one could have a firmer confidence in yourself, or cherish a more unwavering faith in the perfect triumph of her Country's cause.

With the highest respect,
I am faithfully yours,
Geo. W. Briggs

This may be the only birthday gift Lincoln ever got from a constituent while he served as president, since there are no similar presentations to be found in the Lincoln Papers. When he received socks from the same Mrs. Bartlett the year before, Lincoln had replied as follows (there is no record of an acknowledgment to the birthday gift of 1865). (Lincoln's reply, *Coll. Works*, VII: 331)

Mrs. Abner Bartlett   Executive Mansion,
My dear Madam.   Washington, May 5, 1864.
   I have received the very excellent pair of socks of your own knitting, which you did me the honor to send. I accept them as a very comfortable article to wear; but more gratefully as an evidence, of the patriotic devotion which, at your advanced age, you bear to our great and just cause.

   May God give you yet many happy days.

Yours truly
A. Lincoln

Grateful for Lincoln's Christianity and Reelection

Troy, Rensselaer Co. N. Y.
Feb. 7, 1865.

Mr. Abraham Lincoln
Our Beloved and Honored President.
   Ever since you have been our President I have wanted to write to you, when I would read so many things of you that I loved and admired so

1865

much; and I have thought very many times "I wonder if he is not a christian;" lattely [*sic*], I have felt that you must be one, when I have read your Proclamation, and your appointments for national Fasts. But this evening I took an "American Messenger" to read, when my eyes fell upon a paragraph that delighted me more than all the rest. My heart overflowed with gratitude to God, and with increased love and support for our God-given President—for I had very often prayed for you, as all Christian people have. But I have not explained about the paragraph. Shall you be offended at all if I enclose it; then it will explain itself. I cut it out to keep it, but I will give it another reading, and treasure its contents in my heart.

I do so thank God for it all; and for making you our President the second time. God has helped you or you never could have lived through what you have; of course, He will stand by, and uphold you; and be assured there are thousands of warm true hearts all over this noble country who love and honor you, and pray for you, too, every day. Ah! Mr. Lincoln the nation's hopes are centered in you; the national heart beats loyally for you. God bless you fully and richly!

Now, I have taken too much of your most valuable time; presuming, perhaps, in me to think of asking our President to give a moment to the reading of this poor letter, but I did have to write to you; you know now that here is one more heart that thanks God you are a christian, and <u>our President</u> Again.

One of your people.
Sarah T. Barnes

No reply has been located, but this endearing letter was carefully preserved in the president's papers, along with the newspaper clipping to which it refers. The article reported that Lincoln first became a true Christian when he "went to Gettysburg, and looked upon the graves of our dead heroes who had fallen in defence of their country."

Requesting One Last Photograph

Brady's Gallery
352 Penna. Ave. Wash.
[Received March 2, 1865]

Mr. Pres.

Dear Sir

I have repeated calls every hour in the day for your Photograph and would regard it as a great favor if you could give me a sitting to day so that I may be able to exhibit a large picture on the 4th. If you cannot call today Please call at your earliest convenience and very much oblige.

Yours truly
M. B. Brady

As this terse plea suggests, the famed photographer Mathew Brady knew Lincoln well enough to propose that Lincoln sit for a new photograph at a time when the President was no doubt preoccupied with his reinauguration, just two days away. Brady had photographed Lincoln on many occasions, beginning with a widely reproduced February 1860 photograph that Brady believed was "the means of [Lincoln's] election" to the White House. But Lincoln had sat for Brady's onetime employee, Alexander Gardner, now proprietor of his own studio, only a month before receiving Brady's request, and Lincoln was probably not inclined to visit another gallery so soon thereafter. On March 7, the persistent Brady tried a different approach, writing to Mary Lincoln that he would be "very much pleased to make" photographs to display at a forthcoming charity fair in Chicago. The organizers of the event proposed "elegant portraits of the President and his lady" to be made by "permitting Mr. Brady to make some good negatives." Ironically, Lincoln had by that time acceded to the requests of yet another photographer, Henry F. Warren, and posed the day before for two new photographs on the south balcony of the White House. The unusual confluence of events—Lincoln's likely preoccupation with his swearing-in when Brady first proposed a sitting on March 2 and the arrival of Henry Warren on March 6—conspired to deny the country's best-known photographer the opportunity to create what would have been the last studio photograph of Abraham Lincoln. He never again sat before the cameras. (Letter, Library of Congress Manuscripts Division; Ed. note, Carpenter, *Six Months*, 47; Hamilton and Ostendorf, *Lincoln in Photographs*, 214-15, 223-31)

1865

An Admirer's "Epistle"

Sir,

   your excellency, I see by the newspapers is well. And may the great invisible all Ruling Spirit, protect you, and decree that you enjoy good health for years yet to come.

   I took the liberty to address a few words to your excellency two or three times several months ago, the last, Before this, was in last October,—And what I wished and anticipated, in regard to your excellencies' Election, and your self, and countries' welfare has come to pass, thank the great Spirit, the Red Mens Idol, and the White Mens god,—your excellency listens, to so much talk on evry topic interesting and un interesting, and <u>letters</u> of the same Calabre, that any one posted in half the knowledge of high, and, low, human nature, will almost shrink from writing, or speaking to your excellency in these times of acting and not talking.—I have only in the fullness of My good feeling, and love, from my heart sincere, towards your excellency, written this Epistle, to your excellency, And for no other perpose [sic] than to express my self sincerely, and honestly.

   —And now I have Relieved my mind, I close my Remarks, by saying that I hope good health and prosperity, will attend your excellency all the way through to the end, let it be longer, or shorter.

> If god stands by your excellency and, laws,
> Let the devel and the Rebels, smack there Jaws,
> Neither will be able, to satesfy there appetite—
> For when good is set Before them, They will not, Bite—

I am With high Respect
Ever your excellency obt.
Henry Fletcher (or Owothourna[])]

His, excellency, Abraham, Lincoln
God, Bless him

This homely little poem, perhaps written by a Native American, judging by the writer's two signatures and the reference to "the Red Mens Idol," was one of the last such tributes Lincoln ever received. The "great invisible all Ruling Spirit" which the correspondent invoked to protect Lincoln "for years yet to come" failed the president—within five weeks, he was dead.

1865

A Todd Seeks Reappointment

Lexington Ky March 8 1865

His Ex. A. Lincoln—President

Will you do me the kindness to reappoint me Post-master
L. B. Todd

This request from Lyman B. Todd may have been the last appeal for patronage to arrive on Lincoln's desk from his wife's family. The president obliged by re-appointing Todd, inspiring the following letter.

[March 16, 1865]

My Very Kind Friend—

Mr. Lincoln—

I have just observed in the "News-Papers" that I have had the Honor of being re-appointed "Post-Master!"! here—By this, I acknowledge the receipt of another favor from <u>your</u> hand—another evidence of your confidence in me—for which I desire, hereby, to return you, my grateful acknowledgements and heartfelt thanks—Hoping that I may ever prove worthy thereof—and praying that Heaven may long continue its choicest blessings upon You and Yours—

With Love to Cousin Mary, and indulging the Hope of seeing You soon

I am Truly Your Grateful Friend
L. B. Todd

Lexington Ky
March 16th 1865

1865

North Carolina Freedmen Want Rights

Roanoke Island N.C march 9th 1865

Mr. President

Dear Sir

We colored men of this Island held a meeting to consult over the affairs of our present conditions and our rights and we find that our arms are so Short that we cant doe any thing with in our Selves So we Concluded the best thing we could do was to apply to you or Some of your cabinets   we are told and also we have read that you have declared all the Colored people free bothe men and woman that is in the Union lines and if that be so we want to know where our wrights is or are we to be Stamp down or troden under feet by our Superintendent which he is the very man that we look to for assistents, in the first place his Proclamation was that no able boded man was to draw any rations except he was at work for the Government   we all agreed to that and was willing to doe as we had done for $10,oo per month and our rations though we Seldom ever get the mony

the next thing he said that he wanted us to work and get our living as White men and no apply to the Government and that is vry thing we want to doe, but after we do this we cant satisfie him   Soon as he Sees we are trying to Support our Selves without the aid of the Government he comes and make a Call for the men, that is not working for the Government to Goe away and if we are not willing to Goe he orders the Guards to take us by the point of the bayonet, and we have no power to help it   we know it is wright and are willing to doe any thing that the President or our head Commanders want us to doe but we are not willing to be pull and haul a bout so much by those head men as we have been for the last two years and we may say Get nothing for it, last fall a large number of we men was Conscript and sent up to the front and all of them has never return   Some Got Kill Some died and When they taken them they treated us mean and our owner ever did   they taken us just like we had been dum beast

We Colored people on Roanok Island are willing to Submit to any thing that we know the President or his cabinet Say because we have Got since enough to believe it is our duty to doe every thing we Can doe to aid Mr Lyncoln and the Government but we are not willing to work as we have done for Chaplain James and be Troden under foot and

---

Get nothing for it we have work faithful Since we have been on the Island we have built our log houses we have Cultivate our acre of Ground and have Tried to be less exspence to the Government as we Possible Could be and we are yet Trying to help the Government all we Can for our lives those head men have done every thing to us that our masters have done except by and Sell us and now they are Trying to Starve the woman & children to death cutting off they ration they have Got so now that they wont Give them no meat to eat, every ration day beef & a little fish and befor the Ten days is out they are going from one to another Trying to borrow a little meal to last until ration day Mr Streeter will just order one barrell of meet for his fish men and the others he Gives nothing but beaf but we thank the Lord for that if we no it is the President or the Secretarys orders this is what want to know whoes orders it is, one of our minister children was fool to ration house and Sent off and his father working three days in every week for his ration

Roanoke Island N.C march 9th 1865

we have appeal to General Butler and Genl Butler wrote to Capt James to do Better and Capt James has promies to do Better and instead of doing better he has done worst and now we appeal to you which is the last resort and only help we have got, feeling that we are entily friendless, on the Island there numrous of Soldiers wives and they Can hardly get any rations and some of them are almost starving

we dont exspect to have the same wrights as white men doe we know that are in a millitary country and we exspect to obey the rules and orders of our authories and doe as they say doe, any thing in reason we thank God and thank our President all of his aids for what has been done for us but we are not satisfide with our Supertendent nor the treatement we receives now we want you to send us answer what to depen upon let it be good or bad and we will be Satisfide

Respectifully yours
Roanoke Island N.C.

This appeal was found in the National Archives together with two additional, fragmentary letters, both dated March 9, 1865. Scholar Ira Berlin has suggested that all were likely written by a black schoolteacher named Richard Boyle, who may have traveled to Washington to deliver them to the Executive Mansion personally. But no evidence has been found that Lincoln or any of the federal

1865

bureaus responded to these complaints. Still, if he read the petitions, the president may have sensed that they raised issues that he would surely have to confront once the war ended. As the final lines of another fragment noted of these former slaves: "All we wants is a Chance and we can Get a living like White men we are praying to God every day for the war to Stop So we wont be beholding to the Government for Something to Eat." (Letters, Colored Troops Division Files, National Archives; Ed. note, Ira Berlin et al., eds., *Free At Last: A Documentary History of Slavery, Freedom, and the Civil War* [New York: The New Press, 1992], 222–27)

A Convicted Spy and Arsonist Pleads for Clemency

[March 14, 1865]

To His Excellency, Abraham Lincoln
President of the United States

Sir

I have been arraigned before a Military Commission, charged with having acted the spy, and guerilla—tried, found guilty, and sentenced to receive an ignominious death. I respectfully <u>request</u> you to review the proceedings of the Commission, and my case, and give your attention to the following statement.

As to the charge of acting as a spy: I have always thought I understood the definition of the term, and assure you <u>most solemnly</u> that I have never acted in that capacity. I am not responsible for being outside the limits of the Confederate States—was brought North a prisoner of war and confined as such on Johnson's Island, from which place I succeeded in making my escape, and as I was entirely destitute of means was <u>compelled</u> to take refuge in Canada. When in New York my conduct was that of any idler, or pleasure-seeker. I visited no fort, arsenal, navy yard, or <u>any place</u> in which a spy could gain information of importance to him, or detrimental to the interest of the country of an adversary. I was not sent to obtain information—did not come for that purpose and had no idea that the mere fact of entering the territory of the United States rendered me liable to the imputation of being a spy. Of the existence of the Act of Congress pronouncing any individual of the armies of a Power at war with the United States "who may be found lurking in any post, fortification, encampment, or <u>elsewhere</u>["] a spy I was entirely ignorant until informed by the Judge-Advocate, during the progress of my trial. I did <u>not</u> fly from New York in the night but when it suited my convenience, left it on a regular passenger train.

As to the second specification: Acting as a spy in the city of Detroit—I can only say that the document signed by me, pledging my honor to make no delay on my way to the Confederate States, and which was produced in my defense, is <u>genuine</u>—I signed, and intended fulfilling its requirements. Wilmington was then invested and the only route left me was through the United States. Honor, duty, and inclination impelled me to rejoin my command as soon as possible and I would have done so had I not been arrested. In disposing of this charge I will state, however circumstances may be against me I have never acted the spy in thought word, or deed, so help me God.

In regard to the second charge: Violating the laws of war. Please consider the <u>character</u> of the witnesses produced against me. It was not shown that I was in the City of New York after the 21st of Nov., four days previous to the fires which I am condemned to die for kindling. Do not understand me as casting any improper reflections on the members of the Commission. I suppose they did their duty as conscientious men, perfectly aware of the responsibility of condemning a human being to death.

Granting the evidence advanced, sufficient for convicting me of this last charge, is not the penalty too severe for the offense? Arson is not punishable with <u>death</u>! An example is not needed for one has just been made in the person of Capt Beall. He was convicted of conducting unlawful warfare and was executed. Is not his fate a sufficient warning to offenders? My blood is not necessary to the welfare of this country. I feel that I do not deserve death. If I have ever taken the life of a human being it was done on the field of battle—not in unlawful warfare. I have been an enemy to your Government since the outbreak of the present unhappy war, but I [have] been an open and honorable man. I am not a spy, or guerilla—holding each character in abhorrence. The first as a mercenary wretch and the last, as one who strikes for plunder and too cowardly to meet his enemy in open combat.

In conclusion, allow me to say, that if my sentence is carried out my life will be <u>unnecessarily</u> sacrificed. The nation of which you are Chief Magistrate, is certainly powerful enough to be generous—to protect itself without resorting to <u>unnecessarily severe</u> measures towards those so unfortunate as to fall into the hands of its authorities. There are ties which bind me to life and render it dear to me.

1865

I throw myself entirely on your clemency and respectfully ask, at least, a commutation of my sentence.

I have the honor to be, very respectfully, your ob'dt serv't

Robert C. Kennedy
Capt. C S A
Prisoner under sentence of death

Fort Lafayette
March 14, 1865

Major General John A. Dix, head of the Department of the East, forwarded this plea for mercy to Judge Advocate General Joseph Holt, head of the Bureau of Military Justice, on March 18. It was Holt who probably sent it on to the president, for the four-page letter was preserved in the Lincoln Papers. But there is no evidence that the president acted to commute Kennedy's death sentence. Although he had written a highly literate request for clemency, Kennedy probably did himself little good by seeking excuse for his disloyalty by citing the letter, rather than the spirit, of federal law.

Proposing a Return to Cooper Union

Chauncey Shaffer
Attorney and Counselor at Law
No. 245 Broadway New York
March 14th 1865

Abraham Lincoln
President of the United States

Sir

In behalf of the Committee for celebrating the anniversary of the Attack on Fort Sumter, We earnestly solicit your attendance to hear an oration to be delivered by the Hon. Chauncey Shaffer, at the Cooper Institute upon the eleventh of April at 7 ½ o'clock P.M.

We have no doubt but what the affair will be a very interesting one. And we only require your presence to make it complete. Hoping to receive an immediate reply—We remain

Your Obedient Servants
Wm. E. Buckingham Chairman
John N. Fisher Jr.   Sec'y

N.B. Please address the Secretary at the Office of Chauncey Shaffer.

1865

The idea of returning to Cooper Union, the scene of his triumphant first appearance before a New York audience back in 1860, must have intrigued Lincoln. But, not only did he resist the impulse to attend, he failed even to reply to the invitation; at least no copy of a response has ever come to light. Lincoln remained in Washington on April 11.

Seeking Pardon for a Murderer

[Probably March 14 or 15, 1865]
To His Excellency, Abraham Lincoln, President of the United States

Sir,

Although an utter stranger to you May I be allowed the liberty of addressing your Honor a few lines, in favor of Henry A. Meck from Pennsylvania, who has a wife and children; said H. A. Meck being at this time under sentence of <u>death</u> in this city by hanging, about the middle of next week or 14th of <u>March next</u>.

H. A. Meck was formerly a Lieutenant in a Regiment of negro soldiers—stationed here. About June 1864—I think—Meck was under the influence of Spirituous liquors, and while in that Situation with some of his black soldiers unfortunately attacked a Sutlers Store here. The Sutler defended his property, drew a pistol and shot Meck, wounding him severely: Meck ordered one of his black soldiers to return the fire, which was done, Shooting the Sutler, who soon deceased—

Meck has been in prison ever Since—I think—and Shows a very Contrite heart, and repentance I expect for the offence he committed.

If it would not be asking too much of your Honor, in extending your Clemency in this case to a reprieve, and pardon of the unfortunate Criminal Meck, he might yet be Spared, to be a useful member of the Community.

With the most profound respect Sir I remain your humble petitioner
I. N. Baylor
Citizen of Norfolk, Virginia

Lincoln had previously reviewed the lieutenant's court-martial papers, endorsing them "Sentence approved" on January 25. But on receipt of this letter he wired General Edward O. C. Ord, commander of the Army of the James.

1865

Executive Mansion
Major General Ord.   Washington, March 16, 1865
    Suspend execution of Lieut. Henry A. Meck, of 1st. U. S. Colored
Cavalry until further order from here. Answer
A. Lincoln

Ord's reply came by military telegraph the same day.

Head Qrs Army, James Mar. 16th 1865

His Excellency A. Lincoln Prest. U.S.
    Orders have been issued suspending execution of Lieut. Henry A.
Mecker 1st U.S. Colored Cavalry until further orders as directed in your
telegram just received.
E. O. C. Ord
Maj. Gen. Cmdg

The final resolution of the case of Henry A. Meck, or Mecker, is not known.
(Lincoln's reply, *Coll. Works* VIII: 357)

Exiled Child Prodigy Longs for Home

Willie Pape, 9 Soho Square London
Pianist to the Royal Family at Marlboro House
By Command of H.R.H. The Prince of Wales
March 29, 1865

Your Excellency,

    I left my native town Mobile Alabama for the purpose of pursuing my
studies under the best masters in Europe, on the 1st of March 1861—
now four years since. On my arrival in New York I was informed by
my Father who accompanied me that our state had seceded from the
Union & that we had better remain awhile before we embarked for England. I remained in the north for two years studying and occasionally
appearing in public for benefit of charities. On my arrival in England
I was permitted to appear at several Grand Concerts, at which the
Royal Family attended, and have been honored by the highest position
attained by an artist—I have written to my Mother many times, and to
my Grandmother, by the way that all letters to the south go, (I dont

---

1865

234

know how that is, only they are deposited in a bag in Bishopsgate street, & prepaid.) but I have not heard a word from any of my family since the mails were stopped—I was fifteen years old on the 24th of last month—and having been absent from Mobile since I was 11 I am very anxious to hear from my mother if there is a means of doing so—I am in daily communication with Her Majesty or the prince of Wales, they are my patrons & friends, and despite the jealousies of native pianists—they award me the highest honors—it has been a source of great dissatisfaction to the Royal Academy that an American should have been so honored—but in this country merit alone gives precedence in the fine arts.

The honor of your answer will make very happy, one, who although raised to so high a pinnacle of favor is at all times unhappy and despondent.

I am informed that property left me by my Grandfather has been confiscated through our absence from the so called Confederate States—Our property was assessed at 25,000 dollars.

[Willie Pape]

To the Hon Abraham Lincoln

The young pianist to royalty enclosed a newspaper clipping headlined, "Honor to an American Artist," reporting on his successful performances in England. But Lincoln, if he ever saw this appeal, was unmoved. The letter was endorsed with a single word: "File." It is conceivable, however, that it did not arrive from England until after Lincoln's death.

A Musical Honor, Composed Too Late

Hoboken N. J. April 1st 1865

To his Excellency Abraham Lincoln

Honored Sir

After having served for two years in the 103d N.Y. Vol. Regt. (Seward's Infantry) I have settled down in my avocation as Music Teacher and during my leisure moments composed a March. Always having been an ardent admirer of you and the principles you advocate, I desire to dedicate the March to you to be called the "Lincoln March."

By granting me permission to use your name so, you would oblige

Your most obedient servant

R. L. Teichfuss

1865

This letter was filed, probably for Lincoln's review upon his return from his extended visit to the Army of the Potomac at the front that April. But Lincoln likely never attended to it. Within days of his return to Washington, he was assassinated. His death unleashed a huge national demand for musical tributes to the martyred president, but for funeral dirges, not marches. Correspondent Teichfuss's composition was doubtless rendered obsolete by Lincoln's murder.

Harold Holzer, Vice President for Communications at the Metropolitan Museum of Art, is one of the country's leading authorities on the political culture of the Civil War era. Holzer has authored, coauthored, and edited ten books, including *The Lincoln Image* (1984) (with Mark E. Neely Jr. and Gabor S. Boritt), *Mine Eyes Have Seen the Glory: The Civil War in Art* (1993) (with Neely), as well as *The Lincoln-Douglas Debates* (1993) and *Witness to War: The Civil War* (1996). He has published more than 250 articles for both popular magazines and scholarly journals, contributed chapters to a number of books, and regularly reviews Civil War books for the *Chicago Tribune*. Holzer served as a consultant to the ABC-TV documentary miniseries, *Lincoln*, broadcast in 1992, and as a historical consultant and on-air commentator on C-SPAN for the re-creation of the Lincoln-Douglas debates in Illinois in 1994. In addition, Holzer lectures widely before Civil War and Lincoln groups throughout the country and has organized Lincoln symposia and national traveling exhibitions of original Civil War-era art. Among the positions Holzer has held are adjunct professor of history at Pace University, president of the Lincoln Group of New York (1991–96), public relations director for the PBS flagship station WNET/13, and special counselor to the Director of Economic Development in the administration of Governor Mario M. Cuomo (1984–92). Holzer has received numerous awards and honors, including the 1996 Manuscript Society of America Award for his book, *Dear Mr. Lincoln*. Currently, Holzer is working on several books including *The Union Image: Prints of the Civil War North* (with Neely), and an album of paintings and sculptures of Lincoln from life.

However unusual it may

sections or to sections if

agitations which have s

so far ~~~~ hope it in

from propriety whatever

say that if in the coun

too often imbue our

south of this capital

I regard with a left

a his domestic safety

State ~~~~ I do the

country or that I no